THE ART OF CONNECTION

365 Days of Abundance Quotes by Entrepreneurs, Business Owners, and Influencers

ROBERT W. JONES AND JOHN VERRICO

THE ART OF CONNECTION
@2025 Robert W. Jones and John Verrico - All rights reserved.

THE ART OF CONNECTION - 365 Days of Abundance Quotes by Entrepreneurs, Business Owners, and Influencers. Published and distributed in Gifts of Legacy LLC: Scottsdale, Arizona.

No part of this publication may be reproduced, distributed, or transmitted in any form or by any means, whether electronic, mechanical, photocopying, recording, or otherwise, including through information storage and retrieval systems, without the prior written permission of the publisher or author. Exceptions are granted only to reviewers, who may quote brief excerpts embodied in critical articles or reviews, provided proper attribution is given.

While the author and publisher have taken great care to ensure the accuracy and completeness of the information contained in this book at the time of publication, they make no representations or warranties regarding its applicability or accuracy. The author and publisher expressly disclaim all liability for any loss, damage, or disruption caused by errors or omissions, whether resulting from negligence, accident, or any other cause.

Right to Market and Promote The publisher and author retain the exclusive right to market, advertise, and promote this publication through any medium or channel, including but not limited to print, digital, social media, and events. Any unauthorized marketing or promotional activities by third parties are strictly prohibited without prior written consent from the publisher or author.

Right to Republish The publisher and author retain the right to republish this work, in whole or in part, in any manner or format, including but not limited to revised editions, anthologies, compilations, journals, calendars or digital adaptations. Contributors acknowledge and agree that their submissions may be included in such future publications without additional consent, provided proper attribution is maintained.

KDP Print – ISBN: 979-8-9914118-1-3
KDP eBook – ISBN: 979-8-9914118-2-0
Library of Congress Control Number: 2024925268

Cover Photo by Ken Rochon, Jr.

@2025 Robert W. Jones and John Verrico - All rights reserved

THE ART OF CONNECTION - 365 Days of Abundance Quotes by Entrepreneurs, Business Owners, and Influencers.

Copies of this book may be ordered directly from: https://365daysofresiliencequotes.com

Robert and John invite you to submit a review of this book: https://www.amazon.com/dp/B0DSK5HGYZ

To contact Robert W Jones
E-mail: **robert@inetrepreneurnetwork.com**
Website: https://365daysofresiliencequotes.com/

THE ART OF CONNECTION

365 Days of Abundance Quotes
by Entrepreneurs, Business Owners,
and Influencers

ROBERT W. JONES AND JOHN VERRICO

Dedication

This book is dedicated to my grandparents. For much of my life, I knew them as old people. In many ways, it is odd to think of them as ever being young. As a child, you see the years; you don't see the tears, the fears, the love, and the laughter. They, too, in their own way, left a remarkable imprint on the world. Recently, my wife and I decided to clear out the garage, and as we were deciding to keep and discard items, including old papers in boxes, we discovered one of my mom's boxes. She had items from her youth, and she had some items including photos and handwritten letters from her parents. It struck me how interesting life is; time is the equalizer in everything.

A couple of days later, I visited my Dad. We had our normal conversation. Then he said, "Robert, I want to show you something." He pulled out a photo of my grandmother when she was 17 years old with her boyhood crush, who was 18 years old. How young, how beautiful, how handsome, how endearing. That young man went off to college, then served during WWII, then got married, and retired as an Air Force Colonel. My grandmother was married, worked on a farm, and had kids. And, then years later, a widow and a widower, the two young love birds married.

Isn't that life? As a child, I saw what my grandparents had become, not who they were. The life that they led is more mysterious than anything. I have been so busy in my life that I have never really stopped and seen who they were when they were. That is why I am dedicating this book to my four wonderfully perfect and flawed grandparents, who, like me, lived life in their own special and incredible way. Lives that were once young and vibrant, to ones that became older and wise, lives lived, maybe is the same way that I will be remembered.

Foreword
Art of Connection

Ever since I was a child, I felt a desire to connect to humanity. My mom taught me to look for the good in people and find the qualities that inspire a belief in meliorism. After I read Tom Sawyer, I understood that relationships could change your success and how efficient you can be. After reading 'With the Sharks' by Harvey Mackay, I was influenced to value the importance of relationships in his Mackay 66 questionnaire on connecting with customers.

I have always been in the relationship business. My previous entertainment career was heavily reliant on networking. I owe most of my success to each book I read about communication, relationships, and sales. But, most of all, I give thanks for the multitudes of connections I made through happy customers who connected me to other events, which led to my company's exceptional reputation.

I stepped back from my deejay business when my mother was diagnosed with dementia. My mother's battle inspired me. When she was cognizant, we talked. It became evident that my mother left her legacy to her children. This reality sparked a strong compulsion to find my purpose in life. I opened up a social network, PerfectNetworker.com, when Facebook, LinkedIn, and Twitter were in their infancy. After three years of connecting with some of the best heart-centered leaders in the world, I changed directions. I opened up a media and publishing company.

During my mom's last days, I promised her that I would write a book. A year after she passed, "Becoming the Perfect Networker... Succeeding 1 Connection @ a Time" was published. The social network I created around this book grew to about 12,000 members and was proof that your network is your net worth.

I became known as a national marketing and promotion expert. More accurately, I mastered my skills to serve entrepreneurs while focusing on increasing brand value and providing service. This journey taught me, 'You can have everything in life you want if you will just help other people get what they want' - Zig Ziglar. The bigger you play, the more you will run into the people who are serious about the above philosophy.

During my journey in the national marketplace, I kept hearing about this gentleman, Robert W. Jones, and a crazy project he was doing to highlight heart-centered leaders for every day of the year in a directory titled 'The Art of Connection.' I finally met him at the Military Influencer Conference thanks to our mutual friend, Daniel Faust. After meeting Robert, it became clear to me that he wasn't simply a man with an extraordinary vision but a man who lived his vision.

Now, as I connect to Robert W. Jones and his heart-centered directory, I reflect on my early days of social network endeavors. I am thrilled about how Robert's creation is needed and how it will compound the efforts of everyone within the book and all those who have the fortune to have it in hand. 'The Art of Connection' will increase the chances of successful connections and value for the whole community.

You hold a book that surrounds the idea of 'Abundance' from 365 different perspectives. An abundance mindset allows you to truly enjoy life and serve to your heart's content while knowing God has your back. Robert's accomplishment is a masterpiece of inspiration, wisdom, and leadership in one manuscript created as a guide to positive change in your life, just as the contributors create a positive difference in the world.

To get the most inspiration, I suggest keeping it within reach as a daily mindset optimization tool. When you resonate with a particular author, use their contact information, follow them, and reach out to them. This compilation is a book about connection, a calling card to connect beyond your usual networking circles. Do you have a networking group, radio show, magazine, editorial, podcast, or the like? Do you need a guest? This book was created as a networking resource for you.

Many of my favorite people in the world are in this book: Exceptional leaders, each in their own right. Each contributor will bring a smile, solutions, and value to you and those you serve. "You will be the same person in five years as you are today except for the people you meet and the books you read." - Charlie Tremendous Jones. With the use of this powerful book, 'The Art of Connection,' you can reduce the five years and connect more quickly outside your comfort zone.

I challenge you to participate in this fantastic community unconditionally, then watch your abundance soar along with your attitude, balance, purpose, and zest for life. Happy connecting!

Ken (Dr. Smiley) Rochon, Jr. Ph.D

Acknowledgments

In many ways, 2024 was a breakout year for the Art of Connection book series; we were found by quite a few major brands in the publishing, speaking, and entrepreneurial industries. And with being found, so to speak, I must say that I'm very grateful. Although it is not just me that they appreciate, it is the team of people who have really given support, inspiration, and hard work to make this book a reality. My family is always an important part of helping me get through this book.

I want to acknowledge my mom, Dr. Virginia Correa, who has supported me from behind in this book and book series from day one. She has been a driving force in every way, from taking calls to writing emails, helping authors with quotes, and helping create ideas for author content. It is her dedication that helps many of the heart-centered and like-minded business professionals create words of wisdom in the pages that are offered to the world.

Known as the "Quote Coach," she helped many of the entrepreneur authors create the words that started their pages in this book. Her guidance is found throughout the book through the many people she inspired. She also worked tirelessly to follow up and help me reconcile and tirelessly made phone calls and texts on my behalf.

I also would like to acknowledge the beautiful and wonderful wife, Shawn Renee Jones, who has journeyed with me through now is the 5th book in the Art of Connection series. She has helped with calls, texts, and emails. She is the accountability partner that is needed for success. I told her, "It is hard to believe that it's been half a decade" of creating books that provide inspiration, support, and hope to other entrepreneur authors around the world who are still navigating through the embers of COVID-19.

In 2024, I also attempted something different called The Iron Author, which was a competition that allowed any contributing author of book #5 to become an affiliate and partake in a competition where the winner would be awarded by having their name on the front cover of the book. With this competition, several people contributed amazingly by bringing contributions from around the world from contributors with a variety of backgrounds and occupations.

Mr. John Verrico, the winner of the Iron Author competition and cover coauthor, brought in over 35 contributing authors, creating a fantastic section of people. Without his help, this book would not be as diverse or as deep as the quality of the people I've written about within these pages.

Very Special Thanks!

I would also like to acknowledge Susie Finley; she brought over 30 authors into this book and helped create a diverse and amazing quality that highlights the contributions within it. Lastly, a very special thanks goes out to Marc Beilin, who came in at the end of the competition and contributed nearly 30 authors to the fifth book. John, Susie, and Marc helped me bring this book to the marketplace, and I'm genuinely grateful and thankful for them.

Special Thanks

Special thanks go out to Lori Osborne and Laura Lee Kenny, who arrived late in the Iron Author competition, as well as Ken Rochon, Jr. and Perfect Publishing. Tiffany M. Myles and Christine Kipp, these amazing and wonderful affiliates, also deserve special thanks as they each brought in four or more contributing authors to volume 5 of the Art of Connection book series.

The Book Team

My thanks also go to the book team of Natalie McQueen, my publisher, Buddy Thornton (aka Human AI), my editor, Dan Khuu, our QR Code technologist, and Lori Osborne, our website directory creator, along with Tony Amonetti, who he and I curated the database and system called automanuscript to be able to collect and create a manuscript from the data that we've received from all the authors. It does make it an efficient team to bring such an extensive skill book to the market.

I would also like to thank Sanet Van Breda, Bonnie Lierse, Diana Ringer, Joanne Angel BarryColon, and Laurel Pendle. Our support team, Victor J, our digital specialist, Shawlyn, our amazing phone warrior, and our new team member, Suzanne LaFlamme, since she helped keep much of the communication afloat when I was out of pocket. Lastly, thanks to our special services team: Jennifer Farrar, my author circle community partner, and David Goldberg, our venue partner.

Endorsements

Jana Short - jana@janashort.com
"The Art of Connection: 365 Days of Abundance" is a daily invitation to embrace love and thankfulness. It's a joyful journey, a radiant almanac of positivity, and a testament to the power of abundance. As readers embark on the next 365 days, let this book be the guiding light that fills each day with joy, love, and abundance.

Lesley Klein - lesleyaklein@gmail.com
This book is a great collection of 365 points of Abundance to focus on daily, as well as a NETWORK of people to Connect with from a variety of backgrounds! Robert W. Jones, the creator of the book series, has produced the perfect tool to RAISE your vibration so you can thrive and the perfect resource to NETWORK with high-vibing, Abundance-oriented, Heart-centered people! Pure Brilliance! A winning combination that will ripple out gratitude to the Universe and provide a Connection for those who reach out to the Authors.

Kenneth Hill Jr - kennhilljr@gmail.com
WOW! I'm not much of a reader, but I want to read every page! Whether you start reading from the beginning until the end or pick a random page each day, it isn't easy to put this book down. It is an amazing part of each author's life that makes you want to learn more and more! I will purchase the entire series of "The Art of Connection" so that I don't miss a single gem that this series has to offer. This is a "must-have" for your library!

Suzanne LaFlamme - slaflamme1@gmail.com
"The Art of Connection: 365 Days of Abundance" is not just a collection of quotes from random people. It features quotes from amazing business owners, entrepreneurs, and influencers sharing their profound insights about life, business, and people. Each page offers hope, inspiration, and support not only to business professionals but to people from all walks of life. I am grateful to be a part of this book as I was able to dedicate a page to my mother (November 22nd), who passed away a year and a half ago. It is very uplifting to be able to share the wonderful experiences I learned from my mother and get to share them with everyone else in the world! Every time I read through the book, I've learned from many talented individuals about what they are grateful for, making it a truly uplifting experience! This is a book I highly recommend you buy! You will get inspiration 365 days of the year!

The Art of Connection

Table of Contents

Name	Page	Name	Page
SueZee Finley	1	Michael Fritzius	29
Laurel Pendle	2	Doug Giesler	30
Raveen Arora	3	Pamela Scott	31
Nikki Barrett	4	Candy Motzek	32
Vicky Melendez	5	Joellyn Wlazlowski Martin	33
Lauren Mazzoleni	6	Becca Heissel	34
David Doerrier	7	Bonnie Verrico	35
Maggie Bellevue	8	Rich Parsons	36
Jessica Moody	9	Kenneth Hill Jr	37
Lilia Bogoeva	10	Jay Abraham	38
Patricia Anderson	11	Marilyn Richards	39
Laura Lee Kenny	12	Christine Hiebel	40
Mike Raber	13	Rachel Harrison	41
Tara Pilling	14	Kathleen Edinger	42
Nina V Garza	15	Teresa Cundiff	43
Janet Vigil	16	Sherry Gideons	44
Virginia Oman	17	J. Robert Santana	45
Bonnie Zaruches Lierse	18	Ashley L. Whitlock	46
Jenn Haston	19	Lloyd Heath	47
Carol Koppelman	20	Mika Cross	48
Anthony Trucks	21	Nefertiti San Miguel	49
Alyse Rynor	22	Jacquelin Kenny	50
Preston Weekes	23	DJ Barton	51
Diana Hooker	24	Katherine Kim Mullin	52
Jennifer Capaldo	25	Zabdy Love	53
Anne Mayer	26	Katie Evans	54
Ira Koretsky	27	Marla Press	55
Michael Lang	28	Catryn Becker	56

Michelle Snyder	57	Grace Gwitira	88
Laurissa Krishock	58	Joseph Chipokosa	89
Denise Meridith	59	Ella Pahopin	90
Traicey Finder	60	Jamie Rapkiewcz	91
Lori Osborne	61	Vanessa Abraham	92
David Waltzer	62	Regina Spencer	93
Gene-o Cole	63	Michelle Carlen	94
Ezinne Ozurumba	64	Kenyatta Turner	95
Sarren Scribner	65	Jesse Orlando	96
Yanick Séïde	66	Melissa Geracimos	97
Patty Hedrick	67	Cynthia Beckles	98
Michael Noyes	68	Sal Cavaliere	99
Rani Thanacoody	69	Rahul K. Maharaj	100
Vickie Gowdy	70	Joy Beck	101
Joe Lander	71	Lisa van Roode	102
Joanne Salvador	72	Maureen Ranks	103
Maria Mantoudakis	73	Lisa E. Gongaware	104
Caroline Passmore	74	Suzanne Söderberg	105
Christine Kipp	75	Eric Ranks	106
Kelly Hull Aho	76	Anyssa Figueroa	107
Soojin Kim	77	Marion Hill	108
Heather Eileen Harris	78	Tammy DeMirza Lawing	109
Carla Jansen van Rosendaal	79	Brian Hawkins	110
Angelika O'Rourke	80	Christa Rose	111
Brian Swanson	81	Cindy Edington	112
Scott Allan	82	Denzel Smalls	113
Theresa Russell	83	Miles Murdocca	114
Glenda Roberts	84	Nicola Smith	115
Tonya Swainston	85	Jeff Villwock	116
Paul Weigel	86	Denise Ackerman	117
Rani Thanacoody	87	David Brinker	118

Chris Coraggio	119	Brenda Thanacoody	150
Ann Brennan	120	Barb Markey	151
Karen Trapane	121	Kathleen Carlson	152
Lori Osborne	122	TonniLea Larson	153
Carrie Mosley	123	Holly Enzmann	154
Jessica Jorgensen	124	Michelle Gass	155
Robert W. Jones	125	Roy Moore	156
Joseph Fang	126	Becky Norwood	157
Christina Christy Kruse	127	Tres Chapman	158
Andrew Elliman	128	Bobbi Wilcox	159
Lila Bakke	129	K.M. Ringer	160
Drina Fried	130	Jodie Santandrea-Ruano	161
Marylou Leonard	131	Todd Lingel	162
Ken Greene	132	Kevin McDonald	163
Mary Zennett	133	Wendy B King	164
Nancy Nance	134	Kenny Rochon	165
Barbara Goodman	135	Ken Rochon, Jr.	166
Amy D. Spring	136	James Edinger	167
Yvonne E. Gamble	137	Andreea Parc	168
Tricia Parido	138	Craig Darling	169
Maria Matias	139	Shannon Morrison	170
Brenda Kilhoffer	140	Melody Vachal	171
Jim Connors	141	Mary Van Alstyne	172
Vincent Leonti	142	Joseph Blake, Jr	173
Monika Jakubiak	143	Barbara Hazelden	174
Howard Brown	144	Jennie James	175
Kevin Mayer	145	Brent Kesler	176
Karsten Alva-Jorgensen	146	Amber Golden	177
Edie Sangiorgio	147	Regina La France	178
Hannah Kesler	148	Deidre Lopez	179
LaDonna McAbee	149	Larry Linton	180

Name	Page	Name	Page
Daniel Pedemonte	181	Daniel Knight	212
Jeffrey Morris	182	Shawna James	213
Ginny Correa-Creager	183	Erica Crouch	214
Cowboy Joe Marques	184	Jennifer Miller	215
John Verrico	185	Caroline Biesalski	216
Julie D'Ann	186	Leann Coakley	217
LaBarbara Dhaliwal	187	David Knepp	218
Brett Cotter	188	Lydia G. Fougères	219
Jennifer Farrar	189	Andy Tanner	220
Tawni Acosta	190	Mary Gaul	221
Sam Knickerbocker	191	Tricia Livermore	222
J. Lumen	192	Sanet Van Breda	223
Suzi Freeman	193	Naheed Oberfeld	224
Becky Estby	194	Kristin Hannum	225
Corina Blake	195	Susan Flerchinger	226
Naheed Oberfeld	196	Mary E. Knippel	227
Yousef Qabazard	197	Rachael Hudson	228
Ophir Adar	198	Radavie Riom	229
Daniel Simon	199	Ching Fong Sin	230
Troy Hipolito	200	Jaclyn Zoccoli	231
Laura Ballet	201	Audrey Kerger	232
Elisabeth Garner	202	Therese Johnson	233
Natalie McQueen	203	Mary J Robinson	234
Shirley Turner	204	Wesley Swainston	235
Linda Mac Dougall	205	Greg Goddard	236
Jana Short	206	Tanner Seehausen	237
Rebecca Babcock	207	Sherry Anshara	238
Doris Lum	208	Nicola Smith	239
Sylvia Baffour	209	Rabea Katharina Stenger	240
Debbie Steagall	210	Clifford Starks	241
Sarah Clark	211	Althea Samuels	242

Kara Atkinson	243	Gina Matteson	274		
Pat Young	244	Buddy Thornton	275		
Ira Rosen	245	Colleen Strube	276		
Kylah Waits	246	Robert Enzmann	277		
Laura Piel	247	Ophir Adar	278		
Annie Deckert	248	Mayra Hawkins	279		
Crystal D. Turner-Moffatt	249	Melissa Geracimos	280		
Uchenna Faumuina-Eze	250	J. Robert Santana	281		
Tina Koopersmith	251	Diana Hooker	282		
Daniel Pedemonte	252	Dana Schon	283		
Maurice Montoya	253	Georgette Combs	284		
Maris Segal	254	Jeff Marconette Jr.	285		
Robert Thornton	255	Tammy DeMirza Lawing	286		
Char McCreadie	256	Ken Ashby	287		
Mattie Murrey	257	Suzanne LaFlamme	288		
Rizah Valdez	258	Mishianand Mack	289		
Ayden VanWie-Hameria	259	Michelle Mras	290		
Stuart Gethner	260	Laura Lee Kenny	291		
Kimberly Lechnick	261	Chris Naugle	292		
Leonard DeCarmine	262	Nathan Keller	293		
Fernando Sanchez	263	Lauren Miller	294		
Annette Dernick	264	Diana Ringer	295		
Myra Murphy	265	Alex Vitillo	296		
Deborah Kym	266	Joanne Angel BarryColon	297		
Nathalie Botros	267	Lana Stevenson	298		
Nico Stringfellow	268	Sherlyn Halloran	299		
Satie Narain-Simon	269	Lesley Klein	300		
Kathi Hall	270	Ro Gonzalez	301		
Doug Giesler	271	Karla Garjaka	302		
Debra Lee Murrow	272	Heather Orlando	303		
Gabriella Kipp	273	SueZee Finley	304		

SueZee Finley	305
Andrew Paul Skoog	306
Wendy Sellers	307
Hank Longo	308
Niurka Castaneda	309
Julie Jones	310
Art Blanchford	311
Nancy Itokazu	312
Sofia Pinky Magana	313
Shad Hardy	314
Laci Waddill	315
Holly Berry	316
Laura Cobb	317
Bethany Newell	318
Nyasha Hulse	319
Ruth Dorsainville-Hulse	320
Bruce Hulse	321
Kimberly Yvonne Humphreys	322
Yvonne Schimmel	323
John Verrico	324
Tammy Workman-Lopez	325
Martina Wagner	326
Lynn Banis	327
Lady Jen Du Plessis	328
David Doerrier	329
Mamie-Jean Lamley	330
David Goldberg	331
Brent Goddard	332
Marlaina Williams	333
Nancy Sievert	334
Emmeline Saavedra	335
Geri Geasland	336
Susan Kerby	337
Roy Moore	338
Carrie Van Amburgh	339
Marc Beilin	340
Daniel Faust	341
Leslie Kuntz	342
Beth Robins	343
Britton Murrey	344
Karen Clark-Reddon	345
Tiffany M. Myles	346
Angel Marie Monachelli	347
Maureen Poirier	348
Alejandro Lopez Hernandez	349
Lucie Rosa-Stagi	350
Christopher Arnold	351
Mary Gilbert	352
Ericka Avila	353
Joan Patterson	354
Nicola Smith	355
Caydence Wong	356
Daniel Schneider	357
Phyl Franklin	358
Shawn Jones	359
Adrianne Size	360
Rutherford Pascal	361
Courtney Brown	362
Stephen Turner	363
Allison Hammond	364
Amethyst Kinney	365

January 1
SUEZEE FINLEY

Just Hit Play!

THOUGHT

You were born with an abundance of gifts, talents, and, oh yes, magic! In fact, a NASA study on original creativity found that 98 percent of four to five-year-olds scored at the "genius level" of imagination; by the age of fifteen, twelve percent and adults come in at just two percent.

When I was a kid, I loved Gene Kelly and would sing and dance in the rain (yes, I am that old!). I believed my heart held magical music inside that played when I tapped on it as golden light, stars, and music notes swirled around me.

I held that childlike wonder well into my forties, but like many, I fell prey to stress and, later on, illness and thought "my music" was gone forever—

But magic has a way of finding its way back.

Through sound therapy, I discovered my path home.

During my first session, a wave of energy washed over me, from head to toe, and as I drifted into that space between waking and dreams, I saw them again - the lights, the musical notes, dancing just as they had in my childhood. Then came a gentle whisper, "Your music is always inside you; all you have to do is Just Hit Play!"

The genius, the magic, the creativity - it never leaves. It's waiting there for you to Just Hit Play!

QUESTION

What is your magic, and do you allow yourself to access it? If not, what do you believe stopped it, and what steps can you take today to help bring it back? Are you ready to Just Hit Play?

AUTHOR CONTACT INFORMATION

SueZee Finley, Founder of Acoustic Therapeutix
Website: https://acoustictherapeutix.com/
Email: suezeequest@gmail.com
Social: https://www.linkedin.com/in/suezeefinley/
Tags: Author, Speaker, Sound Therapy, Happiness, Retreats

January 2
LAUREL PENDLE

*True abundance is not just about wealth but
the richness of purpose, compassion,
and generosity that flows through our lives.*

THOUGHT

Abundance is more than material wealth; it encompasses a profound sense of purpose, passion, and unwavering generosity that adds richness to our journey. When we embrace abundance as our "north star," we unlock a mindset where success isn't solely measured by financial gains but by the enrichment of our endeavors and the lives we touch.

In business, an abundance mindset fosters innovation and resilience. Organizations can thrive when they operate from a belief in limitless opportunities for growth and collaboration. A leader guided by this philosophy sees challenges as stepping stones for growth, turning setbacks into breakthroughs.

Personally, embracing abundance means recognizing that fulfillment comes from more than material possessions. It's about faith, love, living with intention, pursuing passions, and nurturing meaningful relationships. When we prioritize purpose and abundance, we feel a greater sense of fulfillment that transcends superficial measures of success. Having a heart-centered approach becomes a natural outpouring of abundance. Giving back to others and making a positive impact in the world is what life is all about!

QUESTION

What role does a mindset of abundance play in your decision-making and business growth?

AUTHOR CONTACT INFORMATION

Laurel Pendle, Founder/ Owner of LPBC Services LLC
Website: https://laurelpendle.com
Email: Laurel@LaurelPendle.com
Social: https://www.linkedin.com/in/laurelpendle
Tags: Business Coach, Purpose-driven business, Author

January 3
RAVEEN ARORA

True abundance is not measured by what we possess but by our ability to ensure that every member of our family has a place to call home.

THOUGHT

I think Abundance is a State of Mind, Heart, and Soul. Truly, it's about internal fulfillment and gratitude for what we have, not about hunger and greed for more. Abundance is a mental gathering of all we are, who we know and cherish, and the intertwined memories of a lifetime. All of what we perceive about abundance is tied to our past and is a treasure, not a pursuit.

True abundance is about sharing your material and spiritual wealth with those who need help and lack the resources despite doing their best.
My abundant worldview should include my ability to share unconditionally, with no reservations, and every sharing will increase my sense of abundance. Can we feel blessed if we allow those with less to suffer the indignity of being left behind when we can uplift them in every way, especially family?

QUESTION

Where do you draw a fulfillment line between Material Abundance | (Think The Story of Midas) and Spiritual Abundance?

AUTHOR CONTACT INFORMATION

Raveen Arora, Founder of Think Human
Website: https://thinkhuman.us
Email: arora.raveen@gmail.com
Social: LinkedIn.com/in/raveen-arora
Tags: speaker, author, humanitarian

January 4
NIKKI BARRETT

Live your when NOW! "When" may never come, but there's a NOW opportunity in every moment.

THOUGHT

Have you ever had a dream? Not just a dream, but, a dream? One that fueled your hopes and secured the vision of your future. I have! It started in 1991 with a trip to NC that somehow ended up in TN, where it all began. There were mountains with log cabins lining the lake surrounded by beautiful pine trees in a picturesque setting that captured the life; at least for us, it did. For 30 years, we kept that dream alive and watered it by driving from MD, where we lived, to TN every single year. In 2019, we went fourteen times! When the craziness of 2020 came, we rented space at a gated RV community on Douglas Lake and got a little bit closer.

In 2021, we made the move, sold the MD home, drove out of the driveway for the last time, and became full-fledged Tennesseans. Why, you ask, did it take 30 years? Because when always got in the way. When the kids grow up, when the economy changes, when the bills are paid, when we retire, etc. Nine months later, my husband, the love of my life for 31 years, died in my arms. The dream was over before it even began. So today, I say to anyone with ears to listen with a dream of whatever kind, never to let when get in the way of living your dreams, now!

QUESTION

If not now, then when and is it worth the wait if when never comes?

AUTHOR CONTACT INFORMATION

Nikki Barrett, Owner of Nikki M. Barrett, LLC
Website: nikkimbarrett.com
Email: nikkibarrettntp@gmail.com
Social: https://www.facebook.com/nikkibarrettntp
Tags: Author, Speaker, Intuitive Life Design Consultant

January 5
VICKY MELENDEZ

May a deluge of abundance, victory, and joy wash away the inertia, lack, and unhappiness of your former self to enjoy an amazing life!

THOUGHT

In May 2021, I was in the emergency room. Doctors said, "We can't feel her pulse," "Blood pressure is too low," and "Fever is almost 105 degrees." I couldn't breathe and was in and out of consciousness. I was hooked up to machines and received large doses of medicines to combat COVID-19, double pneumonia, and sepsis. Doctors could not assure me I would be okay.

My life was at stake. In my hospital room, I realized I lived my life in inertia. It took my soul and health to a dangerous place. My 36-year marriage had been broken for decades; I was no longer fulfilled with my corporate job, and I put everyone and everything before taking care of myself.

I pivoted and am now single, a certified life coach, and am pursuing real estate investing. My two grandchildren are teaching me to live joyfully. My broken heart is being restored with love and joy. My broken body is healing as I eat correctly, exercise, and rest. Past trauma is being mended, and my Lord Jesus is leading me in all things!

I feel victorious! I'm smiling again, experiencing joy in my spirit, and living in an abundant mindset. As I improve my well-being, my internal reservoir increases, and I am creating overflow!

QUESTION

What three actions can you take to create abundance in your relationship, career, and health? What negative mindsets can you remove? How do you embrace wealth, plentifulness, and prosperity?

AUTHOR CONTACT INFORMATION

icky Melendez, Founder of Ten K Properties, LLC
Website: https://www.365daysofabundancequotes.com
Email: vemele66@gmail.com
Social: https://www.facebook.com/vicky.leon.71?mibextid=LQQJ4d
Tags: Life Coach, Real Estate Investing

January 6
LAUREN MAZZOLENI

Focus on the glimmers each day, which are small moments that trigger feelings of joy, calm, and safety.

THOUGHT

I can think of a lot of times in my life when I struggled with my mental health. Sometimes, my mental health was impacted by relationships, trauma, work, school, and, well, life. In those dark times, I used my mind to push through those challenging moments. I am a big fan of EFT (Emotional Freedom Technique), reiki, Tai Chi, and visualization.

Trust me, rewiring deeply rooted thoughts isn't an overnight practice. It takes a lot of patience and practice to overcome limited beliefs and see the light in a dark tunnel. Be gentle with yourself. Doing the inner work is hard, but it's worth it. It pays off in life and business.

I've learned how important it is to take care of yourself in and out of the busy entrepreneurial world. The best investment you can make is in yourself.

I'm grateful for the people who have taught me self-compassion and self-love, which were foreign concepts to me prior to my healing and breaking the cycle of abuse.

Even at my lowest points in life, I found a huge glimmer in helping someone else struggling and providing them with the right tools to get them through. I hope this excerpt touches someone positively. You're never alone.

QUESTION

What are your glimmers?

AUTHOR CONTACT INFORMATION

Lauren Mazzoleni, Founder/Owner of HolisticFit Branding
Website: https://www.holisticfitbranding.com
Email: lauren@holisticfitbranding.com
Social: https://www.linkedin.com/in/laurenmazzoleni
Tags: branding, health, fitness, sports

January 7
DAVID DOERRIER

Talking and Telling ain't Training or Selling

THOUGHT

Despite my unwavering commitment and tireless efforts, my training results were not meeting the mark. I was renowned for my meticulous presentations and comprehensive explanations, but I sensed a missing element.

Then, a profound realization dawned on me: "Talking and telling ain't training or selling." This self-made quote sparked a transformation in my career, leading me to explore its essence and apply its wisdom.

I discovered that effective training is not just about imparting knowledge; it's about fostering active engagement. I initiated every interaction by actively listening, asking questions, and genuinely trying to comprehend their specific concerns. This discovery allowed me to tailor my presentations and pitches to meet their unique needs. It's not just about what I can offer but about what they truly need.

As I embraced these insights, my career flourished, and my training sessions became highly sought after. I found abundance not just in professional success but in the fulfillment that came from engaging, understanding, and connecting with others. My journey became a testament to the power of genuine communication, inspiring others to follow in my footsteps.

QUESTION

Can you recall a time when simply conveying information wasn't enough to achieve your goals? How did you handle it?

AUTHOR CONTACT INFORMATION

David Doerrier, Founder of Present Your Way To Success
Website: https://presentyourwaytosuccess.com/
Email: david@pywtsuccess.com
Social: https://www.linkedin.com/in/daviddoerrier/
Tags: Confidence, Brave, Public Speaking, Engagement

January 8

MAGGIE BELLEVUE

*To arrive at your oasis of abundance,
you will have to pursue your life purpose with single-minded intent.*

THOUGHT

Vital as the pursuit of purpose is, most of us are just not deliberate enough to dig deep for those genuine yearnings of our heart that come wrapped as the beautiful package called purpose. It is critical to pause and take stock instead of spending our entire lives jumping from one unfulfilling venture to the next. Finding your true life purpose is such a critical mission because it is your only guaranteed path to happiness and contentment.

Your life purpose allows you to contribute to the continuing evolution of humankind and to receive worthy compensation in return. Allied to your purpose are your core values in each area of your life. To live with purpose is to live with intention. "Living intentionally" means you have a plan, and so you intentionally allow your values to guide you as you set goals for your life.

There is always intention behind any activity. Even the commonplace act of breathing is for the physiologic intent to live. Your purpose is not under the obligation of being your cash cow. The ultimate motivation is not always fortune or fame. Sometimes, it is merely the exultation and independence of your spirit.

QUESTION

What is the major definite purpose for your existence?

AUTHOR CONTACT INFORMATION

Maggie Bellevue, CEO of Treasures International
Website: www.Maggiebellevue.com
Email: bellevuemaggie@gmail.com
Social: https://www.facebook.com/Maggiebellevue?mibextid=LQQJ4d
Tags: Speaker

January 9
JESSICA MOODY

Abundance comes from the value you provide, not the qualities you have.

THOUGHT

The focus on manifesting success has created confusion in the entrepreneurial world. It is said that if you tell yourself you have abundance, you will have abundance. Many say that you don't have abundance because you don't believe it. The gurus want you to state daily affirmations like, "My wealth grows every day" before it will come true.

While it's true that people who are stuck in self-doubt may hesitate to take risks to build their businesses, abundance is an outward response to work, investment, and growth. Think about someone who has a garden. They want it to grow and flourish, so they sit in the house imagining a fruitful garden and proclaiming that it will grow. That person could do this for years, and yet there will never be a garden, growth, or the abundance that comes from the hard work of getting dirty in that garden. Belief in abundance is awesome, but it's fruitless without real work, which is difficult and time-consuming. Truthfully, gardeners don't need to tell themselves that they will be fruitful; their hard work proves that they are fruitful. Abundance comes from the hard work of providing value, not just saying you are valuable.

QUESTION

How do your hard work and dedication lead to your opportunity for abundance?

AUTHOR CONTACT INFORMATION

Jessica Moody, Educational Consultant of Entrepreneur Educators
Website: https://jessicalmoody.com
Email: hello@jessicalmoody.com
Social: https://mybook.to/artofconnection5
Tags: Educational Consultant, Instructional Designer

January 10

LILIA BOGOEVA

Crush Inner Demons; Live In Freedom!

THOUGHT

The struggle within is a tale as old as time. But how can we crush inner demons and win freedom? There's no one formula, but here's a powerful battle plan:

1. Know thy enemy - Observe the damage those inner demons cause, notice how they do it, and catch them red-handed in your natural habitat.

2. Face the enemy - Avoiding inner demons will only feed them until they get all the power. That sucks- you need the power! Show those mental monsters you're not afraid!

3. Plan your attack - Inner demons are strong and clever; however, you can outsmart and overpower them with a solid strategy, powerful weapons, and the courage to fight for yourself!

4. Work smart - you have what it takes, but it will take everything you have. Strategize on when to fight, recharge your batteries, and find new resources. It takes strength, endurance, and flexibility to emerge victorious!

5. Embrace mistakes - Two wrongs don't make a right, but 2,000 wrongs can make everything right. I did all sorts of wrong in my inner demon battles to find what works and what doesn't.

6. Go, Fight, Win! - Fail and restart from experience. Fine-tune your battle plan, sharpen your weapons, and slay those inner demons with no regrets!

QUESTION

How will you crush your inner demons?

AUTHOR CONTACT INFORMATION

Lilia Bogoeva, Multi-Media Artist & Empowerment Coach of Lilia The Inner Demon Crusher

Website: https://www.liliademoncrusher.com/

Email: info@liliademoncrusher.com

Social: https://www.youtube.com/@LiliaTheInnerDemonCrusher

Tags: empowerment coach, multi-media artist

January 11
PATRICIA ANDERSON

*If I walk all the way through this lesson,
I will receive permanent healing.
Abundance comes from finishing lessons.*

THOUGHT

I watched my father die when I was eight. I was sensitive to every physical and emotional pain he felt as he died. I felt my mother's pain and terror as she tried to save him. I was aware of my brother's bravery, pain, and quiet strength. I knew my father was going where I couldn't. I could feel the panic that he was going to be where I could not help. At some point, I couldn't feel anymore.

As we followed the ambulance, I felt a tidal wave of emotions come flooding out, and I couldn't stop them. I was crying uncontrollably. It was too much for my mother. She needed me to stop. I didn't know how. I felt shame because no one else was crying. I felt broken and unable to stop my intense feelings.

Days afterward, I watched them. Eventually, I decided she was right. I didn't need to feel it all. I would learn to stop feeling. At 30, being numb through alcohol and drugs stopped working. I was afraid the ocean of hidden emotions would drown me, but I read the counselor my "goodbye letter" to my father. I saw the vivid image of my father on the floor begin to fade. The mental sirens stopped. The pain began to subside. I felt it all the way through. I was free. I never had flashbacks again.

QUESTION

Are you willing to go to any length to be free from your suffering and receive your abundance?

AUTHOR CONTACT INFORMATION

Patricia Anderson, Owner of Patricia Anderson
Website: https://www.awaken-heal-inspire.com
Email: 0ameth00@gmail.com
Social: https://www.facebook.com/patricia.anderson.543/
Tags: Naam Yoga Therapist, Coach, Healing Facilitator

January 12
LAURA LEE KENNY

Time is your most significant factor in building financial security, so what money you keep and invest is more important than your annual income.

THOUGHT

Abundance means having more than I need, with plenty to share with others. We all know that abundance starts with gratitude for what we have, and most of us strive for Health, Relationships, and Money in this order. Like building a house without a strong foundation first, it won't be strong enough to survive Mother Nature's wrath.

Now, as a Baby Boomer and number three of twelve children, our family knew what it was like to do without at times. We definitely learned to appreciate what we got.

One of my greatest pleasures in life was being a Certified Financial Planner for over 20+ years, guiding my clients to reach their financial goals and securing a nest egg for retirement while giving them peace of mind during challenging times.

Nearly 70 percent of our results come from a focused, positive mindset, defined goals, and following your blueprint.

Now, as a Money Mindset Mentor, I'm on a mission to guide clients to make better choices, step into their Power, and Take Control of their lives and finances, even if they have struggled their whole lives with debt and fear! We are all meant to be abundant. Let's connect!

QUESTION

*Since your success is absolutely guaranteed,
"What would you really love to Be, Do, and Have"?*

AUTHOR CONTACT INFORMATION

Laura Lee Kenny, CEO of Blue Diamond Club LLC
Website: https://LauraLeeKenny.net
Email: Support@LauraLeeKenny.net
Social: Https://linktr.ee/LauraLeeExpert
Tags: Podcaster, Money Mindset & Literacy, Author

January 13
MIKE RABER

*By ourselves, we can do amazing things,
yet together, we can climb the highest mountain.*

THOUGHT

Are you living a life of abundance? I've found that when we proclaim our intentions around what we want and see it as already done, it will be given to us: A parking spot in front of where we are headed, someone offering to help without being asked, or something needed showing up at the right time. Or do you follow the mindset of, "I'll believe it when I see it?" Scarcity vs. abundance thinking.

I've spent the previous five years working on a vision I had, making what felt like very little progress. The vision gave me the action steps to build a community of 100 million people. However, I couldn't see the end game. Then, one night, I had a dream that woke me up in a cold sweat. The end game was clear as day, and I had absolute belief it was as good as done. I went to work on solving what I still didn't fully understand. Over the next seven months, everything needed to bring it into reality revealed itself.

Imagine a 24-hour-long concert covering 24 time zones, spanning 146 countries and 100 different youth ensembles performing in their native language and culture in the name of peace, with a request to pause for one hour and to meditate in prayer or enjoy the music. Join us.

QUESTION

Would you please sign the appeal showing your support for a 24-hour pause of peace? If you had a magic wand, and anything was possible, what would you breathe into existence?

AUTHOR CONTACT INFORMATION

Mike Raber, CEO / Founder of 100 Million Strong SPC
Website: www.100millionstrongspc.com
Email: MIKE@100MILLIONSTRONGSPC.COM
Social: https://www.facebook.com/onehundredmillionstrongspc
Tags: Pauseforpeace, Speaker, Businesscoach, 24hourpfp.com

The Art of Connection

January 14

TARA PILLING

*Real change is an inside job; get the inside right,
and the world will follow. Expect miracles along the way!*

THOUGHT

If there are aspects of your life you're unhappy with, change them! Real change begins within. The outside world reflects your internal state. Align your innermost thoughts, feelings, and actions, and everything improves. A life focused on betterment is fulfilling. Many people remain controlled by their programming—genetic, environmental, or circumstantial—becoming victims of these influences. I call this a "hell realm," a condition we've been programmed into. However, with daily reflection and mentorship, anyone can change. As my mentor Bob Proctor says, "Change is inevitable; personal growth is a choice." You have the power to choose! As spiritual beings, we are here to grow, expand, and express our true essence. You are designed to lead your life and to love every part of it. Real change does come from within. Is it easy? Some days, no. But it's possible, and it paves the way for a life of purpose and potential. You are the victor of your life, here to serve the good, for God, for love. Remember, everything contains both good and bad; what you focus on is up to you. Your focus and choices will determine what grows. It truly is an inside job.

QUESTION

Let your spirit express itself through you. Grow! Express! Are you ready to take the lead in your life? Are you ready to move towards those big goals and dreams and be the leader you're looking for?

AUTHOR CONTACT INFORMATION

Tara Pilling, Chief Manifestation & Mindset Success Consultant of Diamond Mind Consulting

Website: https://www.diamondmindconsulting.ca

Email: tara@diamondmindconsulting.ca

Social: https://www.instagram.com/tarapillingdiamondmind

Tags: Proctor, Gallagher, Certified Consultant

January 15

NINA V GARZA

Abundance, like a multifaceted diamond, shines in many forms: wealth, health, relationships, love, spirituality, and more.

THOUGHT

According to the Cambridge Dictionary, abundance is defined as a situation where there is more than enough of something. Often, when we speak about abundance, we refer to financial wealth and the freedom it brings. However, this is only one facet of abundance. Many people confuse abundance with prosperity. While they are different, they work together to create a "wealth consciousness." This mindset helps attract abundance, leading to prosperity in all areas of life—physical, emotional, mental, and spiritual.

Spiritually, abundance goes beyond money. Once our basic needs are met, abundance means appreciating life while feeling joy, strength, and balance in mind, body, and soul. It's about trusting that life, or a higher power, provides what we need. The universe itself is abundant and continually expanding. Recognizing this can help you attract wealth and prosperity, bringing positive change to your life.

QUESTION

Are you happy with your life? How do you envision abundance in your life? Is it through spiritual growth, vivid health, or financial prosperity?

AUTHOR CONTACT INFORMATION

Nina V Garza, Owner of Inner Light Discovery LLC
Website: https://ninavgarza.com
Email: nina@ninavgarza.com
Social: https://instagram.com/ninavgarzaofficial
Tags: Inner Light, Spiritual Healing, Dowsing

January 16

JANET VIGIL

We are rich beyond measure. We are all trust fund babies, each of us heirs to this miraculous abundance called Life.

THOUGHT

As a Doctor of Acupuncture, I'm reminded of the body's extraordinary abundance: a miracle that humbles and amazes me with each patient I see. We are born trust fund babies, granted an inheritance of potential regardless of our life circumstances. Within this body, hundreds of billions of cells regenerate each day, creating a cycle of renewal that extends from our skin to our liver, bones, and brains. Within each cell, a whole universe is at work! Mitochondria churn out energy, ribosomes make proteins, and a myriad of networks provide structure and communication. Every minute, millions of cells die and are replaced in a brilliant, self-sustaining system. At the subcellular level, neurons fire at lightning speed, electrical and biochemical signals cascade, and magnetic pulses align to create the flow of information and energy. This bounty enables resilience, healing, and connection and reminds me that life isn't happening to me; it's happening for me and through me. The way I see it, we don't create our lives but are rather trustees of them. This inheritance of life's abundance, meant to be treasured and shared, invites us to honor the gift of existence and be grateful for everything.

QUESTION

Life invested everything in bringing you here—billions of cells, countless systems, infinite potential. How are you choosing to manage and grow this sacred inheritance?

AUTHOR CONTACT INFORMATION

Janet Vigil, Doctor of Acupuncture & Asian Medicine of Mountain Goat Acupuncture
Website: https://www.mountaingoatacupuncture.com/
Email: mountaingoatacu@gmail.com
Social: https://www.instagram.com/mountaingoatacu/
Tags: Acupuncturist, Herbalist, Coach, Wellness Expert

January 17

VIRGINIA OMAN

*Abundance has very little, if anything,
to do with money.
True abundance has to do with health and joy.*

THOUGHT

When most people see the word "abundance," they think of money or things purchased with money. I can tell you that in my 70-plus years of living on this planet, I have learned a very valuable fact I wish I had fully comprehended much earlier in my life. Abundance has very little, if anything, to do with money. True abundance has to do with health and joy.

We are given this one chance at life, and it goes by very quickly. Therefore, we should do all we can to make it the best quality of an experience we can. Take care of your health, as good health leads to happiness and the ability to live a fulfilling life. Seek out what brings you joy, spark, and a sense of contentment. Then, make sure your life is filled with those things on a regular basis. A great way to start getting a sense of what abundance is: focus on what you are grateful for. Focus on what you can give to others, not on what you want to receive. We are all put on this planet to take care of each other in peace, love, and compassion. Be peace. Be love and be compassion. If you live with this as your focus, the true essence of abundance will always be yours.

QUESTION

*What activities bring you joy and fulfillment,
and how often do you do these activities? What small steps can you start to implement in your life to bring you more health and joy every day?*

AUTHOR CONTACT INFORMATION

Virginia Oman, Owner, Founder of Virginia Oman - LCMHC, Transformational Coach

Website: https://virginiaoman.com/

Email: contact@virginiaoman.com

Social: https://linktr.ee/virginiaoman

Tags: virginiaoman, transformationalcoach, wellnessmaster

January 18

BONNIE ZARUCHES LIERSE

There are generations of God's unborn children whose lives can be shaped by the moves you make, the things you say, and the actions you take forever!

THOUGHT

Abundance of love and make better choices. I have six precious grandkids, from one to thirteen, that I love and adore more than life itself. When I look into their soulful eyes and beautiful faces, I wonder at this. Parents and role models will impact kids more than someone else's words as long as the child respects and understands what the parents or role models are saying.

Know that teachers, mentors, and coaches can have an impact on your children. Young children, especially toddlers, duplicate what others say. Be aware of who they are mimicking, funny or not.

Know the sources from which it comes. It is okay to ask the child where it came from. I deeply realize how innocent kids are, including mine, who are grown. They are exceptional parents themselves. We have to think twice about the words we choose, decisions & choices we make. Listen well! I'm always working on that myself. Please know how vulnerable our kids are today and be conscious of how everything is impacting them. They are listening to what everyone says, even though their parents or role models would not align with that person. Kids and toddlers take everything to heart. Protect their precious minds & hearts.

QUESTION

Are you willing to reevaluate how you express yourself to your children through words and actions?

AUTHOR CONTACT INFORMATION

Bonnie Zaruches Lierse, Real Estate Agent of Pearson Smith Realty
Website: http://pearsonsmithrealty.com/agent/bonnie-lierse
Email: blierse@gmail.com
Social: http://linkedin.com/in/bonnie-zaruches-lierse-b9767111
Tags: Real Estate Agent Northern VA

January 19
JENN HASTON

Rest Is A Right. It Is NOT Something You Earn!

THOUGHT

Did you know that last year, 46 percent of Americans did not take their earned vacation time? It's not hard to understand, given our culture of hustle and grind, and let's meet that bottom line. Picture this. You are in a meeting with your boss, and they can tell you look tired, and you say, "Oh no, I am fine; I have this project/product/launch/deliverable I need to finish," and then You think to yourself, of course, I plan to rest. Still, I must meet this deadline first, then I will rest.

But then what happens? You go to the next thing, and the vicious cycle starts all over again. It's kind of like saying you will budget for savings at the end of the month when there is money left over, and you know what happens? You never find more money, just like you never find rest. You have to be intentional about scheduling your rest. I realize there are times when you can't make the time, so get ahead of it. Be intentional and put time on the calendar to "rest." Rest Is A Right. When you make the time to put yourself first, you are rejuvenated; you approach all your interactions with fresh eyes and a brand-new perspective. Think About It. Then Do It.

QUESTION

Life will undoubtedly get in the way. But what can you do today, right now as you read this, to plan rest for yourself? Take a moment, schedule it, and make it as non-negotiable as any other priority.

AUTHOR CONTACT INFORMATION

Jenn Haston, Founder of Haston Helping Hands
Website: www.hastonhelpinghands.com
Email: thebossofbalance@gmail.com
Social: https://www.instagram.com/thebossofbalance/
Tags: Speaker, Facilitator, Author, Content Creator

January 20

CAROL KOPPELMAN

If you live in an abundance mentality, even through challenging times, the road becomes clear, and your connection with God becomes even stronger.

THOUGHT

I usually practice abundance thinking, but 2023-2024 has been incredibly challenging. In one year, I lost my father and became a part-time caregiver for my elderly mom. My husband had major surgery and then a fall, requiring me to be a full-time caregiver to him for a short time while still providing care for my mother.

Just one of these challenges in a year is hard, but four in a row left me completely depleted and stressed, about to give up.

Luckily, I have a robust emotional support system. One friend suggested that I do the following every day: breathwork, prayer, and, for five minutes each day, list what I'm grateful for.

Breathwork rebooted my parasympathetic nervous system, prayer fused me with God, and gratitude writing netted hundreds of items. I was already living in abundance!

I live in a beautiful house, and my bills are paid. We have neighbors and friends who have been an excellent support network, especially during and after my husband's hospitalizations.

I am healthy, which was very important amid my mother's transition from wife to widowhood and my husband's hospitalizations.

To live in abundance, we must be grateful. The two are inextricably connected.

QUESTION

How can I embody abundance so that I can encourage others?

AUTHOR CONTACT INFORMATION

Carol Koppelman, CEO of CPK Solutions LLC
Website: https://cpksolutions.com
Email: carol.fuccillo@gmail.com
Social: https://mybook.to/artofconnection5
Tags: International Bestselling Author, Influencer

January 21
ANTHONY TRUCKS

I have done too much work in the dark to lose in the light.

THOUGHT

You cannot attain or sustain anything in life above your current identity. So, you must shift your identity and become the person capable of attaining and sustaining what you desire most. What I call a "Dominator's Identity," by definition, means to govern and control. This identity is not bought, given, or stolen. It is only earned, and it is earned in the dark.

Only when you have attained the transcendent and most abundant form of your heart, mind, and soul away from prying eyes and through the most challenging effort ever given, all while being your only cheerleader at times, are you entirely prepared. When you emerge from that darkness, you will have achieved something significant and become something great. Your "Dominator's Identity" is ready to take on anything, any time, and anywhere to succeed.

QUESTION

Do you believe you have worked so hard that you deserve everything you want so much that you'll tirelessly fight until you have it?

AUTHOR CONTACT INFORMATION

Anthony Trucks, CEO of Dark Work
Website: https://darkwork.com
Email: atrucks@anthonytrucks.com
Social: https://instagram.com/anthonytrucks
Tags: Speaker and Number 1 Dark Work coach in the world

The Art of Connection

January 22

ALYSE RYNOR

*Stay aware of your deepest beliefs,
for they drive or block your flow of abundance.*

THOUGHT

While attending a class on prosperity, our instructor had us close our eyes and hold out our arms in answer to the following question: "How big is your bowl?"

I spread my arms out as wide as they would go. My bowl was quite large, and I wanted it to hold a lot. However, upon opening my eyes, I noticed that some of my classmates had their hands closer together, forming the size of a small cereal bowl.

The instructor explained that the Universe is abundant and happy to give us much of what we desire. But it can only provide what our bowl can hold.

This exercise was a metaphor for our beliefs. The size of our bowl indicated whether our thoughts were based on lack or abundance.

Our beliefs are born out of life experiences, usually early ones. You can repeat, "I am rich," hoping to see money magically flow into your bank account. But, if your unconscious thoughts differ, perhaps passed on from family struggles, someone who told you that rich people were mean or selfish, or you got the message that you weren't worthy enough, it can block your flow of abundance.

Explore your unconscious beliefs. Write them down. Challenge them. Then, shift your thinking.

Your abundance awaits!

QUESTION

How big is YOUR bowl?

AUTHOR CONTACT INFORMATION

Alyse Rynor, Founder & Owner of Soul Choice Counseling
Website: https://www.alyserynor.com
Email: alyse.lcsw@gmail.com
Social: https://www.linkedin.com/in/arynor/
Tags: Integrative Psychotherapist

January 23
PRESTON WEEKES

You receive abundance at the level you are at, and abundance is infinite.

THOUGHT

Everything you need right now exists around you. If you are a business person, many of your ideal clients are probably within a five-mile radius of where you are right this second. All the money you ever need is likely within a five-mile radius of where you are right now.

Almost everything you could ever want, need, or achieve is right by you, or the tool to access it is. If you are honest and think back through your life, abundance has actually been around you your whole life, even as a child. Maybe you didn't experience it, but it was around you. If you didn't experience abundance, you were just not a person capable of seeing it, understanding it, or accessing it. But it did exist. You may ask yourself, "Why don't I have everything I want then?" I am here to tell you abundance is real, expanding, and perpetual. You can have everything you want right now. It is all around you in infinite amounts. You need to become a person who can see it, understand it, and access it. People who have abundance have it because they have become people who can experience it. Understanding this deeper will lead to abundance beyond your comprehension today.

QUESTION

What will you do to be abundant in the world right now?

AUTHOR CONTACT INFORMATION

Preston Weekes, Founder of 10 Step Books
Website: https://10StepBooks.com
Email: preston@operationsx.com
Social: https://www.linkedin.com/in/energyguy
Tags: Books, Systems, EQ, Business Growth

January 24
DIANA HOOKER

At least we're together!

THOUGHT

As my family was embarking on a road trip, we had to make several stops before we began.

At the pharmacy, a car drove by with their car alarm going off. The pharmacist needed more time, so we searched for a mailbox. When we returned to the pharmacy, the same car went by again, and their car alarm was still going off. "Beep! Beep! Is that a mailbox?"

Next, we picked up some fast food; as we drove away, we realized that they had only given us spoons to eat our salads. "Beep! Beep! Is that a mailbox? Do you have any forks?"

Throughout the trip, we got stuck in one traffic jam after another. "Beep! Beep! Is that a mailbox? Do you have any forks? At least we're together!"

Even with all the mishaps, that was one of our best family road trips ever. And to this day, any time we are stuck in traffic, stopped at a long light, or faced with some other adversity, we remember that road trip and exclaim our family motto: "At least we're together!"

Taking those simple moments, creating a special memory that lives long after time has passed, and building a bond with my family are priceless.

QUESTION

What memories are you creating that bring you joy, happiness, and love?

AUTHOR CONTACT INFORMATION

Diana Hooker, CEO of The Living Your Greatness Company
Website: http://livingyourgreatness.net/
Email: Diana@LivingYourGreatness.net
Social: https://www.linkedin.com/in/diana-hooker-04517594/
Tags: Speaker, Author, Coach

January 25

JENNIFER CAPALDO

Make the most of what you have and take action from where you are right now!

THOUGHT

What a simple yet profound principle. It reminds us that true power lies not in waiting for ideal conditions but in embracing and using resources currently at our disposal.

Often, we become stuck in a cycle of longing for more: more time, more resources, more support. We wait for the stars to align before taking action. Yet, progress begins with acceptance of our current situation and determination to make a difference from right there. By using what we have right now, we transform limitations into opportunities.

Consider each step taken with intention, even if small, advances our journey. It's consistent, mindful actions that shape our path. By focusing on what we can control, our thoughts, our actions, and our attitudes, we empower ourselves to create meaningful change.

From where you are, you have a unique viewpoint. You possess invaluable skills, experiences, and insights. By doing what you can with what you have, you acknowledge the power within you to take action, no matter how small it may seem.

Begin Today: embrace where you are, leverage what you have, and take bold steps forward. In doing so, you unlock the potential to transform your own life and the world around you.

QUESTION

What are you facing today that could benefit from this approach? I encourage you to take a deep breath and then boldly answer those three questions above.

AUTHOR CONTACT INFORMATION

Jennifer Capaldo, Owner of Transformational Breakthru
Website: www.transformationalbreakthru.com
Email: jennifer@transformationalbreakthru.com
Social: https://www.facebook.com/jennifer.capaldo
Tags: Transformation Coach, Speaker, Writer, Life Coach

January 26

ANNE MAYER

When you challenge the borders of your self-imposed box, you open yourself up to a world of abundant possibilities and boundless joys.

THOUGHT

This quote encapsulates the liberating essence of my life and work—a reminder that embracing authenticity and pushing boundaries can lead to greater personal and professional fulfillment.

Early in my career, I tried to fit into organizational cultures that didn't quite align with who I was. At times, I was told I was either too much or not enough — too direct or not direct enough, too assertive or not assertive enough, too cautious or not cautious enough, and so on. These experiences taught me how to navigate the boxes others expected of me while recognizing when it was time to move beyond those confines. Each time I challenged the imposed limits, I discovered new opportunities that brought greater fulfillment and led to tremendous growth.

Inspired by trailblazers who have challenged conventions and broken barriers, I'm deeply committed to empowering others to craft strategies for their success. Whether navigating the complexities of professional landscapes, considering a career pivot, or envisioning a fulfilling post-career life, I encourage you to challenge your boundaries. In doing so, you might craft a new box—or choose a path that doesn't require a box at all!

QUESTION

If you dared to step outside your box, what might be different in your life?

AUTHOR CONTACT INFORMATION

Anne Mayer, Founder and Principal of Box Not Required Coaching and Consulting
Website: https://BoxNotRequired.com
Email: AnneMayer@BoxNotRequired.com
Social: www.linkedin.com/in/anne-mayer
Tags: outsidethebox, careercoach, leadercoach

January 27
IRA KORETSKY

*People who like to dream big,
help other people dream big.*

THOUGHT

Storytelling is the secret sauce of organizational abundance. Storytelling is the spark that ignites inspiration, the fertilizer that grows gratitude, and the glue that binds teams together. When we intentionally weave tales of success and possibility throughout our organization, we create abundance ripples, touching every corner of our lives.

"What stories should we tell?" Share the saga of the sales team turning a potential client's "no" into a "yes" through creative problem-solving. Spotlight Jana in customer service, who went above and beyond, turning a client into a loyal fan. Celebrate Chi's fresh perspective, which led to game-changing innovation. These narratives become the DNA of a culture rich in abundance thinking.

Make storytelling a ritual as natural as grabbing your morning coffee. Transform all-hands meetings into story swaps. Turn one-on-ones into opportunities to exchange ideas. Spice up internal newsletters with a "Story of the Week." Create a shared network folder to collect and spread these stories.

By fostering a culture of storytelling, you're not just sharing information, you're sharing inspiration. You're sharing abundance-abundance that benefits everyone.

QUESTION

How can you create abundance ripples in your organization today? What stories will you share to inspire, to express gratitude, or to introduce new possibilities?

AUTHOR CONTACT INFORMATION

Ira Koretsky, CEO of The Chief Storyteller®
Website: https://www.thechiefstoryteller.com/
Email: aoc365@thechiefstoryteller.com
Social: https://www.linkedin.com/in/thechiefstoryteller/
Tags: Storytelling, Public Speaking, Coach, Speaker

January 28

MICHAEL LANG

Helping others win doesn't mean you lose... Instead, you'll multiply your wins.

THOUGHT

Have you considered that helping others succeed will also help you succeed? Life is not a zero-sum game where a win by one means others lose. Conversely, we all rise and fall together. When you mentor an employee, they do better work for you. Even when you help strangers, you'll find more referrals come to you.

A potential customer called me recently, asking how to sign up for one of my technology courses. I asked what their goals were in taking the training and realized they already had the technical skills needed to succeed. They were only looking for more training since prior training did not yet result in the right job offer. They were focusing on the wrong solution.

What they really needed was to use their existing skills to find opportunities in a relevant local meetup. Now, when they talk to others in that group, they will most likely tell their story. That will encourage others to contact me if they actually need my services. Can you find similar opportunities to help others?

When you adopt a mentor mindset, you'll find new opportunities come your way that you wouldn't have had otherwise.

QUESTION

What if you found a way to help others, other than a networking group, that could turn around and help you in return?

AUTHOR CONTACT INFORMATION

Michael Lang, Founder of Nexul Software
Website: https://www.gurufyre.com
Email: michael.lang@nexul.com
Social: https://www.linkedin.com/in/michael-lang-1936a33/
Tags: Technologist, Software Developer, Mentor

January 29
MICHAEL FRITZIUS

Live life like you're running with scissors.

THOUGHT

Psalm 18:36 says, "You gave a wide place for my steps under me, and my feet did not slip." Sometimes in life, when you're running fast and pursuing dreams, it'll feel like your feet aren't going to land securely. And it feels like you're running with scissors, so if you slip, that's a career-ending event! But I'm convinced that's the only way to live. When I'm not quite sure when (or even if) my next step will land, this verse goes through my mind. God is absolutely in control and honors the effort. My feet always land safely. It gives me the firm platform to launch from and to keep going.

The times in life that I've felt the most unsure but still have something inside me that's propelling me forward are the exact times that I've had a huge breakthrough: a new relationship, opportunity, upskill, or awakening happens.
It's always right on time, too; not too early before I'm ready and not too late when the critical point has passed. The more I operate at this level, the more success I have, both internally and externally, and this mindset is something I share with people I meet as well who feel stuck, scared, or stymied.

QUESTION

When was the last time you pursued something with reckless abandon?

AUTHOR CONTACT INFORMATION

Michael Fritzius, Founder of podcastify.me
Website: https://podcastify.me
Email: fritz@podcastify.me
Social: https://linkedin.com/in/fritzops
Tags: Podcasting, Podcast Coach, Speaker

January 30
DOUG GIESLER

Faith protects us from the unknown like a shield.

THOUGHT

WTF: "What the faith?" What's your faith in right now? Consider releasing the nature within that resists/avoids certain moments. Embrace the unknown. Champion "becoming". Master this state as an internal framework using "AI": Actualize Initiation!

Self-actualize by keying on internal awareness. Optimize and maximize the "selves" within. Externals materialize as we "become" new, Now! Master becoming as an active transitioning process. Presence via awareness enables conscious perception of time during the unfolding moment. On the crest of the transitional time wave, presence allows change. At that exact "time," we UNlimit the lower "self" that arrives. By letting go of that lower self, we step into the next moment unlimited. "I" Self-actualize into "Now" as my highest and best Self!

Fear, as an example, shows us non-presence associated with the future mind "sets." As presence is regained, fear vanishes because the future "illusion" disappears from the mindscape. Get back to now, and make a new "You" happen fearlessly!

Don't fret over unknown futures; get present, try! You may fail. However, a better thought is I may win. That's using faith wisely. Master this mind philosophy within!

QUESTION

How does your mind handle the "unknown"? New moments are always unknown, so a new "me" must show up at that time. What better time for a new start than now?

AUTHOR CONTACT INFORMATION

Doug Giesler, CEO of Giesler Systems LLC
Website: http://www.unlimityourlimit.com
Email: douggiesler@gmail.com
Social: www.linkedin.com/in/doug-giesler
Tags: Author, Realtor, Personal Coach, Day Trader

January 31
PAMELA SCOTT

You're never too old, and it's never too late to change the direction of your life. You're one decision, one connection from your next opportunity!

THOUGHT

From my personal experience, there is no age limit to achieving success, dreams, goals, and even love. I am living proof and a testament to anyone who has limited themselves in every way. The limits in one area of your life tend to carry over to other areas. It is imperative to network and connect with others who have released those same chains and are now living in their God-given freedom. We often need to see something is possible in order to believe it entirely. Getting in the rooms with influence and seeking mentorship can open so many doors for us. Fear and making excuses will generally result in us not getting to the finish line.

I relocated cross country at age 43, got married at age 44, obtained my real estate license at age 45, and started a business at age 46! I am the representation of someone who had lived in my comfortable, little bubble and had no idea what thinking and moving outside of my box looked like! I did, however, know I was meant for much more, but I had no idea or way to propel myself to the next level.

My story is your sign to dream and go after everything that you never thought was possible!

QUESTION

What is keeping you from dreaming? Some of us have let life get in the way, and our dreams have taken a back seat in our lives. Please don't let this be you. If you're reading this, you have time to do it all!

AUTHOR CONTACT INFORMATION

Pamela Scott, Owner, CEO of your AZ RELO PLUG LLC
Website: https://yourazreloplug.com/
Email: info@yourazreloplug.com
Social: https://www.tiktok.com/@yourazreloplug?
Tags: AZ Relocation Services Owner, Real Estate Agent

February 1

CANDY MOTZEK

*Decide what you want to be KNOWN for.
Every day, ask, 'How would the best show up?'
Then, step up and do that.*

THOUGHT

We all have impressive skills, but claiming our expertise can feel like a big commitment. So often, we waffle in indecision. Sometimes, we tell ourselves, "Don't get too big for your britches." After all, boasting is frowned on, so we tone it down; we don't declare our ambitions; we dull our shine.

But when we do step up, it's so compelling, not because we're boasting but because of who we become as we grow into that aspiration.

One of my peers claims he is the world's best courage coach. Initially, when I heard that, I was doubtful and had all kinds of judgments.

Later, when we spoke, I learned that by claiming to be the "world's best courage coach," he wasn't standing on top of an imaginary competitive mountain pretending to be better than any other courage coach. It was his signal to himself to aspire to greatness.

Now I do it too! I am the world's best confidence coach. Claiming the title of "the world's best …anything" means that every day, I wake up and relentlessly move in that direction. I ask myself, what is the world's best confidence coach? What would I do? How do I feel? What would I do this week? Where can I grow? How do I show up? How can I hone my skills?

QUESTION

What do you want to be known for? What is so meaningful to you that you will stake a claim and persistently embrace that level of growth?

AUTHOR CONTACT INFORMATION

Candy Motzek, Founder of Step Into Success Now
Website: https://stepintosuccessnow.com/
Email: cemotzek@gmail.com
Social: https://www.linkedin.com/in/candy-motzek/
Tags: Podcast Host, Confidence and Business Coach

February 2
JOELLYN WLAZLOWSKI MARTIN

*Live Your Life Ambitiously Now,
and Your Future Self Will Thank You*

THOUGHT

Today, I am 70 years young and it is Ground Hog Day! The idea of living each day the same as every other day will ultimately never be satisfying nor create abundance. Although I was always busy being a mom, working in retail management, learning to trade the stock market, or trying entrepreneurship, I had no real goals to attain abundance. My thoughts usually focused on the goals of others.

The focus changed a couple of years ago when I found myself in the health and wellness space. This pivot proves to show that we are never too old to change course! I enjoy helping others find solutions to what they need answers to. It could be feeling better about their health with natural products or their finances through entrepreneurship. When someone is worried, thoughts are centered more on how to feel better and not how to live.

We tend to think that abundance is only finances and stuff! When changing perspective, we can find abundance everywhere! I find it with good health, a family with a husband, three grown sons and daughters-in-law, eight grandchildren, a home, friends, connections, and opportunities. With God guiding my actions with ambition, more was created than I ever imagined!

QUESTION

Thinking of where you are right now, can you visualize a more abundant future by having more ambition?

AUTHOR CONTACT INFORMATION

Joellyn Wlazlowski Martin, Founder of Joellyn's Health, Wealth and Beauty
Website: https://www.365daysofabundancequotes.com
Email: JoellynW.Martin@gmail.com
Social: https://linktr.ee/JoellynEyeforDesign
Tags: Leader, Digital Marketer, Health, Wealth, Beauty

February 3

BECCA HEISSEL

You don't need to know the 'how'—just share your dream and let the connections guide you.

THOUGHT

My life changed when I shared my dream of becoming a mother with my boss. After years of infertility treatments, I was hesitant to spend $15,000 on IVF. My mentor helped me envision the joy of holding my child, and that shifted my mindset. I now empower others with these principles: decide what you want, believe in it, and share it with others. You don't have to know how, but you must take inspired action every day—even if it's as simple as sharing your dream with one person. Financial clarity is vital, but it's about shifting your mindset to attract the right people and opportunities. When you share your dream, you attract the support needed to achieve it. Everything is possible when you take action and surround yourself with the right connections. By focusing on your goals, sharing them, and taking action, you harness the law of attraction.

QUESTION

What's one action step you can take today that moves you closer to your dream?

AUTHOR CONTACT INFORMATION

Becca Heissel, Founder of Business Owners Advocate LLC
Website: https://businessownersadvocate.com/
Email: becca@businessownersadvocate.com
Social: https://www.linkedin.com/in/beccaheissel/
Tags: Business coach, speaker, Accountant

February 4
BONNIE VERRICO

Never wish your life away - a life fully lived is a fulfilled life.

THOUGHT

When I was small, my mom used to caution me not to disregard what I had by overlooking it and constantly wishing for more. When I asked why I had to do chores or had to forego a special treat, she gently reminded me how fortunate I was to get to clean my room because I was lucky enough to have a safe place in which to sleep and plenty of toys to be put away. She reminded me how fortunate I was to get to have a choice to give up a treat because, as a family, we worked hard and had the means to have not only enough but a variety of food. What she was teaching me was the power of a positive perspective.

There is a vastly different effect on our psyche when we say:

"I have to clean my room" (drudgery, punishment, lackluster…)

"I get to clean my room" (adventurous, accomplishment, exciting…)

What a powerful concept! Many of us have so much, maybe not the same things we see that others have, but things that make life wonderful, easier, and possible. Rather than devaluing the abundance we already possess (material and otherwise), imagine the enriching impact on our lives if we realize, accept, and celebrate it. Remember, it's not what you have; it's what you get to do with it!

QUESTION

Instead of letting challenges pin you down, can you find the strength and courage to recognize and appreciate what you have, who you are, and what you can do and turn those challenges into victories?

AUTHOR CONTACT INFORMATION

Bonnie Verrico, Office Administrator of John Verrico - Share Your Fire
Website: https://www.johnverrico.com
Email: admin@johnverrico.com
Social: https://www.linkedin.com/in/johnverrico
Tags: Speaker, Coach, Leadership, PersonalGrowth

February 5
RICH PARSONS

Abundance, much like success, is something that must be defined and assessed by the individual seeking it.

THOUGHT

Abundance typically refers to having a plentiful amount of something, whether tangible or intangible. Some people seek abundance in their monetary situation. In contrast, others seek abundance in their relationships, personal fulfillment, professional growth, or spirituality.

There is no right or wrong area to seek abundance; it ultimately comes down to an individual's values, priorities, and goals. The good thing about abundance is that it does not have to be singular in focus.

As I consider my experiences, I realize I have enjoyed abundance in many aspects of my life. However, a commonality throughout is connections with others.

My military career brought opportunities for many connections, with the most special one being my beautiful bride. Had it not been for my assignment to Ellsworth AFB in Rapid City, SD, in 2006, I wouldn't have experienced the level of abundance and personal fulfillment I have been blessed with since.

While I certainly feel that I have been blessed with the finances necessary to live a comfortable life and achieve success in other areas of life, none of it would mean anything without my special person to share life with.

God has an abundant plan for my life!

QUESTION

In what area of your life do you seek abundance? Don't forget to consider relationships and connections with others.

AUTHOR CONTACT INFORMATION

Rich Parsons, Founder of Your Success Books
Website: www.yoursuccessbooks.com
Email: rparsons@highercallingconsultingllc.com
Social: https://www.linkedin.com/in/rich-parsons/
Tags: Publisher, Coach, Speaker, Author

February 6
KENNETH HILL JR

Is that all you got? My abundance stems from a lifetime of experiences.

THOUGHT

The word "abundance" can be a little tricky. Can your perception of this word determine how you define it? Let's explore perception.

When others would say, "I have seven cars," you would think, "Wow, they can drive a different car every day of the week." Or when you hear, "I've been to twenty-three different countries, so I have experienced things you could only wish for," you wonder if they are right. After all, when you thought of abundance, you were taught that it was a massive list of things you have or what you have done. When you flip through your mental Rolodex, it is easy to tally the heartache, pain, misery, and failures that you endured, and even those create abundance.

What if you learned that your survival through those challenging times saved countless lives? It can be humbling to discover that when someone "just wanted to talk," you listened. When others approach you about their most dire moments, you are unafraid to share vulnerable occasions during your journey.

QUESTION

From my perspective, my memories are my abundance, but what about you? How would you characterize abundance?

AUTHOR CONTACT INFORMATION

Kenneth Hill Jr, Owner of U. S. Hapkido Alliance, LLC
Website: https://www.differentpathmartialarts.com
Email: kennhilljr@gmail.com
Social: https://www.facebook.com/profile.php?id=100005963259316&mibextid=ZbWKwl
Tags: Instructor, Ability, Awareness, Social Skills

February 7

JAY ABRAHAM

The primary basis for the entire preeminence strategy is a keen commitment to empathy.

THOUGHT

When you integrate empathy into your business strategy, you fundamentally shift from a mindset focused on transactions to one that's all about transformation. You're no longer just pushing products or services; instead, you're solving real problems, addressing deep-seated pains, and fulfilling the aspirations of your clients. This approach doesn't just make you another option on the market; it establishes you as the go-to choice.

Empathy allows you to connect on a profoundly personal level, creating a relationship that your competitors can't easily imitate. It's about stepping into your clients' shoes, seeing the world through their eyes, and then offering solutions that directly address their unspoken needs. This kind of connection builds loyalty, cultivates trust, and fosters a partnership that elevates your business beyond the competition.

Empathy isn't just an add-on to your strategy; it's the driving force behind genuine preeminence. It's what takes a business from merely getting by to being genuinely transformative, making it indispensable in the lives of those it serves.

QUESTION

How are you currently integrating empathy into your business strategy?

AUTHOR CONTACT INFORMATION

Jay Abraham, Founder and CEO of The Abraham Group, Inc
Website: https://www.abraham.com/
Email: info@abraham.com
Social: https://www.linkedin.com/in/jayabrahamofficial/
Tags: Marketing Expert, Proven Business Leader

February 8
MARILYN RICHARDS

Abundance comes when we trust God, letting faith guide us through darkness and transform pain into purpose, revealing life's true richness.

THOUGHT

I became a Christian at 12 years of age, though I didn't grow up in a Christian home. My stepdad was my first witness to faith. He was stern and emotionally distant, and he often kept adult magazines in the house. Despite this, he was a great provider who loved my mom. His salvation later in life was an answer to years of prayer, showing that God's redeeming love brings abundance, even after hardship.

As a veteran and trauma survivor, I've learned how faith transforms pain into purpose. My dad, a Vietnam veteran, lost his first daughter after she was severely burned and died at 2 years old. He became estranged from his only son and later found love again after his marriage to my mom ended. When he remarried, my younger sister was born, giving him a new purpose. His story reflects the abundance of God's grace, reminding me of John 10:10, where Christ promises life in its fullness.

Louie Zamperini, a former Olympian-turned-POW, shows the same resilience. His story, like my stepdad's salvation, proves faith can open the door to abundance, even in the darkest moments. Jeremiah 29:11 reminds us that God's plans, even in difficult times, give us hope and a future.

QUESTION

In difficult times, how have you found purpose and healing? Are you open to exploring the abundance that comes from growth, even when the path feels uncertain?

AUTHOR CONTACT INFORMATION

Marilyn Richards, Owner/Founder of Echo Tango Sierra LLC
Website: https://www.echotangosierra.com
Email: marilyn.richards79@icloud.com
Social: http://linkedin.com/in/msrichards
Tags: Military Transition Guide

February 9

CHRISTINE HIEBEL

*Abundance is not just about what we have,
but what we're willing to see in every moment.*

THOUGHT

Abundance isn't a destination. It's already here, right here, right now. It's in the moments you embrace, the lessons you learn, and the mindset you cultivate. It's not about waiting for that perfect moment to show up or that big win to come knocking. No, it's about recognizing the wealth you've got in your life right here, right now. When you focus on what is showing up today, you'll see abundance show up in ways you never expected.

We all get caught up in the chase, thinkin' that the good stuff's always just a little bit ahead of us: the next deal, the next opportunity. But the truth is, abundance isn't a someday thing; it's here now. In the people you're close to, the lessons you've learned, and those small, everyday moments that take your breath away.

When you make the shift to abundance, you will start to see opportunity everywhere. Even the challenges, setbacks, and tough times all become part of your growth. And when you get that mindset locked in? Well, that's when life starts unlocking itself. The riches of life are always available, just waiting for you to see them. And when you do? The world starts reflecting that abundance back at you, bringing even more of it into your life.

QUESTION

*How can you shift your focus today to see the abundance already surrounding you?
What's one thing you can do right now to invite more of it into your life?*

AUTHOR CONTACT INFORMATION

Christine Hiebel, Founder of Free Money U
Website: https://freemoneyu.com/
Email: christine@ameliaislandmicrogreens.com
Social: https://www.linkedin.com/in/christinehiebel/
Tags: For-Profit Grant Writing Coach

February 10

RACHEL HARRISON

When we let go of the illusion we can control anything outside of us, we open the door to reclaiming our power and aligning with our authentic selves.

THOUGHT

We may want happiness; however, we spend so much time and energy trying to manage outcomes or change others that we find ourselves exhausted and dissatisfied. This attempt to control everything outside of ourselves disconnects us from our true power, authentic selves, and the happiness and peace we seek. Real happiness begins when we turn our attention to ourselves and our healing, letting go of control and opening to the flow of life and our unique soul's calling.

Soul Recovery is a spiritual path to a happy and healthy life where we use the tools of spirituality to release all that no longer serves us, remember our wholeness, and align with our higher selves. The 9-Step Soul Recovery process offers a powerful guide to this inner journey of awakening, recognizing our suffering is caused by our current perceptions, and beginning to release and heal the stories that were created from our past experiences. Through compassion and forgiveness, we embrace updated beliefs, rewriting our story from a place of authenticity and empowerment in union with the Higher Power. We become aware that by healing ourselves, we are contributing to the healing of the world.

QUESTION

What would change in your life if you updated old beliefs and let go of control?

AUTHOR CONTACT INFORMATION

Rev Rachel Harrison, Owner of Recover Your Soul
Website: https://www.recoveryoursoul.net/
Email: recoveryoursoulnet@gmail.com
Social: https://www.instagram.com/recoveryoursoulpodcast/
Tags: Spiritual Coach, Speaker, Podcast Host

February 11

KATHLEEN EDINGER

*Abundance is not the number of possessions you own.
Abundance is who you have in your life and
how you live your life. Abundance is your mindset.*

THOUGHT

What is abundance? It is wealth on the inside, not wealth on the outside. Let me explain. It is so easy to compare what we have in life to what other people have. It is easy to be envious and jealous if we allow yourselves to go down that path of thinking. We keep striving for the way we think our lives should be or the amount of material possessions we should own. Instead, we should strive to clearly see what we have right now and realize all the blessings that God has provided for us.

Abundance is not about how many things we own, how much money is in our bank account, or the size of our house. Abundance is much bigger than material things. It is the essential things, like our health and the people we have in our lives.

If we allow ourselves to step back from the chaos of our lives, all of the technology and media, and genuinely look at what we have in our lives, our many blessings will come into sharp focus. Abundance is all about our mindset and what we value as being important. A healthy mindset focuses on what is truly important to us. Keeping this focus will guide us on the path we are supposed to follow and not someone else's path.

QUESTION

If you could step away from the chaos today, how much abundance would come into sharp focus? Can you write down three abundant blessings each day and review them as a reminder?

AUTHOR CONTACT INFORMATION

Kathleen Edinger, Owner of TeaScapes
Website: www.teascapes.com
Email: Kathleen@enjoyteascapes.com
Social: https://www.facebook.com/enjoyteascapes
Tags: tea, certified tea specialist, speaker, self-care

February 12
TERESA CUNDIFF

Don't be so busy counting your steps each day that you forget to notice the ABUNDANCE that surrounds you! Stop and smell the roses!

THOUGHT

What do you think of when you hear the word abundance? I submit to you that what comes to mind is money or wealth or "stuff"! Jesus said in the Gospel, according to Luke, "Take care, and be on your guard against all covetousness, for one's life does not consist in the abundance of his possessions."

We may have abundant possessions, but true joy isn't found there. So, more than just stuff, abundance surrounds you in many different ways if you have eyes to see it! There is the abundance and beauty of nature! Indeed, we take this for granted most days until maybe one evening, a sunset stops us in our tracks. Sunsets are free and cannot be possessed!

How about the abundance of your health? Regardless of the health concerns you have now, you are still above the dirt and can make choices! Which is another abundant thing: Making choices! And you make thousands in a single day! And then there are the people who love you! Do you actively take the time to think about what people loving you means for your life? That love is freely given! Renew your mind and your spirit by dwelling on the abundance around you every day!

QUESTION

What I have for you is a challenge! Just for today, stop with each moment that's possible and observe ABUNDANCE around you. Just for one day! I think you will be surprised! ABUNDANCE is EVERYWHERE!

AUTHOR CONTACT INFORMATION

Teresa Cundiff, President & CEO of Wordy Nerds Media, Inc.
Website: https://www.365daysofabundancequotes.com
Email: teresa.cundiff@mac.com
Social: https://linktr.ee/TeresaCundiff
Tags: proofreader, copyeditor

February 13

SHERRY GIDEONS

Abundance isn't something you chase. It's something you become. Align with the frequency of abundance, and everything you desire flows into your life.

THOUGHT

Abundance is a way of being, not something you obtain. It's about shifting your internal vibration to match the frequency of abundance. The moment you stop seeking abundance from external sources and start becoming abundant within yourself, everything changes. Opportunities, wealth, love, and joy begin to flow into your life effortlessly because you are aligned with the abundance of the universe.

Every person can manifest abundance in their lives. By recognizing that scarcity is only a belief, a mindset, you can dismantle the limitations that hold you back. Scarcity thinking keeps you in a loop of lack and frustration. True abundance is unlimited; it starts with gratitude and flourishes when you trust in the infinite possibilities around you. You don't need to chase after what you desire; you need to become an energetic match for it.

Once you become aware of your power to create and attract abundance, you can apply it to every area of life. Everything you desire is within your reach, waiting for you to unlock it by becoming an open channel for abundance. It's time to stop the chase and start embodying the energy that draws abundance to you.

QUESTION

What would your life look like if you stopped chasing abundance and started becoming it?

AUTHOR CONTACT INFORMATION

Sherry Gideons, Founder of Sherry Gideons International
Website: www.sherrygideons.com
Email: sherry@sherrygideons.com
Social: www.linkedin.com/in/sherrygideons
Tags: Leadership Coach, Empowerment Specialist, Speaker

February 14
J. ROBERT SANTANA

To experience abundance requires serving others out of love with no expectations. It is the overflow of God's provisions and our contentment.

THOUGHT

Abundance is subjective and can be measured by the emotion, mind, spirit, and financial circumstances of a person. Emotional abundance, for me, is when you are striving for your emotional maturity, and instead of being reactive, you are responsive, and you influence your environment instead of the environment influencing you.

An abundant mind is a mind that is growing in knowledge for the sole purpose of renewing your mind and that of others.

Spirit abundance taps into the divine, where the ultimate goal is to live in a perpetual relationship with Christ, and in doing so, others will see the Holy Spirit shine through you. Financial abundance is not necessarily being rich and wealthy but understanding that money is a tool and can be leveraged to live life in contentment and not be governed by it.

QUESTION

Have you been so focused on experiencing lack that it has closed your eyes to the abundance that has been given to you?

AUTHOR CONTACT INFORMATION

J. Robert Santana, Owner of Virtual Online Tax and Services LLC
Website: https://www.voltstax.com
Email: rsantana@voltstax.com
Social: https://www.facebook.com/voltstaxservices/
Tags: Tax Advisor, Entrepreneur, Business Coach, Author

February 15

ASHLEY L. WHITLOCK

Abundance is not just about having more, but is it about appreciating the right now more than your eyes can see?

THOUGHT

When you think of the word abundance, it can mean more than enough. While it is great to think about and crave more than enough, living in the moment of what you have right now is also an essential priority. Thinking about and receiving the entire package, not just what you want but what you need, is essential. Abundance is a process to be lived, not achieved.

Coveting more is also a form of sinful greed, which is when we leap over abundance and into greed. It suggests we can never feel fulfilled or capable of gratitude, that our minds can never be stilled or our hearts contented, and I cannot accept that reality. I believe we have to be happy with what we have, materially and spiritually: our daily existence and the peace within us. My quote teaches you to appreciate what you have to receive more.

QUESTION

According to the quote, "Abundance is not just about having more, but is it about appreciating the right now more than your eyes can see?"

AUTHOR CONTACT INFORMATION

Ashley L. Whitlock, CEO of Whitlock Associates LLC
Website: https://whitlockus.com
Email: info@whitlockus.com
Social: https://www.facebook.com/share/18B6Uwt1pJ/?mibextid=LQQJ4d
Tags: Business Strategist, Educator, Notary, Innovator

February 16
LLOYD HEATH

*Abundance isn't just about more for some;
it's about enough for all.*

THOUGHT

Abundance is often tied to material wealth: ample resources and opportunity. At this critical juncture, we face a troubling truth: nearly half our population clings to divisive narratives, blaming others for inflation and rising costs. These beliefs, fueled by deception, show a misunderstanding of abundance. True abundance isn't about hoarding wealth or assigning blame; it's about gratitude, shared prosperity, and resilience.

For billions worldwide, daily life is a struggle for basic needs, with 3.3 billion people living on less than $5.50 a day. This fact is a reminder of what we, as a nation, often take for granted. If abundance is only about more, we miss its fullest potential. Abundance grows from recognizing our shared humanity and uplifting others. It calls us to reject false narratives that divide us and build systems for all.

As Abraham Lincoln said, "A house divided against itself cannot stand." This quote applies to our nation and the world. We must redefine abundance as compassion over fear, gratitude over greed, and unity over division to create a society where everyone can thrive.

QUESTION

What would abundance look like if it were built on gratitude and unity instead of division and fear?

AUTHOR CONTACT INFORMATION

Lloyd Heath, Owner of Vizalliance
Website: https://vizalliance.com
Email: lloydvheath@gmail.com
Social: https://www.linkedin.com/in/lloydheath/
Tags: Digital Marketer

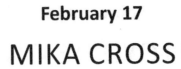

February 17
MIKA CROSS

Our lives become more meaningful when we recognize the impact of our work on others. By humanizing the workplace, we empower positive change.

THOUGHT

For many, our work isn't just a job; it's woven into the fabric of our lives. It shapes our interactions, our purpose, and ultimately, our impact. Whether we're supporting colleagues, serving customers, or pursuing our growth, we carry our work with us, and we can use it to navigate meaningful connections and shared success like a compass.

As workplaces continue to evolve and individuals continue to explore their relationship with work and values around what a job and career mean to them personally, I hope that we all continue to grow and learn to adapt new ways of working together. We must keep the human part of work at the forefront and remember that the way we humanize work is necessary to support the whole person. The more we do that well, with patience, understanding, empathy, and kindness, the better we can empower those who work for and with us to achieve their best work, regardless of how, when, and where work gets done.

QUESTION

When do you feel most empowered to do your best work? What if you were able to contribute to a positive work environment for others and left a legacy of lasting impact just by your behaviors?

AUTHOR CONTACT INFORMATION

Mika Cross, CEO and Founder of Strategy@Work, LLC
Website: https://www.mikacross.com
Email: info@mikacross.com
Social: https://www.linkedin.com/in/worklifechampionoftheuniverse/
Tags: Futurist, Speaker, Executive Coach, Consultant

February 18
NEFERTITI SAN MIGUEL

*Abundance is not about cash flow
but rather resources money can't buy.*

THOUGHT

By intentional design, I am enjoying my version of dream-life, where inner-peace and complete wellness have the most significant value of all, beyond dollars and cents. While cash flow is necessary to pay for monthly expenses, I am more invested in other types of currencies, such as mental and physical health, power of choice, freedom, and respectable reputation.

I let abundance circulate by making any excuse to celebrate my wins, whether it is something of importance in my life, such as receiving the title of Sensei from my Ikebana School, something that brings me pride (I placed in the top three at an international modeling contest in London), future spotlights (I get to share the stage with world-class talent), or pause for a moment and appreciate nature in all its glory! Being in a big city, at times, might feel like living in a concrete jungle, but I never stop basking in the majestic facade of the gothic architecture and iconic landmarks we are known for.

Some of my ways to spread abundant vibes are: Being generous with my time, my words, and my resources. Attention to detail, especially when negligence is at an all-time high, will build relationships, a priceless currency.

QUESTION

How do you measure abundance? And how often do you take inventory of your different currencies?

AUTHOR CONTACT INFORMATION

Nefertiti San Miguel, Founder and Owner of Neurobana
Website: https://www.NefertitiSanMiguel.com
Email: nefertiti.sanmiguel@gmail.com
Social: https://www.facebook.com/NefertitiSanMiguelGlobal
Tags: Floral therapy, mental health, Ikebana art coach

February 19

JACQUELIN KENNY

There are two sides to every story, and when it comes to abundance, the sides are polar opposites.

THOUGHT

The world has an abundance of many things: money and poverty, food and starvation, resources and pollution. Notice how everything I mentioned here has an opposing factor. Just as those examples have opposing factors, many other things do, too. And I think it all comes down to choice.

As a planet, we have more than enough resources to eliminate things like poverty and starvation. But the world is greedy. The world has an abundance of greed. I say this because globally, we have enough resources for those factors, but due to an abundance of greedy choices in our past, it isn't as easy as having these resources and giving them to the people and countries in need. We feel the need to get something in return. We feel as though they owe us for our "generosity."

When I think about the greed within our generosity, I realize that it creeps into our everyday lives. We can't give a compliment without expecting a 'thank you' or wanting them to return the nice words to us. Some may say that it's considered having manners to return the compliment, and it is, but I'd say that it's also greedy to expect it in return. So, when I ask you this, I want you to take a moment to reflect.

QUESTION

Have you ever given something to someone without expecting anything in return, just out of kindness, and if not, can you try?

AUTHOR CONTACT INFORMATION

Jacquelin Kenny, a Student
Website: https://www.jacquelinkenny.beekonnected.com
Email: jacquelin.kenny@hotmail.com
Social: https://mybook.to/artofconnection5
Tags: Student, Dance, Author, Baker

February 20
DJ BARTON

Success is built on the pillars of tools, systems, and leadership and leads to abundance.

THOUGHT

Entrepreneurship isn't just a career path; it's about living life on your terms. For me, freedom to create abundance is everything. It's about dancing to the beat of my drum, building what I want, and not needing anyone's approval. It's about taking care of my own house and focusing on what I can control instead of stressing over things I can't.

When you choose this path, you're committing to a vision that may go against the norm. It's about cutting out the noise and focusing on what truly matters: your family, your dreams, and your legacy. No one's going to hand you freedom; that's something you've got to create for yourself.

Success, to me, comes down to having the right tools, systems, and leadership, but most importantly, it's about having the courage to choose abundance. You don't need anyone's permission to live the life you want. Start by taking care of what's in front of you and building a life that feels true to who you are.

QUESTION

What would your life look like if you played full out, stopped caring what others thought, and started living the life God intended for you?

AUTHOR CONTACT INFORMATION

DJ Barton, CO - Owner of Go Levarti
Website: www.golevarti.com/dj
Email: dj@golevarti.com
Social: https://www.linkedin.com/in/therealdjbarton/
Tags: Travel, DigitalMarketer, sidehustle expert

February 21

KATHERINE KIM MULLIN

Imagine the world you want to live in and step into you.

THOUGHT

Imagination gives us an incredible ability to create and design our lives and businesses precisely as we want them to be.

As a businessperson with an entrepreneurial spirit, I have had great opportunities to serve others, helping them reduce their costs and make money in business while living a complete life.

With Abundance, "all you need is enough." Abundance is here, there, and everywhere around us. How do we access it? Answer: By stepping into you, knowing what you want and who you want to be. There is enough for everybody to live the life of their dreams.

I imagine a world of wealth and connectivity for all. Rich is having the freedom to be who you want and do what you want when you want to do it. While seeking abundance in one area, we often lose connectivity in other areas unless we see the whole picture. It's crucial to focus on enough of what we want, understand what that is precisely, and then have gratitude and appreciation for the gifts we receive, seeing the connectivity of it all. We know that the universe is an excellent storehouse of abundance, and we need only demand our wants and act each day towards that desire.

Sending light and love from my home to yours!

QUESTION

How do you imagine your life?

AUTHOR CONTACT INFORMATION

Katherine Kim Mullin, Founder of Katherine Kim Mullin
Website: https://www.katherinekimmullin.com
Email: katherinekmullin@gmail.com
Social: https://www.youtube.com/@katherinekimmullin9588
Tags: investor, business, lifestyle

February 22
ZABDY LOVE

Abundance is the essence of the soul's presence.

THOUGHT

Abundance is a state of mind and a state of being. It is your soul's essence.
You are abundant because you are undeniably worthy.
Abundance settles in our hearts when we are at ease from the "need" to control or change anything.
Abundance is the aroma the soul releases when living a life of purpose.
Abundance is discovering and understanding the soul's blueprint.
To live in abundance is to call and create into existence what you want that is aligned with your highest good, the highest good of others and the Universe/God.
The frequency of abundance is trust and faith in action.
Meditate, plan, prepare and work. Go in the direction of your vision. Command what you want and heal from low vibrational feelings, traumas, and past life karmas.
Abundance is us releasing into the infinite intelligence, the cosmos,
the source from where our soul derives its power to encompass peace.
Abundance is activating the mind, body, and soul to be whole, unique, and complete.
Abundance is being home.
Abundance is the freedom to be your authentic self.
Abundance is the "Soulsdance."
Abundance is to love and to be loved.
Abundance is The Art Of Connection to the Soul's Freedom.

QUESTION

Do you trust yourself and believe you are worthy to live in abundance?

AUTHOR CONTACT INFORMATION

Zabdy Love, Owner & Founder of ZAB Warrior Coaching & Consulting Services
Website: https://linktr.ee/zabnow
Email: zabwarrior@gmail.com
Social: https://www.facebook.com/zabdy.montenegro
Tags: Transformation & Spiritual Coach, Speaker, Author

The Art of Connection

February 23

KATIE EVANS

Consistently great client experiences are created by repeating thoughtful actions that have become systematized, not through accidental encounters.

THOUGHT

Building an amazing customer experience doesn't happen by chance; it requires intention and dedication to processes that are clear, repeatable, and adaptable. Each interaction a client has with our business is an opportunity to reinforce trust and satisfaction. When we rely on random actions or on-the-spot decisions alone, the client experience becomes unpredictable. But when we create systems, whether it's for how quickly we respond, how we handle inquiries, or how we follow up after a sale, we turn a would-be, one-time positive experience into a standard that can be repeated. These systems ensure that we meet and exceed the expectations of our clients every time, allowing us to surprise and delight without risking inconsistency. Consistency builds credibility, and credibility builds loyal clients and the referrals they send us naturally. Repeatable systems empower teams, make training more effortless, and even reduce stress by removing the guesswork, allowing us the peace of knowing we are delivering quality service every time. Creating great systems that bring customers joy and confidence each time is the foundation of any lasting business relationship.

QUESTION

What systems could you create and implement to ensure every customer has an exceptional experience with your business every time?

AUTHOR CONTACT INFORMATION

Katie Evans, Owner/Lead Agent of The Living 48 Real Estate Team
Website: https://www.living48realestate.com/
Email: Katie@Living48re.com
Social: https://linktr.ee/living48re
Tags: Real Estate Agent, Speaker, Productivity Trainer

February 24
MARLA PRESS

When you are a giver, AND you are open to receive, you will magnetically attract all the abundance your heart desires.

THOUGHT

We are taught it is better to give than to receive, and in some ways, this is true. Yet, we all need to receive opportunities, love, attention, feedback, and the many riches life has to offer. If you are always in giving mode, you may miss out.

Communication is also about giving and receiving. Whether speaking one-on-one or on a stage to many, the best speakers know how to receive their audience. They receive reactions, opinions, and, most importantly, energy. Even when you can't see your audience, you can receive their energy.

When you speak from your heart and gut and stay open, you will connect on a deeper level, and you will receive all the riches, tangible and intangible, life has to offer.

It's a beautiful thing that the cover of this book features the sunflower. Sunflowers often grow taller than other flowers. They reach for the sun, yet they don't take away from any flowers nearby. Be the sunflower and enjoy shining in the sun.

QUESTION

Are you willing to stay open even when it hurts? If so, you will also be open when all the great things find you. I can show you exercises to be in receiving mode, stay open, and attract abundance.

AUTHOR CONTACT INFORMATION

Marla Press, Founder and Chief Public Speaking Coach of Speakers on Fire Academy
Website: https://marlapress.com
Email: m.press@marlapress.com
Social: https://linkedin.com/in/MarlaAPress
Tags: Public Speaking Coach, Speaker, Author

February 25

CATRYN BECKER

Abundance is easy.
Focusing on what you actually want is the tricky bit.

THOUGHT

Why do we pray, wish, hope, and dream for Abundance? Often, it's because we harbor a deep fear that something is lacking in our lives. Society views abundance in positive terms, but in reality, the term is neutral. It simply means more, and it is often entwined with the practice of manifestation. Many people focus on manifesting abundance yet don't specify a target for that abundance. When it doesn't materialize as expected, we feel we have failed or that manifestation doesn't work. We actually live in a world inundated with abundance: An abundance of distractions, stress, anxieties, and regrets. None of that is something that we pray for, yet it abounds all around us.

From working with hundreds of successful women, I've found that not having the life we want stems from not knowing what we truly desire. Social media and pop culture present us with an idea of what we are "supposed" to want, but when I dive deeper with my clients, it becomes clear that their souls often yearn for something entirely different. Identifying what you truly desire is the first step. You will know you have landed on your heart's true desires when it feels good to say it out loud to other people.

QUESTION

What would your life look like if you could reduce the abundance of stress and distractions from it?

AUTHOR CONTACT INFORMATION

Catryn Becker Founder, People Optimization Specialist of Optimize We
Website: https://optimizewe.com
Email: catryn@optimizewe.com
Social: https://www.linkedin.com/in/catrynbecker/
Tags: speaker, business coach, life coach, retreats

February 26
MICHELLE SNYDER

Symbols often have deep meanings that can influence how we see the world and ourselves.

THOUGHT

When I first ventured into the realm of symbols, my perspective shifted profoundly. Symbols are the foundation of human connection—they capture history, tradition, and knowledge, weaving them into the story of who we are and where we come from. These timeless markers hold secrets, whispering to those with the curiosity to explore their depths. Understanding the migration of symbols alongside cultures and uncovering the tales they tell is like discovering hidden treasure.

Sacred texts, rich with allegory and symbolism, offer layers of meaning that lead to enlightenment and revelation. Great works of art, too, are infused with symbolic codes—messages left by the Masters, passed on through hidden teachings and the underground stream of knowledge. Symbolism is a universal language, connecting the past with the present and revealing the profound truths of human experience. Decades of immersion in this symbolic world have taught me its power to transform the way we see and understand the world. There is a vast universe waiting to be uncovered—one that speaks through the silent, enduring voice of symbols.

QUESTION

Do you know how many symbols you see every day?

AUTHOR CONTACT INFORMATION

Michelle Snyder, Owner of The Symbologist
Website: thesymbologist.com
Email: michelle@thesymbologist.com
Social: https://www.facebook.com/MichelleSnyderSymbologist
Tags: Author, Symbologist, Speaker

February 27

LAURISSA KRISHOCK

*Instead of saying I have to or I need to,
my mantra is I GET to.*

THOUGHT

It was 11:30 pm when I got home from waiting tables. After I sent the babysitter home, I jumped in the shower. As the water cascaded over me, I sank down and began to sob. I was so tired and overwhelmed with the thought of another 24 hours with no sleep because I had to study for a college exam scheduled early the following day, clean two houses, and work another shift at the restaurant.

I managed to pull myself together and finish my shower. I walked into the kitchen, put on a pot of coffee, grabbed my textbook/notes, and went to my desk.

Before I started studying, I went to my son's room and sat on the edge of his bed, watching him sleep so peacefully. He was my reason why!

He was just what I needed to remind me that I did not have to do anything, but I get to do many things.

I get to provide for my family and pay for my college education by working three jobs.

I get to study hard so that I can get a college degree and make a difference in the world.

I get to pull my son seven miles in his burley behind a bike when the car doesn't start, which is often.

I get to start a family business called I am ready so others will be ready for whatever life throws at them.

I get to!

QUESTION

When you are feeling overwhelmed with challenges, ask yourself these questions:
What have you got to do that made a significant impact in your life?
What do you get to do because of those things?

AUTHOR CONTACT INFORMATION

Laurissa Krishock, Founder of IAMREADY, LLC
Website: https://Iamreadyworkshops.com
Email: Laurissa@iamreadyworkshops.com
Social: https://mybook.to/artofconnection5
Tags: Teen Driver, Teen Safety Skills, Capable Driver

February 28
DENISE MERIDITH

The only worthwhile abundance to be cherished in your life is the multitude of other people you have helped enjoy more productive and happier lives.

THOUGHT

It is that time of year, the last day of February, when someone (is it you?) says to me, "Why do we have to have a Black History Month? We don't have a White History Month."

I laugh and say, "Yes, we do; they're called January or March or April or May…"

Time changes society's view of what is worthy of recognition. That is definitely the case with the concept of "abundance." In the Christian Bible, the "abundant life" is a beautiful existence full of good feelings and emotions, not necessarily outwardly visible or quickly earned, and which were bestowed by God, not other men. Today, "abundance" is still a "positive" concept, but it is obtained and manifested in very different ways.

Starting tomorrow, as we say hello to Women's History Month (you can borrow the same answer I use for questions about February), I hope you help others enjoy an abundant life of Love, not Luxury; Peace, not Popularity; Humility, not Hate; Faithfulness, not Favoritism; and Wisdom coming from God, not just Google!

QUESTION

What is one thing you did (or plan to do) today to make someone else happy and, thus, enhance both your lives' abundance?

AUTHOR CONTACT INFORMATION

Denise Meridith, CEO/President of Denise Meridith Consultants Inc
Website: https://www.denisemeridith.com
Email: denise@denisemeridith.com
Social: https://www.facebook.com/denise.meridith.7
Tags: Executive Coach, Black History, Women Business

March 1

TRAICEY FINDER

Abundance begins when you align your thoughts with gratitude, your actions with purpose, and your heart with generosity.

THOUGHT

Gratitude, as a practice, can transform the way we approach our lives and goals. When practiced consistently, it fuels the journey toward achieving our goals and bringing the life we dream of into reality. Gratitude is a powerful catalyst; in fact, it is the secret to personal transformation.

Building gratitude into your daily ritual shifts your mindset from scarcity to abundance and sets a positive tone for the day. It adjusts how your brain works, fostering a mindset that looks for opportunities and solutions. This positive perspective feeds resilience and helps keep your mind connected to your deeper purpose. Over time, the practice of gratitude can create a ripple effect, infusing energy into your dreams and building the motivation to stay the course when challenges arise.

Gratitude is more than a reflection on what we already have; it's a way to engage with life's potential and possibilities. This mindset can be powerful in keeping your dreams alive and providing the strength to achieve them, even when faced with obstacles. I hope you will incorporate a daily practice of gratitude, letting it be a source of inspiration and a tool for maintaining momentum on your journey.

QUESTION

What is one step you can take today to let gratitude fuel your hopes and dreams, keeping you aligned with your higher self?

AUTHOR CONTACT INFORMATION

Traicey Finder, Owner of Vibe-Tality
Website: https://vibe-tality.com
Email: traicey.finder@gmail.com
Social: https://vibe-tality.com
Tags: vibecoach, mindmanagement, clearthenegative

March 2
LORI OSBORNE

Abundance is so much more than what you have; it's a state of mind.

THOUGHT

Have you ever met someone who appears to have nothing but is one of the happiest people you have ever encountered? You have also probably seen people who seemingly have everything, but it is never enough.
To me, these examples demonstrate the power of an abundant mindset.

Those who find joy in what they have, regardless of the quantity, live in true abundance. They understand that happiness and contentment come from within, not from what we have. It's a choice to live in and appreciate the present moment, prioritizing relationships and experiences over the endless pursuit of "more." Conversely, the constant drive for more, without ever feeling satisfied, leads to a life of emptiness and misery, no matter how much outward success is achieved. By embracing an abundant mindset, we are able to see potential over limitations, to give generously without fear of lack, and to live fully, knowing the most significant wealth is already within us.

This mindset shift has been life-changing for me, genuinely taking me from a scarcity mentality to one of gratitude and possibility. The result has opened so many doors to opportunities and creativity and has given me a true sense of abundance.

QUESTION

Do you live in an abundant mindset, or are you stuck in the endless pursuit of "more"?

AUTHOR CONTACT INFORMATION

Lori Osborne, Founder & Chief Solution Architect of BizBolster Web Solutions, LLC
Website: https://www.bizbolster.com/
Email: lori@bizbolster.com
Social: https://www.linkedin.com/in/loriaosborne/
Tags: Website Developer and Digital Marketer

March 3
DAVID WALTZER

*God is omnipotent(abundant), and God is love;
therefore, love is abundant, so Abundance is the truth.*

THOUGHT

After I realized that the Abundance Mindset was the way,
I stopped competing with others and started collaborating with them.
Wicked Awesome Happy Hour (WAHH) was and is an inclusive group of people who possess at least one foundational belief in common: the Abundance Mindset.
There is more than enough for all of us to achieve monumental success
without taking anything from anyone else. Another thing that's a part of
the Golden Rule with one thing added. Do unto others as you would have them
do unto you, without expectation of return.

The people in my circle seek to achieve collaboration over competition
before self-interest. If you ask why, it's because working together to achieve
success supercharges abundance. God implores us to be intentional
while building community through consistent positivity.

QUESTION

Whether you are in Abundance or Scarcity in your actual life, where do you feel it is better to live in your mind? In scarcity or Abundance?

AUTHOR CONTACT INFORMATION

David Waltzer, Founder of Wicked Awesome LLC
Website: https://wickedawesomeconnections.com
Email: dcwaltzer1@gmail.com
Social: https://www.facebook.com/profile.php?id=100018774735625&mibextid=ZbWKwL
Tags: Christian, Veteran, MoneyGuy, Connector

March 4
GENE-O COLE

*Love was designed to be a forever emotion,
so don't let yours suddenly stop.*

THOUGHT

Our society often finds reasons to hate our neighbor instead of embracing the opportunity to love our brother. We choose judgment over compassion and walk away rather than staying to understand the unknown. This tendency, left unchecked, has led us to overlook the abundant love surrounding us.

Abundance in love means it isn't limited to one person; it's an infinite resource available to everyone. We are blessed with endless love, which we will never lack. Love is not a scarce commodity; it is a perpetual wellspring that nourishes and sustains us.

Around the world, many are less wealthy, yet they possess an abundance of love that can fill the largest oceans. They understand that true richness lies in the depth of love, not in material possessions. I aspire to swim in these oceans of love rather than settle for a shallow lake filled with insignificant things.

Let us take full advantage of this overflow of love. It's time to move away from the shallow ponds of superficiality and dive into the deep, boundless oceans of love available to us. By doing so, we can enrich our lives and the lives of those around us, fostering a more compassionate, understanding, and loving world.

QUESTION

Why choose to judge and hate rather than embrace the abundant love available to us; how can we shift our perspective to take full advantage of this limitless love to enrich our lives and those of others?

AUTHOR CONTACT INFORMATION

Gene-o Cole, Self of Gene-o
Website: https://gene-o.com/
Email: geneocole@gmail.com
Social: https://www.instagram.com/geneomusic/
Tags: Speaker, Motivator, Artist, Author, Friend

March 5
EZINNE OZURUMBA

Abundance happens in a moment!

THOUGHT

Think about it! When one seed is planted, many seeds are harvested at once during harvest time. That, my friend, is abundance. What is not seen is the multiple minor progressions the seed made consistently to multiply abundantly. The seed had to transform to become something more than it was. It had to get rid of its old self, to die to what was and draw from something far more significant than it. It embraced the pain that the process brought. Learned from stops and turns. Gained from the reward of consistency. Then, abundance!

It is the small, consistent steps that you take in life and business that make the difference. Small steps add up to big moves. On the road to abundance, you will face a lot, feel down sometimes, and want to give up. All you are working towards happens in a moment. So, move, celebrate your wins, learn from your mistakes, and continue to be abundant!

QUESTION

What small step are you taking now towards abundance?

AUTHOR CONTACT INFORMATION

Dr Ezinne Ozurumba, Owner of Havilah Health
Website: www.myhavilahhealth.com
Email: info@drezinneozurumba.com
Social: https://www.linkedin.com/in/drezinneozurumba
Tags: Functional Medicine, Thyroid Health Coach, Speaker

March 6
SARREN SCRIBNER

*Cherish the abundance in your life,
whether it be health, wealth, family, or love.
For you are only here for a moment–make it count.*

THOUGHT

To me, abundance is multifaceted. The above quote emphasizes the importance of appreciating the abundance present in our lives, in whatever form it manifests itself. To remember, we should value the new day we have been given, the roof over our heads, the food on our table, and the people seated at it as well. It reminds us that each person's plate may look different, and that's okay, for that is their journey. We should appreciate our current bounties and be encouraged to recognize and value the blessings we have, as life is fleeting. Our time here is limited–a blink. By cherishing what we currently have, we live more fully, with more meaning, and with a sense of purpose. Ultimately, it is a call to be present, to be grateful and intentional in how we experience life and interact with those around us.

QUESTION

What specific practices can individuals incorporate into their daily lives to cultivate a greater sense of gratitude and appreciation for the abundance they have?

AUTHOR CONTACT INFORMATION

Sarren Scribner, Author of Sarren Scribner
Website: https://linktr.ee/sarren.scribner
Email: sarren.scribner@gmail.com
Social: https://linktr.ee/sarren.scribner
Tags: Author

March 7

YANICK SÉÏDE

*We invite abundance when we approach life with an
open mind and let go of worries about scarcity.*

THOUGHT

Abundance, what do we mean by that? When we talk about abundance, most of us think of material wealth. It is often depicted by the cornucopia, also known as the horn of plenty. However, it includes more than that. We usually are unaware of the abundance surrounding us, which may give us a sense that we are lacking. Abundance is present in many ways: the love and support we give to others or that we may receive, the bonds we create with others, and the growth resulting from overcoming challenges are signs of abundance.

In my coaching practice, I've seen transformation when clients shift from a scarcity mindset to an abundance mindset, unlocking new possibilities and personal growth. Abundance is not about having everything you want but realizing that you already have what you need to thrive. Each day is an invitation to explore new possibilities. When we live with an open heart and mind, we create space for even more opportunities, joy, and fulfillment.

Words can be powerful. I hope these inspire and encourage you to seek and appreciate abundance beyond material pursuits but also in the richness of your relationships, experiences, and personal growth.

QUESTION

Where in your life have you already experienced abundance,
and how can you open yourself to recognizing even more of it in your relationships,
personal growth, or daily experiences?

AUTHOR CONTACT INFORMATION

Yanick Séïde, Founder & CEO of Chrysalis Women Empowerment
Website: https://chrysaliswomenempowerment.ca
Email: yanick@chrysaliswomenempowerment.ca
Social: https://www.linkedin.com/in/yanick-s%C3%A9%C3%AFde-8588b645/
Tags: Life Coach, Career Coach, Women, Speaker, Author

March 8

PATTY HEDRICK

*Celebrating International Women's Day honors those
who paved the way, giving us hope and strength to move f
orward through challenges and triumphs.*

THOUGHT

Nursing has been in my veins since I was a young child. My first job was working in the cafeteria of a nursing home, serving meals to the residents and cleaning up afterward. The woman loved sharing their stories and "pearls of wisdom." I would often finish my shift and stay and visit afterward. They would share their favorite memories but also their regrets. The residents would tell me always to be true to myself, follow my heart, and not let others stop me from who "I was meant to be."

This movement still makes me proud to be a woman and to support and celebrate International Women's Day. Regardless of the consequences of their actions, all of these women believed wholeheartedly in themselves and their causes.

And their beliefs and willingness to step forward changed our history and provided opportunities for their daughters and future generations.

Honoring those who have forged away to celebrate women throughout the years has provided us with a roadmap to help us achieve our goals and forge a new path.

QUESTION

*How does celebrating International Women's Day inspire us to unite
as women and reflect on how far we've come in redefining what it means
to actively and confidently age on our terms?*

AUTHOR CONTACT INFORMATION

Patty Hedrick, Founder of Med-Legal Healthcare Consultants, Inc.
Website: https://pattyhedrick.com
Email: pattyhedrick@gmail.com
Social: https://www.linkedin.com/in/pattyhedrick/
Tags: Speaker, Coach, Consultant, Author, Nurse

March 9
MICHAEL NOYES

Stop Chasing the Shiny Objects in Life When You Can Apply Polish to the Dull Spots

THOUGHT

Abundance means recognizing and appreciating the wealth of resources, opportunities, and relationships around me.

Adopting an abundance mindset allows me to focus on the long-term advantages of nurturing relationships versus concentrating solely on the immediate benefit -"The Sale." I built trust-based relationships with my clients, which resulted in more referrals, broadened my network, and opened up new possibilities.

Adopting an abundance mindset has increased my business. I deliver value to each client through a consultative approach rather than a one-size-fits-all method. This mindset allows me to view every client interaction as a unique opportunity.

With an advanced degree in Adult Education, I help clients cross the finish line. Adults learn best by doing, and when adult experiential methods are used, clients are drawn in, resulting in a deeper understanding.

An abundant mindset continuously allows me to learn and grow. Like astronauts studying the effects of life on Mars, Insurance Brokers are on a continuous quest to discover next-generation insurance products that can sometimes have a profound impact on their lives.

QUESTION

As an Insurance Agent/Broker, what impact will you have on servicing clients' needs if you are of the mindset that you already possess everything you need? Will it move the needle either way? If so, how?

AUTHOR CONTACT INFORMATION

Michael Noyes, M.A. Owner of Mike Noyes Your Insurance Guy
Website: https://www.healthmarkets.com/local-health-insurance-agent/mnoyes/
Email: mjnoyes@cox.net
Social: https://www.facebook.com/HealthMarkets.Mike.Noyes
Tags: Health Insurance Broker, Health Insurance Agent

March 10
RANI THANACOODY

You are the treasure that you are seeking.

THOUGHT

'Abundance is not something we acquire. It is something we tune into,' as said by Dr Wayne Dyer. It comes from developing a connection with our heart, where we can feel and experience more emotions and be able to listen to our inner voice. A wounded heart that is full of anger, hatred, sadness, hurts, fear, and judgment cannot give and receive. A wounded heart can only survive each day and live in a very small space. Healing our hearts enables us to be more authentic to ourselves.

When our hearts are healed and opened, we are more receptive to giving and receiving from the world around us. Healing our hearts creates an expansion within us to create new thoughts, feel our emotions more deeply, and develop our capacity to manifest. We can create the life we want only by going within us.

Abundance is a gift available to all of us. Abundance starts with using your keys to open your treasure chest that is within you through healing your inner wounds and opening your heart. Because all that you are looking for in the world can be found inside of you. You are the treasure that you are seeking.

QUESTION

What if today, you put yourself first and you take the first step to living an abundant life?

AUTHOR CONTACT INFORMATION

Dr Rani Thanacoody, Founder of AmazingYou, Clinical Hypnotherapist of AmazingYoubyRani
Website: https://marsvenuscoachrani.com
Email: thanacoodyr98@gmail.com
Social: https://www.instagram.com/thanacoodyrani/?hl=en-gb
Tags: ranithanacoody, thanacoodyrani, amazingyoupodcast

March 11

VICKIE GOWDY

Abundance is that quiet confidence you show in life that helps pave your life journey.

THOUGHT

In the chaos of our daily lives, we often equate abundance with money and material possessions. However, true abundance transcends mere accumulation of goods; it is a state of mind, a quiet confidence that permeates our very existence. That quiet confidence teaches us more about ourselves, who we are, and what we are capable of.

I have had many challenges along my path, but I have learned to embrace them. I know that even the journey ahead will have its challenges, and I will also be filled with the abundance of an extraordinary life ahead. The essence of abundance, to me, is a serene belief in your ability to navigate life's journey with grace and purpose.

Money and material possessions will come and go, just like many other things in life, but the journey you pave with quiet confidence will last a lifetime. When we can embrace quiet confidence, it will open us up to the unlimited possibilities that life has to offer and create an incredible path of abundance. The best thing is that you created this all on your own by believing in yourself.

QUESTION

When was the last time you took time to yourself to get away from the chaos and embrace the life and path you have created?

AUTHOR CONTACT INFORMATION

Vickie Gowdy, Owner of Vickie Gowdy
Website: https://vickiegowdy.com/
Email: vickie@vickiegowdy.com
Social: https://www.linkedin.com/in/victoria-gowdy-9092a793/
Tags: Virtual Assistant, Executive Virtual Assistant

March 12

JOE LANDER

Your Legacy is something you live NOW, not just leave SOMEDAY!

THOUGHT

Is your Legacy something to be determined in the distant future when your time on this planet is done?? The truth is that your Legacy is much more profound and pressing than that. Your Legacy isn't just about the echoes of your existence when you're gone. It's about the mission you uncover to be uniquely yours that contributes to an enhanced quality of life for others and brings you a sense of purpose, joy, and contentment. It's not about the monuments or accolades that may come later but about the lives you meaningfully touch today.

Living your Legacy means consciously choosing new action that powerfully springs forth from your deepest values and contributes to the well-being and joy of others. Ultimately, living your Legacy is an act of loving kindness, rooted in the wisdom of your life experience, that causes positive change because of what and who you inspire.
By living your Legacy now, you get to experience the fulfillment that comes from knowing you're part of something bigger than yourself, a meaningful contribution to the world. This active, intentional approach to living ensures that your Legacy is something you leave behind, something you live and breathe each day.

QUESTION

What is the Legacy you'd like to create and see in the world while you're still here to witness your impact?

AUTHOR CONTACT INFORMATION

Joe Lander, Owner and CEO of The Life You Love Coaching
Website: https://thelifeyoulovecoaching.com
Email: Joe@thelifeyoulovecoaching.com
Social: https://linkedin.com/in/joseph-m-lander
Tags: Legacy Coach

March 13

JOANNE SALVADOR

*Abundance is all around us;
all you have to do is look.*

THOUGHT

In this ever-changing world, I've found that everything we need lies in the abundance nature offers. Beauty, art, creativity, music, well-being, freedom, peace of mind, all essentials for enjoying life exist here. The signs are there if you know how and where to look. Simplicity is key.

Roam through secluded landscapes and sense their ancient secrets through the mists of time. Every hidden secret is a story waiting to be told; many may have faded from memory yet still linger and endure. Whether by light into dark or day into night, the sun, moon, stars, plants, and animals reveal the enchanted layers of our environment.

Following the rhythm of weather patterns, shapes in drifting clouds, the scent of rain on the breeze, blossoming flowers, dancing leaves, and sparkling crystal snowflakes is pure magic. The natural world is vast and boundless, filled with wisdom. Here is fulfillment that transcends the ordinary and mundane to a unique and extraordinary life. By embracing nature's abundance and all it offers, the possibilities are endless.

QUESTION

*What I desire in appreciating abundance is my personal holy grail fulfilled.
As for other people, what do they seek, and what are their wishes?
I ask them: What is it you want as abundance in your life?*

AUTHOR CONTACT INFORMATION

Joanne Salvador, Founder of Shaitan Studio
Website: https://www.365daysofabundancequotes.com
Email: Circe13@optonline.net
Social: https://www.facebook.com/joanne.salvador.180
Tags: Egyptologist, Antiquities Dealer, Fine Arts Teacher

March 14
MARIA MANTOUDAKIS

Your past may have shaped you, but your past does not define your future and who you are.

THOUGHT

Imagine coming out to drive your car after a heavy snowstorm. You start cleaning the back of your car, and the rear windshield is clear. However, you are in a hurry to get to your appointment, so you decide to drive the car while your front windshield is totally covered with snow. You begin slowly driving your car, using only your rearview mirror as your guide. What an unbelievable scenario!!! You would never do that!! If you did, it would only be a matter of time before you crash.

Yet when I look around, I see people living their hectic lives, rushing and going at full speed, while their only focus is their rearview mirror, their past. In our mind, we replay past events, we replay what people said, we replay what people did, and we take the conclusions we drew from these events as the core of what drives us today.

QUESTION

Are you ready to create the future of your dreams with a clear windshield?

AUTHOR CONTACT INFORMATION

Maria Mantoudakis, CEO and Founder of ReCreate Success Now, LLC
Website: recreatesuccessnow.com
Email: mantoudakis@yahoo.com
Social: https://www.linkedin.com/in/maria-mantoudakis-6979a/
Tags: Life Coach

March 15

CAROLINE PASSMORE

Empowering your decisions with clarity and confidence in your finances is what I hope to help every business achieve.

THOUGHT

An accountant is a strategic partner when it comes to helping business owners make financial decisions and helping business leaders make informed choices by providing precise and actionable insights. The intent is always to strive to present complex financial data in a transparent and comprehensible manner that transforms intricate information into accessible analyses. Building trust between the accountant and the stakeholders is imperative. In the end, this will foster a collaborative environment where informed decisions can be made.

My role as the accountant is to be the guardian of the company's financial health. This duty is essential for maintaining a high standard of integrity and accuracy in the financial documentation. It is a role that transcends traditional number-crunching to become a strategic pillar in decision-making and business success. It motivates us, as accountants, to strive for excellence, embrace innovation, and recognize ourselves as essential partners in every organization's journey toward financial clarity and confident decision-making.

QUESTION

How would having a strategic financial partner impact your ability to achieve your business goals?

AUTHOR CONTACT INFORMATION

Caroline Passmore, Expert Accounting Financial Professional of CRP Specialists Inc
Website: https://crpspecialists.com
Email: caroline@crpspecialists.com
Social: https://www.facebook.com/caroline.rpassmore/
Tags: Accounting, FP&A, Financial Planning, Speaker

March 16
CHRISTINE KIPP

Love in abundance is the greatest treasure, always closer than we think: in every smile, hug, and compliment, the greatest of God's gifts.

THOUGHT

Princess Victoria was born into a lavish life of wealth and recognition; amidst all of the opulence, her life was very isolated. She was destined for a lonely life. One day, in the gardens, she met Eleanor, a portrait of poverty and the daughter of a palace gardener. Eleanor connected with Victoria through her radiant smile that exuded pure joy and affection. Kindness enveloped them as Eleanor reached for Victoria's hand, transcending protocol, wealth, and status, leading her to dance and giggle along the garden paths.

Princess Victoria was awakened to how love nourishes the soul, surpassing all riches. Victoria's life gained meaning in that moment, a connection that was the key to unlocking a treasure-house of love. Even after Victoria was crowned Queen, she remembered the transformative dance in the garden. Inspired by a peasant girl's caring, she became known through the ages for her lavish aid to children in need. She found plentitude in giving and receiving love and caring for others, not gowns that adorned her or a jeweled crown on her head. Imagine the abundant impact we will make if we all are like Eleanor and take a moment each day to share a smile or act of kindness!

QUESTION

In your daily journey on a quest for abundant love, the greatest of God's gifts, how many people can you impact every day with a smile, act of kindness, encouragement, forgiveness, or support?

AUTHOR CONTACT INFORMATION

Christine Kipp, Founder and CEO of Nurture Our World of Nurture Our World
Website: https://www.nurtureourworld.net
Email: chriskippntc@gmail.com
Social: https://www.facebook.com/NurtureOurWorld.net/
Tags: Malawi Aid, Cyclone Freddy Relief, Kids Who Care

March 17

KELLY HULL AHO

*You are forever lost to the energy of abundance
if you only view it in terms of money.*

THOUGHT

Abundance is simply the overflow of energy (or Light) remaining after meeting your basic needs. This extra energy flows next to your heart's desires or passions. Purpose and passion are inextricably intertwined. The trick is learning to accept this fundamental principle, in esoteric terms, that all the power that ever was or will be is here now. Infinite abundance first flows through you, then into the world around you.

Any block to accepting this available energy keeps you from directing abundant flow beyond your basic needs and into your life's purpose. Limitations, either self-imposed or accepted from others, trap you in a lack mindset, cutting you off from the eternal flow of energy.

As the creator of your reality and the life you live, changing your mindset about abundance will lead to increased flow. This critical shift requires a deep commitment to healing. The mystery school tradition of initiation provides a foundation of healing and the tools necessary to transform limiting beliefs into understanding and wisdom for the ultimate abundance mindset. The path to know thyself is the path to accepting that you are powerful beyond measure.

QUESTION

*Pause a moment and consider: What is causing your resistance
to accepting the flow of abundance?*

AUTHOR CONTACT INFORMATION

Kelly Hull Aho, Co-Founder of Empowerful Life
Website: https://www.empowerfullife.com
Email: kelly@empowerful.life
Social: https://linktr.ee/kellyhullaho
Tags: Spiritual Guide, Energy Healer, Esoteric Training

March 18
SOOJIN KIM

Abundance of health is the greatest gift one can possess; it's the foundation of happiness that everyone aspires to be. Health creates abundance.

THOUGHT

From the age of 30 to 43 years old, I had numerous health challenges. There were many times I could and should have died, but it was not my time, and I'm still here for a reason, to be in this book, perhaps. In two of those years, I was so sick that I became homebound and in bed, except to go to the doctors or the hospitals. For five-plus years, I was on heavy-duty prescribed narcotic medications. I suffered from one form of pain and health complications to another, and I was an empty shell version of myself, just existing and not actually living. I had a husband who was a good provider, a house in a great town, and three beautiful, healthy children. Yet, my life was lacking abundance. I learned the hard way without health, abundance does not exist. With an abundance of health, anything and everything is possible. Health is abundance.

As a Wellness Advocate, I want to inspire other Entrepreneurs to make their health a number one priority, as health is the authentic abundance. Inflammation is the main culprit of just about all illnesses; I want to help others address their inflammation problems with a solution that is scientifically proven to be effective against inflammation.

QUESTION

What could be more paramount than an abundance of health in your life?

AUTHOR CONTACT INFORMATION

Soojin Kim, Partner of Zinzino
Website: https://www.Soojinhealth.com
Email: kim13soo@yahoo.com
Social: https://www.instagram.com/Soojinhealth
Tags: Nutritionist, Wellness Coach, Wellness Advocate

March 19

HEATHER EILEEN HARRIS

The abundance you have in your life is reflective of how you love and prioritize yourself.

THOUGHT

What you believe about yourself sets the tone of what you will accept and allow into your life. For much of my life, I believed I was not enough for anyone to love and that I was not worthy of love. These false beliefs set the stage for me to settle for relationships that did not support my best. Fortunately, I was blessed with two friends who helped change all of that for me and opened up my world to new possibilities.

Dr. Landon Poppleton, a friend since childhood, taught me that I am loveable precisely as I am. Knowing me most of my life, he has seen me at my best, my worst, and as a complete hot mess. Through all the storms and celebrations in life, he reminds me that I am enough and worthy of all the love and happiness I desire and more.

Dr. Sylvester Hanna taught me the importance of prioritizing myself and the power of unconditional love. Everyone has pain and struggles, but if I genuinely want to help others, I must first help myself. He taught me that I am worth prioritizing and that beauty evolves when I trust myself, listen to myself, and show myself the same unconditional love that I show others. Everything begins with the self.

QUESTION

How would your life change if you loved and prioritized yourself more?

AUTHOR CONTACT INFORMATION

Heather Eileen Harris, CEO and Founder of Gratitude From The Heart, LLC
Website: https://gratitude4u.com/
Email: hello@gratitude4u.com
Social: https://www.facebook.com/heather.w.harris.58
Tags: Holistic Life and Wellness Coach, Resilience

March 20

CARLA JANSEN VAN ROSENDAAL

*STOP…FOCUS…Wherever you were, Wherever you are,
You can always go…where you want to be!*

THOUGHT

What I've learned most in life is that we live according to what we (often unconsciously) believe. The stories and negative thoughts in our heads steer our lives and experiences.

Why? We're like radio stations: each thought has a unique frequency that we send out, attracting people and situations that match it, just like tuning into a specific radio FM frequency.

When life isn't going your way, if you're not living your dream and keep attracting what you don't want, it's likely because you're sending out the wrong frequencies through negative thoughts and stories.

To discover the stories you're telling yourself, start by observing your daily life: What isn't going well? Who or what makes you unhappy? What do you keep attracting that you don't want? Track these patterns and reflect on your role in them. You've likely attracted these things without realizing it.

Use your power and take responsibility for your life. Stop blaming others or circumstances—you are the one who has to change. When you shift your thoughts and stories, your feelings change, and you change your frequency, attracting what you truly desire.

Start today, the beginning of Spring, and allow yourself to bloom beautifully.

QUESTION

How fast would your life change if quantum technology could show your blocking stories, enabling you to transform them quickly? Shift your frequencies and effortlessly attract what you truly desire.

AUTHOR CONTACT INFORMATION

Carla Jansen van Rosendaal, Founder of Carla Jansen van Rosendaal Life-Mind Creation
Website: https://life-mindcreation.com/
Email: info@life-mindcreation.com
Social: https://linktr.ee/carlajansenvanrosendaal
Tags: Burnout and Mindset Coach, Speaker, Author

The Art of Connection

March 21

ANGELIKA O'ROURKE

*You already hold all the answers within.
Trust your inner voice that guides you on the unique
path that life has laid out for you.*

THOUGHT

When I was younger, I believed others had all the answers, so I followed their advice, thinking they knew better. But I often felt miserable and wondered why things rarely worked out in my favor. Over time, I realized that if I had trusted my inner voice more, I might have been better off. Yet, it was convenient to hand over responsibility; if things went wrong, I could always blame someone else.

Deciding to trust myself and take charge of my life took courage. It meant accepting responsibility, mistakes, and failures. But once I made that choice, everything changed.

Life isn't about being right or wrong; it's about experiencing, growing, and learning from my mistakes. Owning my mistakes was liberating. They were mine to make, and they taught me so much.

I am a Biomagnetism therapist who developed a holistic approach to well-being, teaching meditation and coaching holistic practitioners. The common thread is empowerment, helping others connect with themselves and trust their inner guidance.

No one knows your destiny or purpose better than you. True liberation comes from living in alignment with your inner self and trusting life's plan, guiding you every step of the way.

QUESTION

What if you decided to step outside the tight walls of others' expectations and start following the inner voice that has been whispering to you all along?

AUTHOR CONTACT INFORMATION

Angelika O'Rourke, Owner of BME Solutions LLC
Website: https://bme-solutions.com
Email: infobmesolutions@gmail.com
Social: https://www.facebook.com/topbmesolutions
Tags: Business Coach

March 22

BRIAN SWANSON

*Emotions feel good for a moment.
Logic molds your life.*

THOUGHT

We all travel through the world on a curvy road. Every minute of every day, we are faced with decisions. We can elect to deal with each decision with emotion or logic. Emotion tends to lead us down paths that are meant to make us feel good. Occasionally, we let those emotions take over and lead us astray. However, logic has one direction and will keep us on an even plane.

I was raised by parents who adopted me at a very early ae. I grew up knowing I was adopted but not aware of who my birth parents were. Emotions could have ruled my life. Who I am? Where did I come from? Why did my birth parents give me away? And many other questions. If I had chosen to live through my emotions, I would have become a highly emotional adult.

I decided I didn't want to live my life through emotions and worry. I chose to use logic. I told myself, "I was adopted for a good reason, and someday I may find out why." As time would tell, I found both of my birth parents. It has been a fantastic experience with a new extended family.

QUESTION

Do you live your life through emotion or logic?

AUTHOR CONTACT INFORMATION

Brian Swanson, Owner of DJ WildLife
Website: https://networktogether.net
Email: robert@networktogther.net
Social: https://www.facebook.com/djwildlife
Tags: Speaker, DJ, SoundPro, Keynote, Digital Design

March 23
SCOTT ALLAN

With Spirit, we unlock the most genuine power of abundance, not in what we own but in the undeniable truth that love and connection are eternal.

THOUGHT

True abundance is not what you hold in your hands but rather what you feel in your heart. It's the unshakable connection, deep love, and presence that endure long after the physical has faded. In evidential mediumship, we tap into this abundance by connecting with those who've passed. Their messages remind us that love knows no limits, for it transcends life, death, and everything in between. That is the ultimate gift of abundance!

When we connect with Spirit, we're invited to see abundance in an entirely new light. It's measured not by things but by the love we've shared and the bonds we've built. The "undeniable truth" is this: our relationships are eternal. The love, the cherished moments, and the memories we carry are part of a spiritual connection that transcends physical boundaries.

This perspective is a game-changer. It reminds us to celebrate the people in our lives and the love we share. While possessions come and go, it's these connections that give life depth and meaning. When we open to Spirit, we step into an abundance not limited by time or space—a reminder of our place in a vast, interconnected universe where love doesn't end. It transforms and grows.

QUESTION

How would your perspective on abundance transform your thoughts if you focused on the idea that love and connection are limitless, outshining anything in this material world?

AUTHOR CONTACT INFORMATION

Scott Allan, Owner of Psychic Medium Scott Allan
Website: https://mediumscottallan.com
Email: scott@mediumscottallan.com
Social: https://www.facebook.com/MediumScottAllan
Tags: Psychic Medium, Evidential Readings, Mediumship

March 24
THERESA RUSSELL

*If you keep doing what you're doing,
you're going to keep getting what you got.*

THOUGHT

Living life with abundance is all about experiences, opportunities, and relationships; it is not about wealth. This quote is something that I would tell myself when I was younger so that I would stretch myself to grow. To have abundance in your life, you must be willing to make changes; embracing change unlocks potential that is beyond our current circumstances. To make choices as if they already are and declare abundance without any proof.

Evaluating our habits and beliefs periodically to shift our mindset is crucial. You cannot have a scarcity mindset, nor can you stay stagnant, which limits possibilities. Each step out of the routine and every new challenge that you face widens your horizon and multiplies your chances to live life fully.

Be intentional in your pursuit of abundance. Remember that your current habits could be limiting what could be. By leveling up your habits, your life will be filled with richer experiences. There is more out there that we cannot see. Be open to receive and, in turn, be willing to give.

When we harness this abundance mindset, we create a ripple effect, inspiring others to reach for abundance in their own lives.

QUESTION

What is one mindset shift that would allow you to see possibilities where you once saw limitations?

AUTHOR CONTACT INFORMATION

Theresa Russell, Theresa Russell of Theresa Russell
Website: https://www.365daysofabundancequotes.com
Email: trussellpremier@aol.com
Social: https://www.facebook.com/groups/easethrumenopausenaturally
Tags: Speaker, International Author, Menopause Coach

March 25
GLENDA ROBERTS

*The vibrations of your words are sent into
the universe, which seeks out matching vibrations
(positive or negative), returning to create your reality.*

THOUGHT

The mind is a powerhouse. Everything you think and speak carries vibrational energy into the universe. Your thoughts and words manifest back to you; positive attracts positivity, negative - negativity. What you think and say sculpts what you become. Cultivating positive thoughts of encouragement, kindness, and affirmation shapes your life. Like ripples in a pond, positive vibrations extend outward, affecting our own experiences, extending to those around us, and creating effects of joy, love, and abundance. Creating and maintaining a positive mindset involves embracing uplifting daily habits:

1. Express Gratitude: Give thanks daily for the goodness that will come. Start a Gratitude Journal.
2. Constructive Self-Talk: Replace negative self-talk with productive affirmations.
3. Keep Positive Company: Surround yourself with inspiring, uplifting people. Avoid toxic relationships.
4. Meditation: Yoga, meditation, and breathing improve focus and elevate stress.
5. Set Goals: Make goals that are specific, measurable, and achievable, then create a plan of action.
6. Maintain a healthy lifestyle: Exercise, good nutrition, and sleep keep you positive.
7. Serving Others: Engage in acts of kindness.

QUESTION

*What label does the majority of your thoughts wear, positive or negative?
Do you feel the lift of joy and light, or have you fallen into a pit of darkness?
Good daily habits form positive vibrations.*

AUTHOR CONTACT INFORMATION

Glenda Roberts, Owner/Founder of Glenda's Montessori
Website: https://www.365daysofabundancequotes.com
Email: missglendaroberts@gmail.com
Social: https://mybook.to/artofconnection5
Tags: Montessori, Mesa Preschool, Miss Glenda

365 Days of Abundance Quotes

March 26
TONYA SWAINSTON

Learning can be effortless and abundant.

THOUGHT

I've recognized and succeeded in making abundant learning possible earlier and easier than ever imagined!

When I adopted my daughter, I was made aware that the most well-adjusted adopted adults were ones who had known they were adopted at an early age. Without a playbook to follow, I took steps that led my daughter to be one of those adults. The steps that I took became the catalyst for my measurable learning methodology. Throughout her early years, I used multi-layered teaching techniques and routines that led her to know her adoption story at a young age.

The saying, "Once you see it, you can't unsee it," usually has an unfavorable connotation, but children who have been taught using my program and teaching techniques are enjoying this phenomenon positively! They are achieving learning success in ways they never imagined or thought possible. Immersing learners in relatable and memorable visual hooks that evolve with them over time makes learning effortless and abundant, starting in their first year. I am so excited to share my knowledge to help all students achieve measurable, consistent learning success.

QUESTION

What if you could gain the knowledge to make learning easier, measurable, and successful for your child or students?

AUTHOR CONTACT INFORMATION

Tonya Swainston, Founder and CEO of Measurable Learning, LLC
Website: https://www.123SuperEmpowered.com
Email: 123superempowered@gmail.com
Social: https://www.facebook.com/share/zY4hSXBSLobmHbCw/?mibextid=LQQJ4d
Tags: Education Consultant, Early Childhood, Elementary

March 27

PAUL WEIGEL

I am at peace. I know it will be okay.

THOUGHT

Ten years. It's hard to believe it's been so long: 315,300+ seconds. That's how many hours, minutes, or seconds that I've been a cancer survivor. Natalie, my daughter, and I are riding the Great Alaskan Railroad as we are halfway through our trip of a lifetime to Denali National Park and Anchorage.

I had a lifetime of doubt and misery, of aches so deep for so long that I wanted to scream how much it hurt forever, and I wish it all would stop. Now I've got a bucket list of life experiences flowing over and have the absolute wonder of getting the chance to raise a young woman who is already incredible and who I know will do amazing things one day when she's all grown.

My life changed because of her. I was forty-three, a new father, and an Ironman triathlete when I was diagnosed with a cancerous tumor the size of a lemon in my lower abdomen. I wrote a love story for her, which became so much more about how to connect with your child, deal with the anxiety and fear of being blasted with a potentially unfathomable death sentence, and live with the scariest future ever and a toddler to raise, all while believing in the impossible of a limitless future and having the incredible come true.

QUESTION

What do you do to live your best life every day?

AUTHOR CONTACT INFORMATION

Paul Weigel, Owner of Paul Weigel, Iron Dad
Website: https://www.irondadbook.com
Email: paulkweigel@gmail.com
Social: https://www.linkedin.com/in/paulweigelirondad/
Tags: Iron Dad, Livestrong, Speaker, Evangelist

March 28
RANI THANACOODY

You are the treasure that you have been seeking.

THOUGHT

I aim to empower individuals from all around the world to live a more fulfilled and abundant life. Abundance is about having more than you need. You can live an abundant life, and it starts with you and is within you. I will show you how I created abundance in my life by using some simple steps that you can apply to create the abundance that you deserve. You are the alchemist and painter of your life.

The first step is to change your perception and remove the limiting beliefs in your mind. Any perception you cling to about never being capable of acquiring abundance in whatever form you can imagine is a mental block, not a genuine barrier to your eventual success. We can eliminate mental challenges and make your life incredible, full of joyous hope and peace. So, let's make your life abundant and worthy.

QUESTION

What if, today, you put yourself first and take the first step to living an abundant life?

AUTHOR CONTACT INFORMATION

Dr Rani Thanacoody, Clinical Hypnotherapist and Relationship Coach of AmazingYou by Rani

Website: https://marsvenuscoachrani.com

Email: thanacoodyr98@gmail.com

Social: https://www.instagram.com/thanacoodyrani/?hl=en-gb

Tags: ranithanacoody, thanacoodyrani, amazingyoupodcast

March 29

GRACE GWITIRA

A mindset of abundance promotes creativity, innovation, and transformation.

THOUGHT

Abundance means different things to different people. According to the Webster Meridian dictionary, abundance means "an ample quantity." For me, "abundance" means more than enough. Thus, living in abundance means you have more than what you need.

God blesses us so that we can bless others. The talents, knowledge, gifts, and resources that have been bestowed on you are not only given to you for your upkeep but to enable you to serve others.

For example, Sarah had her 70th birthday recently. Instead of having a lavish party and being gifted stuff she already had, she asked her friends and family to channel their gifts to add to the money she already had. This request enabled her to install a well, thereby supplying clean water to a drought-stricken rural community in Africa. Because she was living in abundance, she thought of creative and innovative ways to serve a community by solving their lack of clean water problems -- bringing about transformation in the lives of the villagers.

With the mindset of abundance, you recognize the blessings you have, think of creative and innovative ways to solve problems, overcome obstacles, and inspire positive action – leading to transformation.

QUESTION

What is your definition of living in abundance? Do you believe you are living in abundance now? If yes, in what way can you channel your abundance to serve others?

AUTHOR CONTACT INFORMATION

Grace Gwitira, Founder of Transformation Oasis
Website: https://drgracegwitira.com/
Email: ggwitira@outlook.com
Social: www.linkedin.com/in/drgracegwitira
Tags: Leadership, Speaker, Conflict Resolution, Train

March 30
JOSEPH CHIPOKOSA

*Comparison builds walls against abundance,
but giving crumbles those walls down.*

THOUGHT

The Oxford Dictionary defines abundance as a large quantity that is more than enough. How much is enough is something most people haven't given much thought to. We often think we do not have enough because the next man has a little more in comparison to what we think we have. If abundance is having more than enough (for yourself), then it can only be measured by what one has left to give to others and to nurture our world.

Two concepts to consider then are comparison and giving. They both play crucial roles in shaping our experiences and perspectives as far as abundance is concerned. Comparison, evaluating what you have versus others, prevents us from experiencing abundance, distracting us from gratitude. Giving, in contrast, shifts our focus outward in a positive way. It enriches both the giver and the receiver, or as the old saying goes, "It is more blessed to give than to receive."

When we give, we cultivate gratitude and empathy. Giving encourages a sense of abundance; it reminds us that we have enough to share, which can counteract negative feelings of scarcity and competition. Embracing giving enriches our lives and strengthens our connections with others.

QUESTION

Since giving creates the most positive form of abundance, in what various ways can you think of to contribute to the world around you?

AUTHOR CONTACT INFORMATION

Reverend Joseph Chipokosa, Malawi President/Director of Operations of Nurture Our World
Website: https://www.nurtureourworld.net
Email: josephchipokosa@gmail.com
Social: https://www.facebook.com/NurtureOurWorld.net/
Tags: Malawi, Cyclone Freddy

March 31

ELLA PAHOPIN

Relish in the gift of abundance.

THOUGHT

I had the misguided notion that abundance was having a great deal of possessions and money. I've worked tirelessly most of my life to achieve these items. With all my achievements, there was always a feeling of emptiness inside me. I always believed my thinking was flawed or I was misinterpreting the mindset behind wealth and the happiness it should bring with it. The thinking was flawed.

As I aged, circumstances in life made me understand the old saying, "The best things in life are free." I now realize that I always had everything I needed to feel joy and happiness. I have the ability to love and be loved; I am surrounded by the beauty of the earth, the stars, the powers of nature, and the universe. I am healthy and stress-free. I now appreciate and relish the gift of abundance that was bestowed on me.

QUESTION

Do you appreciate the abundance in your life?

AUTHOR CONTACT INFORMATION

Ella Pahopin, CFO of Pahopin Projects
Website: https://www.365daysofabundancequotes.com
Email: ellapnyc@aol.com
Social: https://mybook.to/artofconnection5
Tags: Speaker

April 1
JAMIE RAPKIEWCZ

Intentional living is the bridge between where you are and where you want to be, built with the bricks of your strengths.

THOUGHT

By using our strengths with intention, we can transform challenges into opportunities and open the door to deeper connections and a more abundant life. This strengths-based approach empowers us to face challenges with confidence and creativity. By living with intention, we not only improve our own lives but also positively impact those around us. This journey fosters gratitude and fulfillment, enriching our experiences and relationships.

Cameron often felt inadequate about her leadership skills and ability to motivate her team. Through self-awareness, she recognized her strength in empathy and chose to lead her team with compassion. By intentionally using her empathetic nature, Cameron became a more trusted, influential, and respected leader. Her team thrived under her guidance because they trusted that she understood their needs. As a result, they were motivated to produce better quality work and take more risks in development. Cameron formed more robust connections with her colleagues, and her team became top performers in their field. This approach brought abundance and fulfillment to her life.

QUESTION

How can you use your unique strengths to face a current challenge with confidence and creativity?

AUTHOR CONTACT INFORMATION

Jamie Rapkiewcz, M.Ed., Co-Founder of SCORES Model
Website: https://scoresmodel.com
Email: scoresmodel@gmail.com
Social: https://www.instagram.com/scoresmodel/
Tags: Life Coaching and Organizational Consulting

April 2
VANESSA ABRAHAM

Facing death sharpens one's values, revealing what truly matters. Reclaim your strength and live your life fully, no matter the odds.

THOUGHT

One day, I was a mother, wife, and full-time speech-language pathologist living a full life. A few days later, I was on a ventilator, fighting for my life against an unknown illness. Facing death sharpened my focus on what truly matters. I've since learned the importance of resilience and finding your voice.

Now, I dedicate my time to helping others recover from medical trauma by sharing my journey through my book *Speechless: How a Speech Therapist Lost Her Ability to Speak and Her Silent Struggle to Reclaim Her Voice and Life,* and through my inspiring speeches. One of the key topics I discuss in my speeches is Post-Intensive Care Syndrome (PICS), a condition that affects many medical trauma survivors who struggle without understanding why.

By sharing my personal experience, I bring attention to this often-overlooked issue, helping survivors feel understood and supported. I also offer solutions like the Neubie device, an electrical stimulation tool that aids physical recovery. I combine my journey with innovative tools to help others heal and live fully. My mission is to empower others to reclaim their strength and voice, no matter the odds, and rediscover their lives.

QUESTION

How can I use innovative tools and approaches, like the Neubie device, to accelerate my physical recovery or help others in their healing journey?

AUTHOR CONTACT INFORMATION

Vanessa Abraham, Owner/Founder of A Neu Healing
Website: www.aneuhealing.com
Email: vabraham14@gmail.com
Social: https://www.instagram.com/speechless_slp/
Tags: Speaker, Author, ICU Survivor, PICS Advocate

April 3
REGINA SPENCER

Embracing your authenticity can increase the abundance of peace in your life.

THOUGHT

Authenticity is seemingly very simple: decide who I am and live true to myself. If only things were so easy!

From birth, there are cultural expectations: Familial pressures. Friend group norms. Economic situations. Workplace dynamics. Societal evolution. All of these combine to shape our behaviors and perceptions from an early age. Frequently, however, these can lead to the development of patterns and beliefs born of necessity, not authenticity.

It can be challenging to separate ourselves from these outside influences. Going "against the grain" of those around us can be anxiety-inducing, especially when it feels threatening to our stability and support. Fear of the unknown often keeps us from embracing our authentic selves. We often find ourselves fearful of what we will lose rather than hopeful of what we will gain.

Identifying authenticity involves reflection. It is essential to set aside everything we have been "told" and examine what only we "know." What feels "right" to us? What creates peace within us? What brings us joy? What allows us to block out the noise? What rings true? Answer these questions without consideration of what others will think or how they will react.

QUESTION

If there were nothing to be lost, only to be gained - what would you change about yourself? Do you find yourself not honoring pieces of yourself out of fear? What is holding you back?

AUTHOR CONTACT INFORMATION

Regina Spencer, Founder & Owner of Spencer & Associates Therapeutic Alliance, PLLC
Website: www.spencertherapies.com
Email: regina@spencertherapies.com
Social: https://www.instagram.com/spencer_and_associates/
Tags: Therapist, Counselor, Mental Health

April 4
MICHELLE CARLEN

*The abundance you desire already exists.
You may not recognize it in its current form.
Be willing to open your eyes, receive it, and give thanks.*

THOUGHT

Abundance is truly a mindset and understanding that everything you need, desire, and hope for is already there. When you live your life in a sphere of abundance, all things are possible and present themselves when you are ready for them. They may not always appear when you think they should, but they will appear when you open your mind to them and are ready to receive them with gratitude.

Also, consider that abundance isn't really about one's fortune, the number of physical possessions, or even fame. Abundance is the quality of your life, the people and relationships you enjoy, the health that gives you another day to live, the time that gives you the ability to grow and improve, and the vision that allows you to see the beauty around you.

Abundance abounds when you choose to view the world from a place of overflowing blessings. This perception is the light and truth of the matter of abundance.

Challenge yourself to find abundance in your life today. Gifts arrive to you daily. Receive them willfully and give them away freely. You will see the abundance expand exponentially.

May you choose to live abundantly every day from now forward.

QUESTION

*What abundance is in your life that you hadn't realized previously?
What caused you to open your eyes and "see it?"
Was it staring at you the whole time you wished for it?*

AUTHOR CONTACT INFORMATION

Michelle Carlen, Founder & President of Alignment Advising
Website: https://www.alignmentadvising.com/
Email: michelle@alignmentadvising.com
Social: https://www.linkedin.com/company/alignmentadvising
Tags: Business Coach, Business Consultant, Facilitator

April 5
KENYATTA TURNER

*Behavioral clarity creates a path
to an abundant reality.*

THOUGHT

"Abundance" is a whole lot of "something." That something is in a plentiful and overflowing supply. More than enough..and then some! When we genuinely understand who and why we are; it transforms how we think about the moment and shows up to ourselves and those around us. The transparent energy emitted by a behaviorally aware human flows with love, positivity, and intentionality. We become equipped to understand how we get what we want for our true selves through the irrefutable universal laws. As a reward, the universe, the ether, catches our deliberate broadcast of purpose, amplifies it, and kicks it back to us with a powerful, abundant force that creates a tsunami of momentum.

This infinite force, defined by behavioral clarity, smashes through limiting thoughts of negativity, scarcity, or aspects of fear. What's left is an abundant reality where we can exude confidence, creativity, and congruency, leading to more abundance, fullness, and overflowing opportunities. Subsequently, the mindset shifts from one of doubt to one of knowing. That is the game-changer, allowing abundant swells of energy to help us materialize all that we have ever wanted and are capable of ourselves.

QUESTION

Do YOU have an abundant reality? If so, how did you find the behavioral clarity necessary to guide you on the right path? If not, how will you find it after reading this?

AUTHOR CONTACT INFORMATION

Kenyatta Turner, MM, BSPC, Founder and CEO of Freedom Empire Consulting
Website: https://freedomempireconsulting.com/
Email: kenyatta@freedomempireconsulting.com
Social: https://www.linkedin.com/in/kenyattaturner/
Tags: Behavioral SuperPowers Coach, Speaker, Author

The Art of Connection

April 6

JESSE ORLANDO

*Do what you love now,
and don't let your dreams pass you by.*

THOUGHT

We only have so much time on this planet, and this quote shows that you should not let distractions or negativity stop you from chasing what truly matters. This quote is a way for me to remind people to think of themselves and do what they want for their lives because doing this will help fulfill their purpose.

In my life, putting what's important first is one of the best things that makes me motivated and focused on my goals and aspirations for myself and my life. Even when life is unclear and challenging, doing what you love feels as if there is energy guiding you. The only way to feel this is to pursue and chase those critical pieces in life to find you further. This quote is a sign that you should live in the moment and take all the available opportunities you have in front of you so when you look back, you are proud of what you accomplished.

QUESTION

What do you love that makes you wish you had done more?

AUTHOR CONTACT INFORMATION

Jesse Orlando, Owner of Orlando's Visuals
Website: https://linktr.ee/jesseorlando
Email: orlandosvisuals@gmail.com
Social:https://www.instagram.com/_jesse_orlando/profilecard/?igsh=Zmc0NHVrbWtnenh4
Tags: digitalmarketer, photographer, videographer

April 7
MELISSA GERACIMOS

It's clear to me that there can be an Abundance of Abundance.

THOUGHT

Can I have an abundance of abundance?

Yes. Perhaps. I think so. Most definitely.

In a year when my young sister-in-law Dina died suddenly, my beautiful granddaughter Olivia was born. I am about to celebrate my first wedding anniversary with the most amazing man, that's abundance with a great heap of humbling, numbing loss.

And yet, I rejoice, and I am grateful for knowing dear Dina, the light and hub of the family. I am smitten with Olivia and my dear husband. And so, I am humble and happy. Can that be?

And yet, it must be, for I am hurtling forward past the filled pages of the calendar, and in the blur of all the days that rush toward some ultimate something, I pause. My mind is still. I think of Dina. Dina, the one who had an abundance of life so well lived and so joyous that it overflowed to the spokes of her hub and onto us lucky many.

And because that baby who is thriving, smiling, and playing, and soon will be crawling, has captured me up high in the light of happiness.

And because the stars aligned to bring my intellectual and silly darling husband to me as fate's good fortune.

Yes, I can have, and so do have, an abundance of abundance.

Yes. Most definitely.

QUESTION

How do you measure the feeling of abundance?

AUTHOR CONTACT INFORMATION

Melissa Geracimos, Thinker of Abundance
Website: https://www.365daysofabundancequotes.com
Email: myv0p11@gmail.com
Social: https://mybook.to/artofconnection5
Tags: Thinker

April 8

CYNTHIA BECKLES

*Embrace the unknown;
abundance lies beyond the door.*

THOUGHT

Have you ever felt that a dream was out of reach? I certainly did. The instinct to flee when faced with fear is common. For years, writing a book seemed like a distant dream; I'm glad I chose to pursue it rather than run away. Despite confidently giving speeches, I struggled to finish my book. I didn't want to be someone who never completed what they started.

With no local events to guide me, I created "Book It," an event bringing aspiring writers together. We had five incredible speakers who shared their publishing journeys, inspiring us to believe we could do the same. Initially, hosting an event for published authors felt strange while my book sat unfinished on the shelf. However, these feelings faded as the event progressed, bolstered by positive feedback from the 30 attendees.

In the end, five attendees published their books. I've contributed to ten best-selling collaborative books over the past five years. This journey helped me complete my journal, "Overwhelm Rewired." It led me to guest blogging and speaking at podcasts, conferences, panels, and summits.

If your dream feels out of reach, take the first step today. Abundance lies beyond the door. Every step is victory.

QUESTION

What's one fear you've overcome in pursuit of your dreams?
How do you push through moments of self-doubt?
What's your next step toward reaching your full potential?

AUTHOR CONTACT INFORMATION

Cynthia Beckles, Owner of OptiSuccess Marketing
Website: https://bit.ly/maximizingmarketing
Email: cindyebeckles@yahoo.com
Social: https://www.linkedin.com/in/cynthiaebeckles/
Tags: Marketing Expert, Strategist, PR, Speaker

April 9
SAL CAVALIERE

*As we perfect our habits of life,
illness will become impossibly impossible.*

THOUGHT

Man is the highest manifestation of this one great ever-present universal energy we call God, Yahweh, and Allah, which is awaiting our intelligent use for still higher and loftier achievements. We were born perfect, even at the genetic level. God wanted us to be healthy, wealthy, and happy.

Man has harnessed the elements, subdued the beasts, and created new flowers and fruits. We have left to the last the earnest consideration of our supreme destiny: the quest of self. We have created poor habits of thoughts, gluttony, and sloth. We are seeing diseases that did not exist 50 years ago and beyond.

As we implement discipline in our thoughts, become conscious of what we consume, and undertake necessary steps to detox our bodies physically, we bring our bodies back to the natural state of healing as God intended. It is easy to get caught up in a fast-paced lifestyle where we grab anything to fill an empty stomach. However, developing proper habits psychologically and emotionally, as well as eating habits and physical activity, makes it more difficult for our bodies to become ill.

Without illness, we achieve more and more abundance.

QUESTION
How do you want to die?

AUTHOR CONTACT INFORMATION

Dr. Sal Cavaliere, DO, Owner and Founder of Dr Blue Zone
Website: https://www.drsalbluezone.com
Email: drsalbluezonedoctor@gmail.com
Social: https://linktr.ee/drbluezone
Tags: Physician, Anti-Aging

April 10
RAHUL K. MAHARAJ

Understanding emotional resources is the heartbeat of mental health, nourishing connections that empower healing and inspire resilience.

THOUGHT

This quote resonates deeply with my passion for mental health advocacy through my books and conferences. Each story shared is a testament to the strength found in vulnerability. By exploring emotional resources, we uncover the tools that allow individuals to connect authentically with themselves and others. (What is meant for you shall never pass you by. What passes you by was never meant for you.)

I emphasize that these connections are not just supportive; they are transformative. It creates a safe space where healing can occur and resilience can flourish. When people come together to share their experiences, they realize they are not alone in their struggles, which fosters a sense of belonging, just as in my book "Untold Stories Hidden Truths."

Through my books, I aim to highlight these narratives, showcasing how understanding one's emotional traumas can lead to empowerment. At my conferences, understanding facilitates discussions that remind us that our shared experiences create a tapestry of hope, encouraging others to embrace their journeys toward mental well-being. I did not have this available to my younger self, but it's here for everyone who needs it in abundance today.

QUESTION

What does your mental health and trauma mean to you?

AUTHOR CONTACT INFORMATION

Rahul K. Maharaj, CEO of Your Life Experiences With Rah Inc.
Website: https://ylewrah.com/your-trauma-talks-2025/
Email: ylewrah@gmail.com
Social: https://www.facebook.com/YLEWRah/
Tags: mentalhealth, rahstaz, ylewrah, trauma

April 11

JOY BECK

Healing begins when we let go of what no longer serves us rather than stuff it within.

THOUGHT

Healing is not about tucking away or ignoring our emotional or physical wounds in hopes no one will see them, or they will magically disappear. True healing requires courage, allowing ourselves to feel, acknowledge, and release these deeply held pains. When we do not fully release negative emotions, they settle within us like heavy stones, often manifesting as stress, physical discomfort, or limiting beliefs that hold us back from living fully. Facing our struggles with compassion, curiosity, and courage lets us heal, let go, and break down the walls protecting our hearts. Healing becomes a journey of rediscovery, freeing our minds, bodies, and souls from past burdens.

As we unpack the backpack of our lives, we find each rock inside represents old challenges, disappointments, or deep-seated insecurities. Often, we are unaware of how much we carry or how these burdens shape our perspectives and actions. We create space for joy and inner peace with each stone we release. Healing becomes an empowering journey to wholeness—a chance to live free from old wounds, reclaim our freedom, and embrace the joy that's always been our birthright.

QUESTION

What are you holding onto that, if released, could bring you more hope and joy?

AUTHOR CONTACT INFORMATION

Joy Beck, Founder of Joyful Options
Website: https://bettercalljoy.com
Email: joyfuloptions@gmail.com
Social: https://www.linkedin.com/in/joy-beck-healer
Tags: Speaker, Holistic Healing Expert, Life Coach

April 12

LISA van ROODE

Abundance is not measured by what we hold in our hands but by the infinite energy we hold in our hearts. Tune into this energy; the universe responds.

THOUGHT

To me, abundance transcends the mere accumulation of material wealth. Once our basic needs are met, true abundance manifests as a profound appreciation for life in its fullness, a sense of joy, vitality, and inner strength. It's about embracing the creative energy of the universe and feeling a deep connection to the infinite possibilities around us. This kind of abundance is not about what we have but who we are. It invites us to leave behind feelings of lack, dissatisfaction, and emptiness. It opens us to the light and love that emanate from a spiritual place.

To understand abundance at a deeper level, we need to explore the concept of frequency. Everything in the universe, including our thoughts and emotions, vibrates at a specific frequency. When we operate from a mindset of scarcity or lack, we are vibrating at a lower frequency. This minimal vibration creates a self-fulfilling cycle where our thoughts and feelings of insufficiency attract more of the same into our lives. However, when we shift our frequency to one of abundance, we align ourselves with the higher vibrations of the universe, drawing more positivity, love, and opportunities our way.

QUESTION

So, how will you choose to tune into the frequency of abundance today?

AUTHOR CONTACT INFORMATION

Lisa van Roode
Website: lisavanroode.com
Email: hello@lisavanroode.com
Social: https://www.instagram.com/lisavanroode/
Tags: healthcoaching, wellnesscoach, liveyourbestlife

April 13
MAUREEN RANKS

*Abundance isn't just about having more;
it's about sharing what you have, knowing that every
act of kindness plants seeds for future growth.*

THOUGHT

Abundance is often misunderstood as merely accumulating wealth or possessions. However, true abundance is not just about how much we possess; it's about recognizing and sharing the wealth that already exists in our lives. When we give—whether it's our time, energy, resources, or kindness—we're not just contributing to others; we're enriching our own lives in ways that extend far beyond material gain.

Every act of giving, no matter how small, has the power to create a ripple effect of positivity. It plants seeds that grow into deeper connections, opportunities, and fulfillment. The more you give, the more you realize that your resources—be it love, knowledge, or material wealth—are not limited. Instead, they expand with every act of sharing. This mindset shift—from scarcity to abundance—opens us up to receiving and appreciating life's many blessings.

So, embrace the power of giving. Recognize that each time you share, you are planting seeds of growth—both in the world and within your soul. Through these acts of kindness, you will witness the flourishing of abundance in your life and the lives of those around you.

QUESTION

How can you use the abundance you already possess to create positive change in your life and the lives of others?

AUTHOR CONTACT INFORMATION

Maureen Ranks, Director of Marketing & Design of 22 Salute Spirits & Coffee
Website: https://22salute.com/
Email: maureen@22salute.com
Social: https://www.instagram.com/mo_ranks/
Tags: Graphic Designer, Assistant

April 14
LISA E. GONGAWARE

Abundance does not equate to the number of material items you own but to the number of individuals who you love and reciprocate that love to you.

THOUGHT

As a teacher, I have a life filled with abundance. There is always enough love in my heart to share with every student I meet. At the beginning of every new school year, I make it a priority to let students know how important they are to me by verbally sharing my feelings.

At first, students may be unsure about hearing how important they are and how they will grow up to become great men and women who will make positive contributions to society. However, as the mantra continues to be repeated throughout the school year, a student's transformation begins. With my consistent love and support as their teacher, the students begin believing in themselves, prompting other positive changes to occur.

The students complete more academic work, have a more positive disposition, and reach out to help others who seem to be struggling. Clearly, experiencing abundance fosters abundance in others. In a world where material things represent abundance to so many, be the change and focus on improving relationships through love rather than collecting items of little value. Consider gifting a loved one with an experience they will remember forever instead of buying a gift they might soon forget.

QUESTION

How would your life improve if you changed your definition of abundance to include the love you share with others?

AUTHOR CONTACT INFORMATION

Dr. Lisa E. Gongaware, Special Education Teacher of Pennsylvania Public Schools
Website: https://www.365daysofabundancequotes.com
Email: shelby2323@aol.com
Social: https://www.facebook.com/lisa.gongaware
Tags: Special Education Teacher, PhD

April 15
SUZANNE SÖDERBERG

Do Your Best and Just Be You

THOUGHT

That is what I heard growing up, as I was constantly comparing myself to my brother. My parents were so wonderful that they encouraged me to be myself. They reminded me that I was myself and no one else.

Don't compare yourself to anyone except yourself from yesterday. Decide who you are and be that person to the fullest. No one else can be you the way you can be you. Each person is unique in their fantastic way. We are not meant to be the same. As they say, being different is what makes the world go around. Can you imagine if we were all the same?

After years of not knowing who I was, I finally decided that I was going to be the "me" I know I am on the inside and shine it to the world. The me that loves me no matter what. The me that is there to listen and help others when they are going through something. The me that is going to live each day as if it's my last and enjoy every minute.

This choice reminds me of a quote from Oscar Wilde - "Be yourself; everyone else is already taken." Do what you do best and be happy doing it. I ended up doing "Me". So go be "You," whoever that awesome person already is.

QUESTION

Who have you always wanted to be? Are you that person?
If you have always wanted to do or be something other than what you are doing, what is stopping you? Go and do it!

AUTHOR CONTACT INFORMATION

Suzanne Söderberg, CDLP, Sr. Mortgage Loan Originator and CDLP of Benchmark Mortgage
Website: https://suzannesoderberg.com
Email: suzanne@suzannesoderberg.com
Social: https://www.linkedin.com/in/suzannesoderberg/
Tags: mortgage, divorce, homebuyer, refinance, purchase

The Art of Connection

April 16

ERIC RANKS

*Abundance is the art of seeing the beauty in simplicity;
cherish the little things with gratitude, and life will reveal its infinite treasures.*

THOUGHT

Abundance isn't just about having a lot of things; it's about noticing the little, everyday moments that make life unique. When we feel gratitude, we start to see the world differently. Gratitude helps us find joy in simple things: a sunny day, a friendly smile, or time spent with family. These are the natural treasures in life that show us how rich we genuinely are.

When we are thankful for the small things, we begin to realize just how much good is already around us. It's not about how much we have but how much we appreciate the ones we love the most. Gratitude makes us see that ordinary moments can be extraordinary. It helps us focus on what we have instead of what we don't.

By being grateful, we can find happiness in every moment, and that's what abundance really means: feeling like we have more than enough just by loving and appreciating the little things in life.

QUESTION

What simple moments or things in your life make you feel genuinely happy? How can you use gratitude to see the abundance and special treasures already around you every day?

AUTHOR CONTACT INFORMATION

Eric Ranks, Co-Founder and CEO of 22 Salute Spirits & Coffee
Website: https://22salute.com/
Email: eric@ericranks.com
Social: https://www.linkedin.com/in/ericranks/
Tags: Speaker, Author, Entrepreneur, CEO, Founder

April 17
ANYSSA FIGUEROA

*Don't let the world feed you the feeling of needing 'more'
to live a full and abundant life; instead,
take a step back and see that you are living it.*

THOUGHT

The world today is run by social media and influencers who are pushing ideas of what your life should look like, what clothes you should wear, what car to drive, and the list can go on and on. There is an overabundance of "stuff" that is always bigger and better than before. While some of these trends and ideas can be helpful and fun to experiment with, there comes a time when it can feel like there is a never-ending cycle of needing to catch up with the next trend or big thing on the market. This fallacy leads us to think of why we aren't going on specific vacations, how we aren't doing fun activities, how we don't have new materialistic items, and why we think it is not enough.

With the vast access to social media, it is easy to compare your life to others and wonder why you aren't living a particular lifestyle. It can easily make you unhappy with the things you do have. It is time to start combating those thoughts in your mind when you start to compare yourselves to others to see the abundance you have in life. Acknowledging the abundance of love, support, and resources you have allows you to feel confident in yourself and feel secure and satisfied with where you are in life.

QUESTION

How often are we letting social media influence our decisions and letting it affect our happiness? Can you name five things that you can already have that you experience an abundance of?

AUTHOR CONTACT INFORMATION

Anyssa Figueroa, Manager of Financial Services
Website: https://www.365daysofabundancequotes.com
Email: figueroaanyssa@gmail.com
Social: www.linkedin.com/in/anyssafigueroa
Tags: Finances, Banking, Lending, Treasury, Merchant

April 18

MARION HILL

*My beliefs dictate my behavior,
and my behavior creates exceeding abundance.*

THOUGHT

The power of abundance comes from reshaping our mindsets and perspectives. Many equate abundance with possessions, influencing their beliefs and behaviors. While there's a common notion that hard work leads to success, tying self-worth to material things can make them feel even more unattainable.

I believe that true abundance is realized when we operate within our purpose. Each of us is created for a purpose, which often involves creating, connecting, and contributing to our communities. Identifying what matters most to you—your strengths, talents, and how you can serve others—defines your purpose.

Once you discover your purpose, your actions will align with it, allowing you to embody your true self. Embrace discomfort, push your boundaries, and let your purpose evolve into your calling.

By flipping the formula—allowing beliefs to shape behaviors rather than possessions—you've embraced an abundant reality. Now, focus on your purpose rather than what you lack, resulting in a more profound sense of fulfillment and abundance.

QUESTION

What is your purpose? Are you operating for your purpose? If not, why?

AUTHOR CONTACT INFORMATION

Marion Hill, Project Director of M.A.N.C.A.V.E Fatherhood Project
Website: https://www.azmancave.org
Email: reggie4377@gmail.com
Social: https://www.facebook.com/AZMANCAVE
Tags: Fatherhood Speaker

April 19
TAMMY DEMIRZA LAWING

*What you want already wants you,
and you are destined to have it!*

THOUGHT

You can custom order something, and the Universe has no choice but to give it to you! It's true, and this has been proven repeatedly by me and my clients. You, too, can learn how to create what you want by understanding that what you want already wants you, and you are supposed to have it, or you wouldn't want it. Owning that fact is just one of the vital recipe points given to me intuitively years ago while overcoming homelessness.

The recipe is simple, but few find it, and it is ultimately in alignment to receive quickly, easily, and miraculously. Getting what you want is knowing what you don't want and clearly defining what you want. The next step is to gain an awareness of why you want it. What does it do for you? How would it feel to have it? The last stage is with confidence custom ordering it to the Universe. Understanding these secrets and sharing them has delighted clients worldwide once they realize that there is a recipe they can follow for anything in life that they desire. And, when it comes, it is always more than what they dreamed or imagined.

Your mind is a brilliant tool. Choosing consciously creates new neural pathways for you to receive!

QUESTION

What is one desire you've held back from fully claiming, and are you ready to embrace the belief that it's not only possible but destined for you?

AUTHOR CONTACT INFORMATION

Tammy DeMirza Lawing, Spiritual Guide of Tammy De Mirza, LLC
Website: https://www.tammydemirza.com
Email: tammy@tammydemirza.com
Social: https://www.youtube.com/@TammyDeMirza
Tags: Author, Speaker, Intuitive, Transformation Leader

April 20
BRIAN HAWKINS

Strength isn't built during comfort, but rising after life hits you hard. True resilience is shaped when we face challenges with grace and purpose.

THOUGHT

I spent my younger life being caught up in what was right and wrong. I had an insensitive and hard-nosed attitude that ruined relationships that were important. I masked it all with substance abuse, cycles of destruction, and devaluing my life. Two years ago, I was on my motorcycle on the freeway, got cut off by a car, went over the car, and then was run over and dragged to the side of the road.

I remember a loud noise, then opening my eyes and looking up at the sky, thinking this was really bad. I could not move my legs, and my whole body was numb. The trauma center at the hospital could not find a broken bone in my body. I was left with a massive hematoma on my leg, a dead shoulder, and a lot of road rash. Going through the shock of this situation, therapy, and many doctors for depression and anxiety, I realized the amount of self-improvement and the need for a drastic change in my life. April 8th, 2024, was the day of the solar eclipse. I took that day to end a vicious cycle and form a new beginning. I surrendered my old self and committed to serving God and living a clean, sober lifestyle filled with daily self-improvement, meditations, and physical fitness. Truly a miracle!

QUESTION

What life situations have you faced that knocked you down; how have they strengthened you? Are you embracing challenges to improve yourself, or are you stuck in what's right and wrong?

AUTHOR CONTACT INFORMATION

Brian Hawkins, Owner and CEO of Hawksfield Productions LLC
Website: https://hawksfieldproductions.com/
Email: brian@hawksfieldproductions.com
Social: www.linkedin.com/in/brian-hawkins-61b66636
Tags: App Developer, Content Production, AI Services

April 21
CHRISTA ROSE

H.O.P.E can be an acronym for Heck Over Pleasing Everyone to Hold On Pain Ends.

THOUGHT

On April 21, I held my husband as he took his last breath. We only knew for two weeks that he had an aggressive form of leukemia. In that short time, I went from being a wife and mother to being a widow and single parent. Who am I now? I had to face the unimaginable pain and loss because I was also recovering from a head-on collision that happened one year, one month, and one day before, so I felt I was now losing my identity. It would have been so easy to give up, and I almost did.

I decided to try hope—an acronym for Heck Over Pleasing Others. For once, it reminded me that even in the darkest moments, there is a future worth fighting for, but that future would only happen if I started taking care of myself first. This choice led to the acronym meaning Hold On Pain Ends. Letting go doesn't mean forgetting; it means finding the courage to move forward. I found the key was gratitude; if I hadn't gone through loss, I wouldn't have valued health and learned true love. I will honor my husband's memory by living fully. The journey ahead is uncertain, but by shifting my mindset from fear to hope, I know I can face it with resilience and fulfill my purpose by inspiring others.

QUESTION

How have you turned moments of loss into opportunities for finding hope in your life, as well as inspiring others?

AUTHOR CONTACT INFORMATION

Christa Rose, Owner of Christa Rose
Website: https://christarose.com/
Email: messagechrista@gmail.com
Social: https://www.facebook.com/christa.rose.967
Tags: BestsellerAuthor, Speaker, Advocate, EnergyWorker

April 22

CINDY EDINGTON

Abundance isn't something to hope for. It's all around you and within you every moment of every day.

THOUGHT

My mission in life is to help as many women as I can rise like a Phoenix from the ashes of divorce. I believe this quote captures the essence of rediscovering abundance in the aftermath of divorce, a period in time that is often accompanied by feelings of loss, scarcity, and emotional turmoil. Divorce, while signifying the end of a relationship, doesn't have to mean the end of joy, love, or abundance in one's life. Instead, this statement invites those navigating the painful waters of divorce to shift their perspective and see that abundance is not something to aspire to but is a perpetual state of being that surrounds and inhabits us. It encourages us to acknowledge and appreciate the many forms of abundance that life offers: our friendships, the beauty of nature, and all of the joys we experience in our daily lives. By opening our eyes and our hearts, we allow ourselves to see, feel, and receive the rich abundance that life continually brings to us. This shift towards recognizing and welcoming abundance is transformative. It can help one move from a state of loss to a state of gratitude and openness and from focusing on what has ended to all the possibilities that lie ahead.

QUESTION

In what ways might opening your eyes and heart to the abundance that surrounds you change your view of loss and open new paths to fulfillment and joy in the wake of a life-altering event like divorce?

AUTHOR CONTACT INFORMATION

Cindy Edington, Owner of Tranquil Heart Wellness
Website: https://tranquilheartwellness.com
Email: cindy@tranquilheartwellness.com
Social: https://www.linkedin.com/in/thwcindyedington/
Tags: Author, Speaker, Transformational Life Coach

April 23
DENZEL SMALLS

You try really hard to see images in clouds only others see, so share the same ideologies with others' perspectives; I do.

THOUGHT

Think back to when you were a child with your friends, looking up at the clouds. One saw a dragon, the other a butterfly, and you a dog. If you could visualize what your friend could do, you try as hard as you could to see things from their perspective, no matter how long it took. You did this with such vigor and curiosity, and when you finally see it, you're excited because you shared a moment with them. If people took that same perspective on life, the world would be in a much better place.

Abundance works like that lazy day peering into the sky with friends; only now do you get to share the significant collection of spiritual, psychological, and tangible accumulation of your lifetime with valued friends. Perhaps maturity has changed the setting, but is the sharing of your abundance any different?

QUESTION

Why do you believe people are so unaccepting of others' perspectives?

AUTHOR CONTACT INFORMATION

Denzel Smalls, Founder CEO of Word of Mouth Productions
Website: https://wordofmouthproduction.com
Email: denzelrsmalls@gmail.com
Social: https://www.linkedin.com/in/denzel-smalls-345130228/
Tags: I/O Psychologist

April 24

MILES MURDOCCA

Small hands can make big waves.

THOUGHT

It's fascinating to see how a child's mind differs from that of an adult when it comes to helping others. Little kids are more willing and eager to lend a hand without hesitation, but as we grow older, something seems to shift. Is it the constant rush and pressure to get places or the distractions that come with adulthood, like technology and busy work schedules?

The simplicity of helping others, whether it be holding a door, offering a kind word, or just smiling, takes little time and effort. Yet, it can make a significant impact on someone's day. We must remember that even the smallest act of kindness can leave a lasting impression.

There is contentment in helping others. You have the power to make a positive impact by your kindness. Be a dog walker at an animal rescue. Start a collection drive for a local shelter. Bake cookies for your local fire department. Deliver used books to a community center. Help a neighbor. Volunteer.

In a world where everything seems to come at a cost, it's refreshing to know that being kind doesn't require any money or resources. It's a choice we can make every single day, and the best part is that we have an abundance of it within us.

QUESTION

What did you love as a child? How can you take that memory and turn it into an act of service?

AUTHOR CONTACT INFORMATION

Miles Murdocca, Founder and Chief Fun Officer of Going the Extra Miles, a 501c(3) organization
Website: www.GoingtheExtraMiles.org
Email: Info@GoingtheExtraMiles.org
Social: https://www.facebook.com/GoingTheExtraMiles2024/
Tags: Chief Fun Officer, Going the Extra Miles

April 25
NICOLA SMITH

*Through the sacrifices of those who came before us,
we are reminded of the abundance of freedom, opportunity,
and connection that surrounds us.*

THOUGHT

Today is ANZAC Day. This day is a reminder of the service and sacrifices made by New Zealand and Australian soldiers in the fight for our freedoms. As we greet the dawn to commemorate their bravery and honor their memory, we can also reflect on the abundance that their sacrifices have gifted us: freedom to live, to choose, and to shape our futures. When we practice appreciation for these, we expand our capacity to see and embrace the abundance we already have in our lives.

It's easy to take for granted the things we wake up to every day—the opportunity to connect with loved ones, the choices we make in our work, and the communities we belong to. Appreciation is an active practice, one that honors the past by recognizing the value in our present.

Today, as I reflect on everything ANZAC day means to me personally, I remind myself to see and honor the abundance that those sacrifices have made possible for me. No matter where you are in the world, I invite you to do the same.

QUESTION

What freedoms and opportunities in my life can I appreciate more deeply today, knowing they were gifted to me by those who sacrificed for them?

AUTHOR CONTACT INFORMATION

Nicola Smith, Founder of The Next Level 'training for the mind'
Website: https://www.thenextlevel.co.nz
Email: nicola@thenextlevel.co.nz
Social: https://www.linkedin.com/in/executive-coach-mindset
Tags: Mindset, Coach, High Performance, Speaker

April 26

JEFF VILLWOCK

Big dreams require a big heart. It requires exceptional perseverance. It requires that we never give up regardless of the obstacles we face.

THOUGHT

What kind of dreamer are you? A "daydreamer" or an "unstoppable dreamer"?

We dream of being like the Kardashians. A race car driver. A top real estate agent selling multi-million homes. We know that none of those dreams will come true. Or if we tried, we fold at the first adversity.

Unstoppable dreamers are different. This kind of dreamer has passion. They have grit. Determination. A spirit that says, "No matter what, I'm going to accomplish this."

My daughter is a perfect example. At age eleven, she told me that she wanted to dance ballet professionally. We had a long talk. I told her that she needed to have the heart of a champion racehorse. Be able to put up with pain. The agony. The disappointments. Was she ready? She insisted she was.

Sometimes, she would come home with busted blisters. I watched her pour rubbing alcohol on her feet. She wrapped a pencil with a towel and would bite down so she wouldn't scream. Now, that's the heart of a champion.

She moved to NYC at age sixteen to dance with the NYC Ballet. Her professional dance career lasted fourteen years. She made her dream real.

Unstoppable dreamers persevere no matter what. They never give up.

That's a real entrepreneur.

QUESTION

What kind of dreamer are you? A daydreamer who says, "Would be nice if …"? Or an Unstoppable Dreamer who will do anything to make it happen? Pain. Disappointment. Roadblocks. Never Give Up.

AUTHOR CONTACT INFORMATION

Jeff Villwock, Founder of Acquisitions Professor LLC
Website: http://www.acquisitionsprofessor.com
Email: jeff@jeffvillwock.com
Social: https://www.linkedin.com/in/jeffvillwock
Tags: M&A Coach, Acquisitions, Buy a Business

April 27
DENISE ACKERMAN

Through my lens, I see an abundance of beauty and emotion. With photos, we freeze moments in time to create a wealth of memories that live on forever.

THOUGHT

Photography is about seeing the abundance of beauty in the world and capturing those precious moments with loved ones. When I pick up my camera, I capture pieces of life. Each shot freezes moments that would otherwise slip away, and I turn them into lasting memories. A portrait isn't just a face; it's a story written in expressions of joy, happiness, sorrow, and resilience.

Every photo we take becomes a part of our history. It's a memory that lives on and tells our story. When my dad went to heaven, what truly mattered was all the wonderful times and beautiful experiences we had together. The photos I took then help me now to hold onto those precious moments and relive them in every detail. They're more than just pictures; they keep the people we love close, even when they're gone.

Photography helps us to appreciate the beauty around us and to preserve memories for generations to come. Each photograph becomes a chapter in our personal history and is a testament to our experiences.

I encourage you to take photos and share your story through images. Every picture is a piece of us that will continue to speak our truth, share our light, and connect us to the world long after we're gone.

QUESTION

Which photo in your collection holds the most meaning for you, and why does it hold a special place in your heart?

AUTHOR CONTACT INFORMATION

Denise Ackerman, Professional Photographer of Lakeside Photography
Website: https://www.lakesidephoto.ch/corporate-photographer-zurich/
Email: denise@lakesidephoto.ch
Social: https://www.facebook.com/denise.ackerman.5
Tags: Photographer, Photography Coach

April 28
DAVID BRINKER

It is never too late to heal your heart.

THOUGHT

Grief is usually tied to the death of a loved one. Grief is also felt at the end of a marriage or other significant relationship. But did you know that grief shows up whenever there is a change in the familiar patterns of life?

These changes may be minor inconveniences, or they may bring significant heartache, pain, and a profound sense of loss. Changes in health, finances, employment, or stages of life can also shake our world. Our emotional struggle can come from what is less visible: loss of support, safety, trust, purpose, or belonging. The cause may be moving, a child going off to college or getting married, friends moving away, retiring, or our social circle falling apart.

Unmet hopes, dreams, or expectations in life lead to grief. Sadly, most of us have not been taught how to recover from the negative impact of significant emotional loss. Unresolved losses move on with us into the future and continue to limit our lives until we find healing.

A more abundant life comes when we discover, name, and voice the emotions connected to our losses. What grievers need is to be heard, not with judgment, comparison, criticism, or pushback, but with compassion.

QUESTION

Instead of recovering from my losses and finding abundance, have I been gathering a lifetime of heartaches, only to keep them like rocks in a backpack, which I take with me everywhere I go?

AUTHOR CONTACT INFORMATION

David Brinker Owner, Certified Grief Specialist of Compassionate Grief Recovery

Website: https://davidbrinkergrms.wixsite.com/mysite

Email: david.brinker.grms@gmail.com

Social: https://www.facebook.com/groups/compassionategriefrecovery

Tags: Grief Recovery Specialist, Speaker, Coach

April 29

CHRIS CORAGGIO

Abundance is believing both: "I have enough" and "there's more than enough for everyone".

THOUGHT

Abundance, as I share in this quote, is not in relation to a physical reality of resource availability but the perspective someone has on their own life.

Abundance is a belief: an internalized truth that we feel in our bones. Abundance gives us the peace of knowing that we already have everything we need to live a fulfilling and beautiful life. At the same time, if we want more, there is always "more" out there. But our relationship to wanting more is "could be nice" instead of "We need that." By the way, abundance refers not just to more resources but also to more people, more opportunities, more variety, and so on.

We also feel abundance in relation to others. When we believe there is abundance, we share; when we believe there is scarcity, we hoard and compete. Abundance is ultimately choosing a way of existing with ease, flow, and harmony with others.

QUESTION

What, for you, is "enough" to have a fulfilling and beautiful life?

AUTHOR CONTACT INFORMATION

Chris Coraggio, Founder of Potencia LLC
Website: https://www.yourpotencia.com
Email: chris.coraggio@yourpotencia.com
Social: https://www.linkedin.com/in/coraggio/
Tags: Executive Coach, Habits Coach, HR Consultant

April 30

ANN BRENNAN

Don't have competitors. Have referral partners, confidants, and friends instead.

THOUGHT

I don't believe in competition. As the owner of a digital marketing agency and the founder of a mental health nonprofit, I have a unique perspective. I see the pressure my fellow business owners are under and the risks they face by going it alone. So, I have made a conscious decision to treat my competition as collaborators, colleagues, and friends. I created a supportive community of business owners who could build each other up instead of tearing each other down.

People often quote a line from The Godfather: "It's not personal, it's business." That line has always bothered me. Business is personal. We should be building relationships, leaning on each other, and cooperating. When we stop seeing our competitors as adversaries and start seeing them as people who need help as much as we do, we can build relationships that benefit us both professionally and personally. Cooperation, support, and even friendship become possible when we embrace this mindset.

QUESTION

How can you build a relationship with your competitors? How can you collaborate and support them?

AUTHOR CONTACT INFORMATION

Ann Brennan, Owner of No Bullshit Marketing
Website: https://nobullshitmarketing.com
Email: Ann@NoBullshitMarketing.com
Social: https://Twitter.com/BrennanAnnie
Tags: Digital Marketer

May 1
KAREN TRAPANE

Abundance is the richness of relationships, belly laughs with friends, and serving others; it's every moment of every day of your life.

THOUGHT

It's easy to see what's "wrong" in our lives. We can blame others for what we don't have, missed opportunities, or all the pain we have suffered. It's easy to live in a mindset of wanting more. Have you wondered why you're working so hard, not getting promoted, and barely making ends meet while others seem to have everything? Do you think abundance equals money?

Abundance, simply put, is more than enough of something. Ever felt so full after Thanksgiving dinner that you had to change your jeans to stretchy pants? That, in a nutshell, is abundance.

Abundance is a feeling that you can access at any time. Practicing gratitude and mindfulness is the quickest route to get you to that feeling. Saying thank you daily for what you have right now, in this moment, is the key to creating the life you have always wanted; therefore, abundance is merely a mindset away.

Dr. Joe Dispenza, a Neuroscientist, said in his book *How to Become Supernatural*, "I think we are greater than we think, more powerful than we know, more unlimited than we could ever dream." If this is true, everything you want is already inside you. Say "thank you" every day and watch your life change.

QUESTION

What are ten things you are grateful for? How can you practice saying "thank you" instead of complaining about what you don't have?

AUTHOR CONTACT INFORMATION

Karen Trapane, Owner of Trapane Group, LLC
Website: www.trapanegroup.com
Email: kt@trapanegroup.com
Social: https://www.instagram.com/kt_trapane
Tags: Life Coach, Business Owner, Artist

May 2
LORI OSBORNE

Abundance or Misery. You choose.

THOUGHT

I am not a spiritual advisor, coach, or healer, but I do believe in the power of our minds. And I believe that we control every aspect of our lives through what we think, believe, and speak. But knowing this to be true in the deepest of my core doesn't mean that it's easy.

I have only recently started grasping the power held in what we believe. Like many, I first started hearing about this concept in 2007 after the release of "The Secret." At the time, I was toward the end of an abusive 18-year relationship with no self-esteem, a mountain of debt, and very little hope for a happy future. What I didn't realize at the time was that the very act of submersing myself in that miserable life was only perpetuating the misery.

Once I was able to free myself from the anger, belittling, and manipulation, I was able to finally see myself as the beautiful person I had never known was there. I was finally able to see how much abundance the Universe has in store for me. I just had to open my heart, start believing it, and start speaking abundance into reality. I have also learned that it is not a one-time thing. It's ongoing, a constant, and a daily choice. Today, I choose to live in abundance.

QUESTION

What one thing can you change today to create more abundance over misery in your life?

AUTHOR CONTACT INFORMATION

Lori Osborne, Founder and Chief Solution Architect of BizBolster Web Solutions, LLC
Website: https://www.bizbolster.com/
Email: lori@bizbolster.com
Social: https://www.linkedin.com/in/loriaosborne/
Tags: Website Developer, Digital Marketer

May 3
CARRIE MOSLEY

*Any time I fail to see abundance in my life,
it simply is because I am not looking.*

THOUGHT

Over a decade ago, on May 3, 2014, I saved my dad's life after a prescription pill overdose. He survived, though just barely, and with a new need for 24/7 care. Those first years after the overdose were incredibly challenging, and the only abundance in our lives at that time was from anger and unresolved trauma.

In time, healing came in the way of afternoon outings, game nights at home, and day trips as a family. As we slowly got healthier, a thankfulness grew in me for life's simplicity: that my dad lived and we were able to forgive each other for hot morning beverages, lifelong friendships, a warm bed, slow Sunday mornings, and a best friend in my husband. These were all things I could have easily overlooked, but in taking a moment to reflect, I saw they meant far more in my healing journey than money or possessions ever could.

You can be in a season of receiving after decades of yearning for more, clawing at anything in life that might bring temporary fulfillment. Just like the red car theory—where you begin to notice red cars after looking for them—you may not see abundance in your life if your eyes aren't open to it.

QUESTION

*Where can you find small sparks of gratefulness leading to
an abundance of good things in your life?*

AUTHOR CONTACT INFORMATION

Carrie Mosley, Co-owner of Mosley Coaching
Website: https://www.mosleycoaching.com
Email: carriepeck@live.com
Social: https://www.facebook.com/share/g/1KSFnbb1RK/?mibextid=K35XfP
Tags: Wellness Coach

May 4

JESSICA JORGENSEN

Living an abundant life starts with finding what fills your soul, training your mind, and recognizing joy in the tiniest moments of life.

THOUGHT

How do you compare your abundance with others? We all do it. Our brain is wired to see what others have and compare it to our own lives. Be it an abundance of things or experiences, our survival, self-esteem, and daily dopamine levels are based on observing those around us and scaling our lives to theirs.

Over the last three years as a full-time traveling digital nomad across the USA, my definition of abundance has changed. The happiest people I have met across my travels focus on experiences and lessons learned from making hard choices to balance their lives and feed their souls.

Abundance is free and available to everyone! We started by leaning into the experiences that fill our souls compared to the challenges we face daily. Intentionally balancing self-acceptance against our old perceptions of abundance was hard. We had very uncomfortable moments and continued being grateful for those challenges until our brains began to recognize abundance as a personal, introspective, and healing process. I promise you the payoff to waking up happily because you know your life is abundant; it is worth every hard decision made. Take your life on and watch your abundance grow!

QUESTION

What soul-filling activity can you add to your agenda today?

AUTHOR CONTACT INFORMATION

Jessica Jorgensen, CEO/Founder of goRoam, LLC
Website: https://goroam.tech/
Email: info@goRoam.Tech
Social: www.linkedin.com/in/jessicascrivnerjorgensen
Tags: Traveler, Adventure Seeker, Speaker, Digital Nomad

May 5
ROBERT W. JONES

*Abundance is the cultivation of
all high vibrational things.*

THOUGHT

When I was a toddler, I thought all things were abundant. My dependency on my family provided the space where my needs were met. I did not take too much stock into what abundance was. For me, it was a well of water that was always on. I expected it. As I grew older and more independent, I realized that abundance was not given. Most of the time, abundance had to be pursued. When I left home, I found that abundance was a privilege.

As I grew older, my understanding of abundance grew as well. Abundance was not so much a physical state; more so, it was a mindset state. From within this mindset, I could cultivate fulfillment, joy, compassion, love, and well-being. All expressions of the essential energy that manifested my true self. I still remember my grandfather saying to this day, "Abundance isn't what you receive; it is the overflow of what you have to give."

When I look at the world around me, I see that abundance in everything. From the air I breathe to the water I drink to the food that I eat to the thoughts, I think there is abundance. There is more than enough for all of us. We must believe that our cultivation curates the highest vibrational things that allow us to do so.

QUESTION

What do you do to curate high vibration?

AUTHOR CONTACT INFORMATION

Robert W. Jones, Founder and Owner of Network Together, LLC
Website: https://www.networktogether.net/
Email: robert@networktogether.net
Social: https://www.linkedin.com/in/inetrepreneurnetwork/
Tags: Speaking, Academy, Entrepreneur, Author, Media

The Art of Connection

May 6

JOSEPH FANG

*Reflect on the Past, Enjoy the Present,
Plan for the Future*

THOUGHT

Learn from past successes and failures so you can improve yourself. Lifelong learning and personal development are the abundance attractors you gift to yourself. Keep in mind there is always more to learn and things to be curious about. Use the lessons you learn wisely.

Enjoy life in the present because when the moment passes, you will never get it back. The one thing younger people have in abundance that older generations regret not having enough of: Time. You can never roll back the clock, so use the time you have each day wisely.

Always plan for the future so you can make your dreams become reality, and remember that the journey has more value than any destination. Live in the moment while you plan so you don't regret not enjoying each memory created and the relationships you might have never built.

QUESTION

What is most important in your life right now?

AUTHOR CONTACT INFORMATION

Joseph Fang, Owner of Agape Consulting
Website: https://www.365daysofabundancequotes.com
Email: josephfangceo@gmail.com
Social: https://www.facebook.com/josephfangofficial
Tags: Financialstrategist, FinancialProfessional

May 7
CHRISTINA CHRISTY KRUSE

An abundant mind finds value in time. Uncovers moments of treasures sublime. You choose the lenses you use to see. How you react shapes who you'll be.

THOUGHT

Have you ever had moments when time froze? Other times when time flew by? Same time, but different. Let's skip to the good part. It has a lot to do with which lenses we live life with. How we feel, our state, and who we are with.

We act on what we believe and not on what we can actually do. The limit often lives inside our imagination. Life is not always easy and can get tough. You can't do it all at once in life, but you can choose your focus and how you react. Life happens, and you control which lenses you view life with.

When your lenses are filled with abundance, it makes you focus on possibilities, not problems. You will find more opportunities than obstacles. Even if you are outside your comfort zone, you will adapt, and what once seemed difficult will become easier. Instead of saying I can't and don't have time, focus on what you can.

Use the words how can I do it and who can help. We have 24 hours daily, and you decide what your priorities are. Most people can find 18 minutes a day, which ends up being 100 hours in a whole year. You can achieve a lot with those hours. Live with gratitude to light your way. Your identity shapes the destiny of your legacy. You have a choice.

QUESTION

Next time you think, "I can't," say, "How can I find time and who can help?" Look at your dreams and prioritize them. Look for possibilities and opportunities. Do it N.O.W.: No Opportunities Wasted.

AUTHOR CONTACT INFORMATION

Christina Christy Kruse, Efficiency Expert of Art of Living Efficiently
Website: https://tinyurl.com/cruisecontroldk
Email: info@artoflivingefficiently.com
Social: https://www.facebook.com/groups/2132042060289169
Tags: Efficiency Expert, High-Performance Speaker

The Art of Connection

May 8

ANDREW ELLIMAN

To make a difference without knowing is the gift of life.

THOUGHT

Having survived an earthquake while attempting to summit Mount Everest, broken a world record for the highest dinner party ever held, and learning to swim at the age of 48 to take on the English Channel, I've gained many valuable insights. Among them, one of the most surprising and profound realizations has been about the people we meet along the way. Whether in the high mountains or the waters of the English Channel, I've encountered individuals whose stories, strength, and kindness have left lasting impressions on me. These connections remind me that our journeys are not just about personal achievement but about the impact we have on each other's lives.

Each challenge has pushed my limits, testing my endurance and resilience, but it has also revealed the power of shared experiences. I've seen firsthand how we inspire, support, and uplift each other, even in the face of adversity. The friendships and bonds formed in these moments become as significant as the goals themselves. In the end, it's not just about the mountains climbed or the seas crossed; it's about the people who journeyed alongside you and the difference we make together.

QUESTION

Ask yourself, what is stopping you from following your heart, and how can you make a difference?

AUTHOR CONTACT INFORMATION

Andrew Elliman, Founder of Stranger Expeditions
Website: https://strangerexpeditions.org
Email: Strangerexpeditions@gmail.com
Social: Https://strangerexpeditions.org
Tags: Motivational Speaker, Adventurer, Explorer, Friend

May 9

LILA BAKKE

Abundance is joy and sorrow in equal parts made alive by imagination and reason, enabling understanding, healing, and partnership.

THOUGHT

"What is 'abundance'?" she asked Tree.

"It is plentitude, an overflowing of a thing," Tree answered. As if to demonstrate, Wind blew through Tree's branches in a tremendous rush, stealing her breath, wilding her hair, and sending the leaves in a raucous frenzy. Her skin tingled, electrified. Weightless, she danced with the leaves, radiant in the golden sun. The joy of these moments strengthened her heart forever.

Humanity frequently talks of Nature but seems not to grasp the importance of her gifts to us. Instead, we plunder her natural resources, imperiling her in selfishness and greed. Our biological abundance contributes to the planet's toxicity and our eventual demise.

It is not too late to rebalance if we allow ourselves to connect to and amplify Nature's countering abundance. Vibrant colors of flora and fauna enchant us. Fireflies dance with. Crickets sing us to sleep. Trees teach us ancient ways. The elements can seduce or destroy us. In them all, Nature speaks to us, "We breathe the same air, drink the same water, walk the same ground. We share the same joys and sorrows."

This choice leads to imagining and then building a path forward of shared unity that does no more harm.

QUESTION

What experience, real or imagined, anchors you? How do you use that to balance the toxicity you encounter? How do you imagine shared abundance and a shared path? How do you project that forward?

AUTHOR CONTACT INFORMATION

Lila Bakke, Author
Website: https://lilabakke.com
Email: lila.bakke@gmail.com
Social: https://linktr.ee/lilabakkewrites
Tags: Author, poet, writer, artist, potter, dollmaker

The Art of Connection

May 10

DRINA FRIED

You can attain a more abundant life when you allow yourself and others to naturally and safely release negative emotions.

THOUGHT

After I was a toddler - until in my early 30's, I was expected to hold in negative emotions (sadness, anger, frustration, fear, embarrassment, and even boredom). Society and my well-meaning parents encouraged it with words such as, "Don't you get teary-eyed!" etc.

Then, a large group of people introduced me to being at peace with the universe, filled with zestful fire, serene with past achievements, and alive with new desires. They sat me in groups; we held hands (for human connection) and took turns. As we released emotions, we'd think of words opposite of the emotional pain. Words worked that brought out more discharge. We learned to stop inhibiting noises, tears, shutters, abundant laughter, and reluctant and animated talking, all while our skins got cold as we released fear, red and warm as we released anger through screams, sobs, tears, and shrieks, just like we naturally did when we were infants. After enough time doing this process (I did this at least once a week for an hour, exchanging equal time listening to somebody else do it.) Result? Able to think clearly, be relaxed and contented, and make more flexible, creative, intelligent responses to each ensuing situation.

QUESTION

Do you remember a time when you released your old negative emotions fully and naturally and ended up feeling much better?

AUTHOR CONTACT INFORMATION

Drina Fried, Owner of Fried Speaking & Consulting, LLC
Website: https://DrinaFried.com
Email: drinafried@iCloud.com
Social: https://www.linkedin.com/in/dr-drina-fried-ed-d-5a991a1a/
Tags: Suicide Prevention, Homicide Prevention, Prevent

May 11

MARYLOU LEONARD

When your life radiates contentment, you have achieved abundance, regardless of your circumstances.

THOUGHT

Some people long for abundance, hoping it will bring them happiness and peace to their lives, for which they are searching. Others feel abundance when they may not have all the world offers them in material possessions. Still, others find abundance in nature or within the spirituality they embrace. Regardless of where I am looking, I see abundance, and it comes in many forms and many ways.

Whenever I am working with my elderly residents, I can hear the feelings displayed in their voices; they are feelings of gratitude for the abundance of every new challenge they face, and they are very willing to share them with me. Their circumstances are only an afterthought. Through the richness of their lived experiences and sharing, I am genuinely blessed with abundance, and my life radiates contentment.

QUESTION

How can all of us continue to reach out to others in the spirit of abundance?

AUTHOR CONTACT INFORMATION

Marylou Leonard, Life Enrichment Assistant of Ashton Creek Health and Rehab
Website: https://www.365daysofabundancequotes.com
Email: marylouleonard28@yahoo.com
Social: https://mybook.to/artofconnection5
Tags: Author of RELEASED/ Palmetto Publishing Co

May 12

KEN GREENE

Abundance is HOPE: Helping Other People Everyday!

THOUGHT

Abundance is a fascinating word. I looked it up in the dictionary, which shows abundance in its simplest form, "more than you need." I thought about this meaning and realized it could mean so many other things. For example, I have a garage full of things: cars and motorcycles. Since I'm only one person, so I have more than I need. My question is, "Is that vanity combined with stupidity?"

Maybe, or perhaps, it is having more than one, like stocking up with food for backup. So, if one breaks down, there is another one to drive. But abundance isn't simply about material things. You can have an abundance of "stuff," but what about friendships or relationships with family? What's more important?

When I was younger, I liked "stuff," toys that were fun to play with. Still, as I got older, I remembered the words my parents told my brothers and me, "Nothing is more important than family, while friends will come and go." My two brothers live in Seattle; we do zoom calls every week on Tuesdays. We visit each other at least once annually; I go to Seattle in the summer, and they come to Phoenix in the winter.

It took me a while to realize what abundance was for me. It's about family!

QUESTION

When you consider abundance, do you see things or people?
Do you see material things or relationships? Or could it be family?

AUTHOR CONTACT INFORMATION

Ken Greene, Independent Agent of US Health
Website: https://www.365daysofabundancequotes.com
Email: Greenemachine.1@netzero.net
Social: https://mybook.to/artofconnection5
Tags: Licensed health insurance professional, speaker

May 13
MARY ZENNETT

Real transformation takes place in people's hearts, one person at a time.

THOUGHT

Much has been written about the transformation of health care from an illness to a wellness model. Yet, so many still do not understand. While institutions compete in the 'race for the cure,' they have left the people they should serve behind. Today, a health pioneer, RFK Jr, brought children's failing health to the forefront on the national stage. Yes, we said failing health. Children's health has been deteriorating to an alarming degree at the hands of toxic food, toxic air, and toxic water, not to mention toxic media. Rates of autism are at an all-time high. So are turbo cancers.

All is not lost. RFK Jr founded Children's Health Defense, a vital resource to educate parents and all who love children with practical ways to enhance children's health. Right now, toxins and corporate capture are killing us as Americans, most especially our children.

And it's time for each of us to do our part. The US has the worst health scores of all industrialized nations. Now, the stage is set for the US to be the best, and It will take each of us. Let's embrace this awakening! It will change the course of human history one person at a time, one heart at a time, and one healthy habit at a time.

QUESTION

What is my role in this transformation of health?

AUTHOR CONTACT INFORMATION

Dr. Mary Zennett, Dr. Mary Zennett of Global Health and Heart
Website: https://ghh.world
Email: awareinspire@gmail.com
Social: https://instagram.com/createahealthyworld
Tags: Health Educator

May 14

NANCY NANCE

*Gratitude helps me see the abundance in
life and celebrate every day.*

THOUGHT

Two melodies played softly in my mind, drifting like distant echoes from a forgotten piano. One, a quiet and entrancing song, carried a whispered warning—never speak the words of the dead. The other offered a sweet, gentle assurance, softly promising it was safe to share the messages from heaven.

The gift of her song came three days after my daughter, Emily Joy, passed. Emily is with me now, guiding me toward my magnificent future through her eyes. My imagination is alive with visions of infinite possibilities, knowing that my angels are managing my manifestations. The powerful knowledge that all of heaven is cheering me on inspires me to dream, plan, execute, and create our legacy together.

Sharing my gifts as a psychic medium, energy healer, breakthrough transformational coach, and author has become my joy each day. I know I was born to communicate with the dead; their whispers come to me both night and day.

I wholeheartedly choose joy and embrace the abundance of life, celebrating each day because I understand that helping others is a way to heal and uplift myself.

QUESTION

How do you find ways to connect with loved ones who have passed, and how do those connections shape your journey of healing and self-discovery?

AUTHOR CONTACT INFORMATION

Nancy Nance, Author, Energy Healer, Psychic Medium of Exponential Joy
Website: https://exponentialjoy.com
Email: muthermayifly@icloud.com
Social: https://www.facebook.com/nancy.chaplin.9
Tags: Psychic Medium, Energy Healer, Author

May 15
BARBARA GOODMAN

*Bring your vision and light into the world.
Believe in the beauty of your dreams.*

THOUGHT

Do you doubt your abilities, procrastinate, or fear failing? If so, you're wiring your brain against living your dream life. Fact: by 35 years old, 95 percent of who you are is set: memorized behaviors, emotional reactions, and unconscious beliefs. The energy-saving brain creates shortcuts, forming neural pathways to make repetitive actions and thoughts automatic. It only knows the familiar; it's the subconscious survival system that keeps you safe, yet it can trap you into patterns of self-doubt.

In this loop, the neural groove deepens and is harder to break with repeated thoughts or behaviors. The good news: the brain is not fixed; it's constantly rewiring itself by neuroplasticity, creating new pathways.

Interrupt old patterns and reverse limiting beliefs to relight your dreams through seven steps: discover and own your unique gifts; appreciate your inner vision and voice; capture and record your dreams; acknowledge your growth; commit to your values; express gratitude and love; take focused action steps daily. Every time you interrupt an old pattern, you weaken it; every time you choose a new thought or behavior, you strengthen it. Commit to rewiring your brain for seven days.

QUESTION

What situations, thoughts, or feelings pull you into old patterns: fear, judgment, feeling unworthy? Write them down to challenge them. Visualize success + replace self-doubt with empowering thoughts.

AUTHOR CONTACT INFORMATION

Barbara Goodman, Chief Creative Officer of Vital + Alive
Website: Https://www.vitalalive.com
Email: barbara@vitalalive.com
Social: https://www.linkedin.com/in/barbaraagoodman/
Tags: Vital Alive, Speaker, Content Strategist, Coach

May 16

AMY D. SPRING

*Abundance flourishes in the quiet moments
we share; a memory, a touch, and a laugh
together can fill our hearts immensely.*

THOUGHT

Abundance doesn't just mean we avoid life's difficulties. Instead, it is found in those quiet everyday moments that are easy to overlook unless we're really paying attention. Pause. It's there in a comforting touch from someone we love, in shared laughter that recalls a fond memory, and in those small but significant signs of connection we too often take for granted.

These moments remind us that true abundance is not about the absence of challenges but about appreciating the beauty and love around us, even during tough times. Let us cherish these whispers of life's richness, which are all around us and never lost. As we navigate our days, remember abundance is about appreciating what we already possess, finding joy in the mundane, comfort in the familiar, and peace in fleeting encounters that resonate deeply within our souls.

This perspective helps us see challenges not as obstacles but as opportunities to deepen our appreciation for the abundant beauty that surrounds us.

QUESTION

*Look around...What simple joys in your life remind you of
the abundance around you, even during challenging times?*

AUTHOR CONTACT INFORMATION

Amy D. Spring, Founder and CEO of Wise-Transitions
Website: https://wise-transitions.com/
Email: amyspring@wise-transitions.com
Social: https://www.linkedin.com/in/amy-spring/
Tags: Wise-Transitions, Elder Care Consultant, Speaker

May 17
YVONNE E. GAMBLE

Plan the next 100 years, and you will know what you are going to do with your life today.

THOUGHT

Short-term goals plan 1-10 years, 40-year direction change plans, 100-year legacy plans. The world has evolved over the millenniums and eras, and the current era is Cenozoic. The world is 4.5 billion years old; day continues to turn into night, trees live, flowers bloom, waters flow, and air circulates while man and creatures thrive. Great plan!

To fully comprehend the 'My100-Year Legacy Plan Book," one simply has to look at the world around them. Wherever you may be in the world, life, career, or business, you adhere to systems, protocols, policies, moral values, and traditions. Why? Because of centuries-old plans, they act as guides to navigate our daily courses of action. Without these directives, everything becomes chaotic and dismal, as the end cannot be seen from the beginning, and vice versa.

100-year planning is a legacy responsibility to achieve your impossible dream while shaping the world in the meantime. 100-year Planning will demand strategic, focused goals, cunning desire, and the will to keep going no matter the odds. You do not plan based on trends, the next big thing, or to capture a market share; you plan 100 years to define the future you want to live in.

QUESTION

For every action, there is an equal and opposite reaction; how long have you planned to be a reactor to your life and not the action of your life?

AUTHOR CONTACT INFORMATION

Yvonne E. Gamble, CEO of SanPete Financial Group, Inc.,
Website: https://www.sanpetefinancialgroup.com/
Email: yvonne.gamble@sanpetefinancialgroup.com
Social: https://www.linkedin.com/in/yvonnegambleleadership/
Tags: Speaker, Venture Capital, Space Funder, Asset Mgmt

May 18

TRICIA PARIDO

*Embrace the power within you to shape your reality.
This is your life, too! It gets to look, feel,
be however you want it to. You get to choose.*

THOUGHT

We all possess an incredible power within to shape our reality and create the life we desire. It isn't derived from external circumstances but from our internal strength and determination. Embracing this power gives us control over how we perceive and respond to the world.

Imagine waking up each day confident that you can handle whatever comes your way. An understanding that you're not a passive observer but an active creator. By focusing on positive energy, practicing mindfulness, and nurturing emotional intelligence, you can navigate challenges with grace and resilience.

This reality is your life; it gets to look, feel, and be however you want. You choose how you experience each moment, interaction, and challenge. It's about the choice to let go of what no longer serves us: negative thoughts, toxic relationships, or limiting beliefs. We can fill our lives with what uplifts and empowers us. The journey is unique to each person, but the principle remains: our internal power shapes our external reality.

I've witnessed many people transform their lives by tapping into this power. They moved past fears, overcame anxieties, and built lives filled with joy, purpose, and fulfillment.

QUESTION

What steps can you take today to harness the power within you, embrace that this is your life too, and begin transforming it into the masterpiece it was always meant to be?

AUTHOR CONTACT INFORMATION

Tricia Parido, Founder | Master Practitioner of Turning Leaves Recovery Life and Wellness Coaching

Website: https://www.turningleavesrecovery.com/

Email: turningleavesrecovery@gmail.com

Social: https://www.facebook.com/tricia.parido/

Tags: Architect of Life Fulfillment and Transformation

May 19

MARIA MATIAS

*Get Intentional with Abundance and Feng Shui...
it's a conscious choice that turns intentions into reality.*

THOUGHT

I decided to get certified in Diamond Feng Shui and Diamond Dowsing. I applied it effectively in my home and businesses, and the results were beyond magical. I have created abundance for myself, my family, my friends, and my clients.

When we think about abundance, we frequently think about money. Indeed, money is an excellent form of abundance. However, abundance comes in many forms. When you have chosen to allow abundance to flow into your life, start by aligning your environment with the desires for prosperity, money, and joy. Create clear intentions for your money and use your space as a tool to manifest those desires.

Deliberately design the southeast corner of your space to attract abundance by placing a money tree, a jade plant, or anything in gold. Invite prosperity into your life and create a loving relationship with it. Many times, we have loose change in our pockets or purses. Put your loose change in a golden bowl in the southeast corner of your space, and every time you have loose change, you know precisely where to put it. This behavior creates a mindful action that opens doors to your abundance and positive energy flow.

QUESTION

*What is your relationship with your money?
And how are you welcoming it into your life?*

AUTHOR CONTACT INFORMATION

Maria Matias, Owner of Maria Matias Feng Shui, LLC
Website: https://www.mariamatiasfengshui.com/
Email: info@mariamatiasfengshui.com
Social: https://linktr.ee/mariamatiasofficial
Tags: Feng Shui, Dowsing Expert, Abundance, Success

May 20

BRENDA KILHOFFER

*Influencers have fame and fortune,
but true power lies in shining your light through
the shadows cast by haters.*

THOUGHT

Everyone wants to be an influencer. An army of "experts" are selling shortcuts to get you there. Do not be distracted. Your message is too essential for shortcuts. It is one that only you can deliver. It might not hit the first time or the hundredth time. But when consistent, you will grow each time you deliver the message. You will refine it and begin to collect evidence that you are on your path.

The evidence won't always be obvious. It may even be apathy, criticism, failure, or hate. That's the evidence that offers you the best opportunities for growth and transformation. Allow it to shape you and mold you. The path may be full of shadows and self-doubt. Those are your opportunities to shine.

In those shadows, you will face a choice. You can draw upon your courage and shine your light, not in condemnation, but with empathy, by highlighting the same shadows in your own life to lead yourself and others out of the darkness.

The message you share when everyone opposes you reveals who you are. Your power lies in the emotions you choose to fight that battle with.

Will you fight hate with hate, vengeance with revenge, or will you answer with empathy, forgiveness, and love?

QUESTION

What distractions, hidden as support, criticism, or hate, pull you into the darkness or prevent you from sharing your message effectively? What action steps can you take to overcome them?

AUTHOR CONTACT INFORMATION

Brenda Kilhoffer, Founder of Equine Learning Lab
Website: www.EquineLearningLab.com
Email: Brenda@EquineLearningLab.com
Social: https://www.tiktok.com/@equinelearninglab
Tags: Coach, Facilitator, Speaker, Retreats, EAL Coach

May 21
JIM CONNORS

*Never underestimate those you meet;
everyone has a story to tell. Genuine connections,
built on trust, will always prevail.*

THOUGHT

This quote really hits home for me. It reminds me that everyone I meet has a story worth hearing. In our busy lives, we often overlook the importance of genuinely listening to others. Real connections happen when we take the time to understand and appreciate each other's experiences.

Getting to know people better means showing empathy and patience. It's about asking the right questions and making others feel valued. Sure, some might take advantage of your kindness, but the real reward is in the genuine, trustworthy relationships you build. These connections are worth more than any material gain.

Believing in this isn't always easy. You'll face challenges and moments of doubt, but it's vital to stay committed to helping those whose stories need to be told. Your dedication will uplift others and bring unexpected joy and fulfillment to your life.

Remember to be mindful of the company you keep, stay alert, keep your head on a swivel, and don't let anyone stop you from reaching your goals. Keep pushing forward despite obstacles! In the end, you'll make a lasting impact or influence the lives of those you touch.

QUESTION

How can you create genuine connections and ensure that everyone's story is heard and valued?

AUTHOR CONTACT INFORMATION

Jim Connors, Executive Producer of JimConnors.net
Website: https://JimConnors.net
Email: jc@jimconnors.net
Social: https://www.instagram.com/talktojc
Tags: Emcee, host, audio, radio, podcast, producer

May 22

VINCENT LEONTI

Physical Health is achievable, but it must be Integrated with Mental, Emotional, and Spiritual Health.

THOUGHT

We are seeking to feel better in our lives. That underlies everything we do. It influences our choices. Those choices influence our health. The seeking can result in "dis-ease." Or we may be exposed to an environmental factor that creates "dis-ease." We think if we take the right medicine or the right supplement, we will be better; we will free ourselves from "dis-ease." But, more is often needed. We must look at how we got to where we are. We must find the root causes.

We must use energy to get out of the cycle of being stuck in inflammation and the cycle of negative emotions that accompany this. Investing mental and emotional energy to realize, believe, and work on the mindset that we can feel better is often the vital step other people miss as they are on their health journey.

But as I continued my journey from Doctor to Healer, I realized that those who get better invariably come to trust they would improve. And those who stayed stuck felt they would never improve until they changed their mind.

QUESTION

Are you willing to invest in your most precious resource, yourself?

AUTHOR CONTACT INFORMATION

Vincent Leonti, Owner of Princeton Integrative Health
Website: princetonih.com
Email: drvince@princetonih.com
Social: https://www.facebook.com/princetonintegrativehealth
Tags: Integrative Medicine, Wellness

May 23
MONIKA JAKUBIAK

*We can all focus on Being Creative.
It's research, risking & making. At that moment, you forget everything.
Your senses engage, and you just make.*

THOUGHT

I'm moved to tears by music or colors. Sometimes, Art makes me feel so alive that I want to hug everyone on the street and shout, "How Great Is This?!"

I'm not sure if it's the work that engages me most or if thinking about what makes the Artist tick is more interesting. Creativity can be non-linear and riotous, but it is possible to decide to create and move towards a vision step by step.

How often do we think, "Today I'm going to get creative. I just have to finish something, and I'll start writing that book or doing that collage," only to end up doing everything else instead? I always salute the artist, as it takes guts to show up, be brave, and take risks. Do you miss times when you're in the flow: making stuff, messing with materials, tools, doodles, and textures? Do you want to find it again? That's what Be Creative Again is here for.

After 20 years in fashion design and creative education, I decided to teach myself how to be creative again. Not how to be creative, because we're all naturally creative. Sometimes, we need a guide or a community. It's possible to formulate your creative process, and I teach precisely that; I will license you to dream big and start making.

QUESTION

*Are you ready to experiment and take risks in your creative journey?
Want to build confidence in your artistic self?*

AUTHOR CONTACT INFORMATION

Monika Jakubiak, Founder and Creative Director of Be Creative Again
Website: https://www.linkedin.com/in/monika-jakubiak-80a42b4/
Email: monikajakubiak@yahoo.com
Social: https://www.linkedin.com/in/monika-jakubiak-80a42b4/
Tags: Creative Educator, Designer, Artistic Facilitator

The Art of Connection

May 24

HOWARD BROWN

Shining Brightly with Abundance!

THOUGHT

How do we achieve a rich and abundant life? Do a self-check to see where you are emotionally, physically, financially, and in relationships. Do not isolate. Let people help uplift you in your time of need. Allow the light of others to shine in and for you.

I will share my morning mantra as I look in the mirror every morning as a two-time stage IV cancer survivor 26 years apart:

- I am blessed.
- I am lucky.
- I am grateful,
- I will choose to be kind.
- I will choose to be giving.
- I will choose to be healing.
- I will choose to be joyful.
- I will choose to be happy.
- I will choose grace for myself and others.
- I will choose not to hate.

I guarantee that you can embrace my mantra or create your own to take the necessary actions to make the authentic, intentional, and positive changes necessary in your life. You, too, will Shine Brightly in Abundance by sharing your light with others.

QUESTION

How are you Shining Brightly for yourself and others each day?

AUTHOR CONTACT INFORMATION

Howard Brown, Mr. Shining Brightly of Shining Brightly
Website: https://www.shiningbrightly.com/
Email: howard@shiningbrightly.com
Social: https://www.linkedin.com/in/howardsbrown/
Tags: Author, Speaker, Podcaster, 2-Time Cancer Survivor

May 25

KEVIN MAYER

Abundance is all around us; the Law of Attraction demonstrates abundance daily!

THOUGHT

When I reflect on how my industry is thriving with plenty of work and clients, I am embracing the abundance available to me while struggling to comprehend why many of my peers claim they are sitting on their hands. One thought keeps surfacing in my mind: Who is right?

During a discussion with another studio owner, I mentioned two of my high-profile clients. One of the clients has been in the industry for decades, and the other owner has never heard his name. I instantly recognized my reflections about abundance and had my answer. If another local owner didn't know the biggest fish in our pond, then he was also clueless about the abundance around him.

Be aware of the diamonds in your surroundings and use the Law of Attraction to acquire them. If not you, then who? Imagine how many giving moments you can enjoy by attracting abundance.

QUESTION

If you are struggling to find what is in front of you, shouldn't you find a mentor to guide you? "When the student is ready, the master shall appear."

AUTHOR CONTACT INFORMATION

Kevin Mayer, Founder and Owner of Arizona Studios
Website: https://www.arizonastudios.com
Email: kevin@arizonastudios.com
Social: https://www.linkedin.com/in/kevin-mayer-arizonastudios
Tags: Video Production, Soundstage

May 26

KARSTEN ALVA-JORGENSEN

Doing What You Love and Loving What You Do unlocks True Abundance.

THOUGHT

Discovering your purpose is essential for living a fulfilling and meaningful life because when you live in alignment with your purpose, you awaken your creativity, leadership, and influence.

I am sure you have experienced the difference between doing something that you love and doing something that you are forced to do. Even your sense of time shifts from 'time flying' to 'time stopping still,' doesn't it?

Simply put, Doing What You Love unleashes not only vitality and joy but also generates focus and action. When we pursue our purpose, we gain the courage and perseverance to dream and act big, and we attract the resources and support needed to fulfill our mission.

My purpose is to help you gain a clear understanding of your essence and unique talents and create a new and expanded vision for your future. In just a few weeks, I will help you see new possibilities for yourself and your life, including how you can make money from doing what you love.

I will also help you overcome obstacles, blocks, or fears and build a new level of trust and confidence in yourself. I will support you with proven processes and tools as you implement your vision and become unstoppable in your path to abundance.

QUESTION

What becomes possible for you, for others, and the world when you know and live your purpose? Will there ever be a better time than today to begin unfolding these possibilities?

AUTHOR CONTACT INFORMATION

Karsten Alva-Jorgensen, Founder and Owner of Executive Growth Circle, Ltd.
Website: https://executivegrowthcircle.com
Email: karsten@executivegrowthcircle.com
Social: http://linkedin.com/in/karstenalva
Tags: Speaker, Life Coach, Executive Coach, Leadership

May 27
EDIE SANGIORGIO

*Abundance is not a destination to be sought
but is a place you come from – it's a state of mind.*

THOUGHT

Acquiring wealth and having abundance has always been a major priority and goal in life for many people, but I think the reason so many struggle in this area is that they don't quite understand that abundance is not something "out there" to achieve. It's a perspective. It's a way of thinking. It's a way of feeling about yourself and the world.

Abundance is all around us if we choose to see it. The world radiates with abundance. There isn't a shortage or scarcity of anything. It's all out there for the taking. When we come from an abundance mindset, then things are much more likely to come to us with more ease. An abundance perspective makes us so much more receptive to anything we desire, whether that is in the form of money or relationships or even desiring an abundance of health and vitality.

So, if you struggle in this area, check in with your attitude about abundance and start making changes there first. You'll be surprised at how willing the universe is to play with you once you have an abundance mindset and a receptive heart.

QUESTION

Do you interact with the world with an abundance or scarcity perspective?

AUTHOR CONTACT INFORMATION

Edie Sangiorgio, Owner of Catie's Corner Cartoon
Website: https://catiescorner.net
Email: edie.sangiorgio@gmail.com
Social: https://www.facebook.com/catiescornercartoon/
Tags: EFT Coach, Writer, Blogger, Author, Speaker

May 28
HANNAH KESLER

*Every moment of indecision is a choice,
but abundance flows through decisive action.*

THOUGHT

Throughout my journey in entrepreneurship and life, I've faced countless crossroads, often paralyzed by fear of making the wrong choice. It was during these moments of inaction that I realized a powerful truth: inaction is a choice. It's the choice to stay stagnant, letting circumstances or others decide for us. Every time we avoid decisions, skip tough conversations, or hope problems resolve themselves, we're choosing to remain stuck. The consequences of this choice are often more significant than facing the situation head-on.

In business, the world is constantly shifting: markets change, trends evolve, and opportunities can disappear in an instant. Avoiding decisions risks missing out on game-changing moments or, worse, becoming irrelevant.

My advice: be present in your choices. Every moment is a chance to shape your future. Even when the road ahead feels uncertain, take a step forward. As the saying goes, "Every moment of indecision is a choice, but abundance flows through decisive action." Moving, even in uncertainty, reveals more than standing still ever could.

QUESTION

What decision in your life or business have you been avoiding,
and how could taking action today shape your future?

AUTHOR CONTACT INFORMATION

Hannah Kesler, 2nd Generation Money Mentor of The Money Multiplier
Website: https://www.themoneymultiplier.com
Email: hannah@themoneymultiplier.com
Social: https://linktr.ee/themoneymultiplier
Tags: Money Mentor

May 29
LADONNA MCABEE

*You Are The Only You, So Go Be
The Best You That You Can Be!*

THOUGHT

This quote is a mindset. So often, we neglect ourselves in the rush to meet everyone else's needs. We wear ourselves thin, believing it's the only way to show love or care. But here's the truth: to give your best, you have to be your best.

You are unique, and the best gift you can give others is a stronger, healthier you. Respect yourself first. That means prioritizing your well-being—not just physically but mentally and emotionally.

When you take care of yourself, you lead by example. Your actions become a reflection of what you preach and teach. By showing others how to love and respect themselves, you inspire them to do the same.

This realization didn't come easy for me. I spent years focusing on others while neglecting myself. I thought selflessness meant putting myself last. But I've learned that giving from a full heart—one that's cared for and whole—is the only way to serve those around us genuinely.

So today, I challenge you: What's one way you can show yourself love and care? Let's lead by example and be the best versions of ourselves—for us and everyone we care about.

Remember, when you shine, you permit others to shine too./a

QUESTION

*Do you prioritize everyone else while forgetting to take care of yourself?
How can you lead by example if you're not at your best?
What's one way you'll start being the best version of YOU today?*

AUTHOR CONTACT INFORMATION

LaDonna McAbee, Networking Expert Owner and Host
Website: https://www.LaDonnaMcAbee.com
Email: ladonnamcabee@gmail.com
Social: https://www.linkedin.com/in/networkingexpert
Tags: Networking Expert, Owner, Host

May 30

BRENDA THANACOODY

Abundance is a frequency that you have to magnetize.

THOUGHT

In order to manifest what you want, you need to generate the abundance frequency. Everything is energy, and so is abundance. And as energy has a frequency, abundance also has a frequency. You need to vibrate with the right energy at the right frequency for you to attract what you want.

Therefore, vibrate the frequency of abundance, generate the emotions, and feel them so you can be at the frequency of abundance.

How will you vibrate at the frequency of abundance?
You do this first by visualizing what you want.

Have clear, colorful, and vivid images in your mind.

The next step is to generate the feeling that you would have should this visualization happen. Feel the emotions. What emotions are being triggered? Is it love? Is it happiness?

The more positive the emotions, the higher the frequency of abundance. So, feel more love, feel more happiness, feel more elation, and feel the excitement! These feelings will make you magnetic!

The more magnetic you become, the faster you will manifest. You will not only be generating the abundance frequency, but you will be a magnet attracting the abundance to you!

QUESTION

What emotions will you feel when you will manifest abundance?

AUTHOR CONTACT INFORMATION

Brenda Thanacoody, Owner of Brenda Thanacoody
Website: https://www.365daysofabundancequotes.com
Email: shela_thanacoody@yahoo.com
Social: https://www.facebook.com/profile.php?id=61561471820325
Tags: Spiritual Coach, Past Life Regressionist, Healer

May 31

BARB MARKEY

Finding my people made a difference in my life and taught me how to make a difference in others.

THOUGHT

Lying on the beach, I watch the sun sink into the horizon; I feel the warm sand tickle my sunburned skin. A cool breeze brushes my face as the day winds down. My thoughts drift and flow like the gentle waves on the shore.

My thoughts are the deep sense of gratitude I feel for the people in my life who've taught me important lessons, and I hope to make a positive difference for others as they did for me.

My aunt, strong and independent, showed me that I could build the future I wanted through intentional hard work. She emphasized that a positive attitude and gratitude can make the world a more beautiful place.

My best friend was a true fighter who always put others first. I admired how she managed her chemo treatments to volunteer at a local non-profit. Even on days when she felt awful, she'd still found time to help someone else. She taught me the importance of selflessness and serving others, even when it's the most challenging of times.

Though they are now gone, their lessons continue to inspire me. I cherish this moment, filled with warm memories of them and the lasting impact they had on my life. It brings me comfort and joy to reflect on how their influence shapes who I am today.

QUESTION

Who has made a difference in your life? How can you make a difference in others?

AUTHOR CONTACT INFORMATION

Barb Markey, Author, Organizational of Did I Forget To Mention
Website: https://www.didiforgettomention.com/
Email: didiforgettomention@yahoo.com
Social: https://www.facebook.com/profile.php?id=100044301714259
Tags: Did I Forget To Mention, Preplanning Book

June 1
KATHLEEN CARLSON

*You get to define abundance in all areas of life,
and when you feel it, really feel it, you get to live it.*

THOUGHT

What is abundance, really? According to Webster, abundance means "an ample quantity: affluence, wealth" or a "relative degree of plentifulness." For much of my early life, the word abundance, and indeed the feeling of It, wasn't part of my vocabulary. The concept felt distant, reserved for the few fortunate enough to know prosperity and overflow in tangible ways.

But as time passed, I discovered that abundance isn't solely about wealth or the accumulation of more. Abundance, I realized, is deeply subjective. Each of us holds the power to define what it means to be abundant. We can choose to experience it not only in our financial circumstances but also in our health, our relationships, and the many other areas of our lives where fulfillment matters.

You get to define abundance, and when you feel it—really feel it—you get to live it. Once we know what abundance means to us personally, we can begin to tap into how it feels and weave that sensation into our everyday lives. Living in abundance is a choice, a daily decision to perceive and embrace the plentitude already surrounding us in whatever form we choose to value.

QUESTION

What small changes can you make today to feel and live in greater abundance in the areas that matter most?

AUTHOR CONTACT INFORMATION

Kathleen Carlson, CEO and Founder of Straight Up Executive Consulting
Website: https://www.straightupsuccess.com
Email: Kathleen@StraightUpSuccess.com
Social: https://www.linkedin.com/in/kathleen-carlson-a05779a8/
Tags: WomenInLeadership, IntuitiveGuide, Speaker, Author

June 2
TONNILEA LARSON

*You can grow old in numbers
but never grow up in your heart.*

THOUGHT

Have you ever had someone so special or dear to you that the very thought of losing them just made your heart hurt deeply? I have had one special person in my life: my paternal grandma. She was the rock to our family and the most remarkable storyteller. I can still remember Sunday dinners, sitting around the table after lunch, and having a history lesson with the family.

Usually, it was more about my grandpa than her family. It always amazed me that she knew so much about his family and could remember the stories passed down for generations. The quote I live by now and tell my grandchildren is from her words. She always acted like a kid with a heart of gold and full of joy. She would often surprise us grandkids by doing silly things and just laughing at herself.

I believe I owe so much to my grandma, the way she lived, the Christian foundation she gave our family, the heritage and legacy she left behind, and to be able to honor her with the gift of writing that she encouraged me with so long ago. I credit the word "Abundance" to my grandma, Gladys Rose Millican. She had her life aligned in Christ, full of His Joy, and Dancing in His Love daily. Today, I know she's dancing with Jesus.

QUESTION

If you could leave one piece of wisdom or give your family a legacy, What would you want to leave behind for them to remember about you or your life?

AUTHOR CONTACT INFORMATION

TonniLea Larson, Owner of TonniLea Ministries
Website: https://tonnilea.com/
Email: tonnileatv@gmail.com
Social: https://www.linkedin.com/in/tonnilea-larson-1b55701b5/
Tags: Host of The Healing Conferences, Event Planner

June 3
HOLLY ENZMANN

*Never underestimate simply showing up with
a golden energy and a curious mind!*

THOUGHT

There is always an advantage to a positive, approachable attitude. I've been passionate about traditional martial arts for over a decade, and the key to growth and success is a smile on your face and an eager, unassuming attitude. When you walk into a room, you should take your time to take everything in, find the beauty, and think of possibilities and curiosities.

The key to a successful transaction is a healthy relationship with your client, and the only way to cultivate that is by listening, considering, and taking action. You wouldn't believe where you could go with your shining energy and curious, courageous mind.

QUESTION

When speaking with people, do you listen and respond or wait for your turn to talk? When you walk down the street, are you looking at the ground or acknowledging and appreciating your surroundings?

AUTHOR CONTACT INFORMATION

Holly Enzmann Real Estate Agent of Berkshire Hathaway HomeServices Commonwealth Real Estate

Website: https://hollyenzmannrealestate.com/home

Email: holly.enzmann@commonmoves.com

Social: www.linktr.ee/h.enzmann

Tags: Real Estate Agent Berkshire Hathaway

June 4
MICHELLE GASS

Has someone ever said to you, "Just do it?"
"What are you waiting for?" "Go for it!"

THOUGHT

I'm almost 100 percent sure someone has! I was in search of a creative job. I stumbled upon my kitchen designer position at Wren Kitchens. I went for it! Days later, I was hired! Always, a new style to present to the client has kept the client engaged & satisfied.

Since this is a sales position, there are ups and downs. During a downturn, emotions run high! Keep your focus on the goal ahead, which will make your mind remain clear. Push the drive within you further! Many emotions are experienced, and my resolve is strengthened daily. A useful one is active listening. Here is when the wants and needs are established. This habit is an essential part of sales; many clients need assistance separating the two to ensure the investment level is always at the back of their minds.

While listening, engage conversationally by asking open-ended questions. Smiling and sharing a joke to break a barrier makes the clients share more about the project. When you have this technique and master it, not only do you have the client highlight the benefits of your product, but they have mastered the art of customer buy-in! This skill is trial and error! Find a way that works for you! Now, Come on, Go For It!

QUESTION

What would you reward yourself with after you've " Gone For It"? Wishing you all the strength that you need to reach your level of success!

AUTHOR CONTACT INFORMATION

Michelle Gass, Kitchen Designer of Wren Kitchens
Website: https://www.wrenkitchens.com/us/showrooms/Commack
Email: Michelle.Gass@WrenKitchens.com
Social: https://www.linkedin.com/feed/?trk=guest_homepage-basic_nav-header-signin
Tags: kitchendesigner

June 5
ROY MOORE

Envision the end, not the beginning.

THOUGHT

During my 20-year tenure in the United States Marine Corps, I've honed the essential skills for coaching and training individuals across various professions through consistent, real-world applications. Often, when faced with a perplexing or stressful situation, some people may feel or become overwhelmed, but why?

Venturing into the unknown can be frightening, not because they lack the skills and knowledge to succeed but rather because readily envisioning a clear path to success becomes difficult. By leveraging a routine and a mental organization process, your abundant victory will become second nature.

At RPM Fitness, that is precisely what we aim to achieve with our clients. Through creating customized plans in the areas of life, leadership, fitness & nutrition, and self-defense, we empower individuals to take the necessary steps to achieve what they believe to be greatness. To maximize our plans and ensure sustained success through a positive paradigm shift, we utilize our four-pronged process to accurately identify the root cause of a concern, validate and acknowledge that our discovery is the actual cause, change the behavior that is enabling the concern, and sustain the change.

QUESTION

How would a well-crafted routine change the way you show up daily?

AUTHOR CONTACT INFORMATION

Roy Moore, Founder and Owner of RPM Fitness, LLC
Website: https://www.rpmfitness.com
Email: roy@rpmfitstrong.com
Social: https://www.instagram.com/rpmfitstrong
Tags: Life Coach, Leadership Coach, Self Defense Coach

June 6
BECKY NORWOOD

*True abundance is found in inner happiness,
peace of mind, grace, self-worth, and a grateful heart.*

THOUGHT

Being abundantly wealthy monetarily does not necessarily mean happiness. Life lessons, including the challenging times, teach us that no amount of material wealth can bring happiness. Material wealth is wonderful, but without happiness, peace of mind, a deep sense of self-worth, and a grateful heart, it loses its flair.

Becoming your own best product, consistently improving your life, and being responsible for your actions and reactions in times, both good and bad, is what hones your experience of life into one worth living.

I find that the vast majority of those who have found and answered their calling found it as a result of events in their lives that were not so joyous. Downright gut-wrenching times that ended up changing the trajectory of their lives, the outcome of which is how they are called to serve in our world.

True abundance comes from knowing ourselves, our self-worth,
and our willingness to invest in ourselves, giving ourselves a big, intentional dream.
It comes from investing in relationships, the kind that are nurtured and cherished.
It comes from happiness, the ability to have and show enthusiasm for life, and smiling more each day. That is abundance at its finest!

QUESTION

What does true abundance mean to you?

AUTHOR CONTACT INFORMATION

Becky Norwood, CEO of Spotlight Publishing House
Website: https://spotlightpublishinghouse.com
Email: becky@spotlightpublishinghouse.com
Social: https://www.linkedin.com/in/beckybnorwood/
Tags: Book Publishing Expert, Spotlight Publishing House

June 7

TRES CHAPMAN

Living a life full of abundance is soothing for the soul.

THOUGHT

Abundance reminds me of having more than I need. This excess can be tangible or spiritual. But what if you don't feel like you're living a life of abundance? There are steps you can take to turn it around. First, clear your mind of negative thoughts and focus on what you have, not what you don't have. Now, you can concentrate on the next steps.

Write down a clear vision of what you want. For example, I want to be a homeowner by September 2028. Believe that you can achieve this challenge. Ask the universe for what you want. This request can be made on a vision board, personal journal, or through prayer. Surround yourself with like-minded people. You deserve support and encouragement, not negativity and doubt.

These next steps will change your current trajectory. Develop a plan and seek assistance to help hold you accountable. You may not achieve homeownership by September 2028, but you will achieve that goal. Material items, friends, and family will not make you happy. You won't find happiness in others. Dig deep within your soul to find fulfillment. Small wins lead to big wins, and you must enjoy the journey along the way. This life of abundance will soothe your soul.

QUESTION

What does a life filled with abundance look like to you?

AUTHOR CONTACT INFORMATION

Tres Chapman, Co-founder of T & K International
Website: http://tkinternational.org
Email: treschapman4@gmail.com
Social: https://www.facebook.com/profile.php?id=100063739073149
Tags: Health & Wellness, Author

June 8
BOBBI WILCOX

Ignite your sparkle...your soul is meant to shine.

THOUGHT

As human beings, we are meant to awaken to our inner sparkle. This sparkle resides within each of us—it's something we're born with. We are all divinely created with a loving essence. We can see and feel this loving essence in the innocence of newborn babies and young children. We recognize it as the inner light we often notice in others, and sometimes, we feel this light within ourselves. Our souls instinctively recognize this light in other souls—it's a connection we all share.

However, as we grow up, many of us—especially women—are taught not to shine this light. We are conditioned to believe that if we let our light shine, others won't like us, will become jealous, or may withdraw their love. It's time to awaken into our true loving nature, embrace our loving essence, and honor our inner light! Our sparkle was never meant to be dimmed—it was meant to shine brightly. Ignite your inner sparkle!

QUESTION

What area in your life do you desire sparkle? If you had sparkle in that area, what would it look like? What would it feel like?

AUTHOR CONTACT INFORMATION

Bobbi Wilcox, Soul-Centered Author, Coach, and Speaker of Blended Families United

Website: https://bobbiwilcox.com

Email: bobbi@bobbiwilcox.com

Social: http://www.facebook.com/bobbiwilcoxr/

Tags: Sparkle Author, Bobbi Wilcox Realtor

June 9
K.M. RINGER

Sometimes, too much is what you need.

THOUGHT

When struggling to get through that demanding project at work, the demons in your head want to take over, or you are fighting for every word on that manuscript sitting on your computer screen, just wanting to give up having a voice to push you through can be so important. Have someone around you who will give aggressive love and support. When you feel as though you can't take it anymore, lean into your support system as they share their abundance of faith in just how amazing you are doing and remind you that you are a fighter, a survivor, and loved. It feels like too much at the time, but you must believe it can give you the motivation and mental fortitude to push forward to break through that wall.

Just because that aggressive love feels like a lot, it doesn't mean you don't need it. Yes, it can feel overwhelming and too much, but that sternness can shake something deep within and push you further into greatness.

QUESTION

Are you going to give up?

AUTHOR CONTACT INFORMATION

K.M. Ringer, Owner of K.M. Ringer
Website: https://kmringer.com
Email: kim@kmringer.com
Social: https://www.instagram.com/kimberlymringer/#
Tags: Romance Author, Cover Designer, Formatter

June 10

JODIE SANTANDREA-RUANO

In the dance of life, open your awareness to the beauty that surrounds us every day. Embrace it with an abundance of gratitude. Live Life Full Force.

THOUGHT

The doctor walked in and said, "You will be put on a ventilator, you will have a trach, and you have one in four chances of survival. You have five minutes to tell your family." My world came to a standstill.

I turned to prayer, spoke to loved ones, and put my fate into the skills of the medical team and God. My body endured an immense ordeal, but the true miracle was when I finally emerged from life support. Although I had a long road to recovery ahead, I was alive. This second chance allowed me to see life through a renewed lens.

I realized what truly matters. I cherish every moment spent with my loved ones, giving hugs, and moments spent with my grandson, which is a blessing I fervently prayed for. I started doing what aligned with me. Don't wait for the 'right' time or circumstance. Don't get to where you say I wish I did that. The past is for reflection, the future is a realm of possibilities, and the present moment holds the essence of living. Many people forget this simple truth, caught up in regrets or worries, so cherish each breath and each heartbeat and embrace each day with passion and an abundance of gratitude. Life is the ultimate gift we have been given.

QUESTION

In those crucial moments, what would you do? Did you live life full force?

AUTHOR CONTACT INFORMATION

Jodie Santandrea-Ruano, Founder of Live Life Full Force
Website: livelifefullforce.com
Email: jodiesantandrearuano@gmail.com
Social: https://linktr.ee/jodiesantandrearuano?
Tags: Speaker, Coach

The Art of Connection

June 11
TODD LINGEL

Who Kares, We Care!! Creating Change, One Life at a Time!!

THOUGHT

"Who Kares, We Care!!" is a foundational statement of who we are and who we should all strive to be. That statement is made up of four key elements: Education, Prevention, Communication, and Support.

Youth today face far more significant challenges with increased peer and social media pressures, impaired driving due to alcohol or drugs, and distracted driving. As we constantly focus on our phones, our youth are becoming increasingly lost amidst the distractions. We can change this with hard work and perseverance.

So, how do we bridge that gap? The key to all good relationships is Communication. But there first needs to be some sense of respect between adults and youth. Respect, whether earned or not, is a crucial component of authentic open communication. Communication can be broken down into three basic types: Verbal Communication, in which we listen to one another to understand their meaning. Written Communication, where we read the meaning, and Nonverbal Communication, where we observe each other and infer meaning. Take time to sit down with a youth today and ask them how they are genuinely doing. Take Charge and Communicate!!

QUESTION

How do you communicate with your kids or peers? Challenge: Schedule time to sit down and communicate without any distractions. Who Kares, We Care!!

AUTHOR CONTACT INFORMATION

Todd Lingel, Founder of Kares Foundation
Website: https://www.ks-kares.org
Email: toddkaresf@gmail.com
Social: https://www.instagram.com/kares_foundation
Tags: Speaker, Youth Services, Victim Impact, School

June 12
KEVIN MCDONALD

Evolving Ideas, One Conversation at a Time.

THOUGHT

Meet Kevin McDonald, a seasoned host of radio and podcast shows since 2003, who has captivated audiences with his engaging and heartfelt approach. With a passion for storytelling and connecting with listeners, Kevin has built a loyal following over the years.

As the founder of a thriving media company called KMmedia.pro, which offers a range of media services designed to enhance and elevate brands and businesses, their expertise in the industry ensures that clients receive top-quality content and strategies tailored to their needs.

Beyond his professional achievements, Kevin is known for his extraordinary and bubbly personality. Driven by a mission to uplift and inspire, he brings positivity and joy into every interaction. Whether on-air or in person, Kevin's infectious enthusiasm and genuine care for others make them a beloved figure in the community. Their dedication to spreading positivity and supporting others in their journey is at the heart of everything they do.

QUESTION

How can one conversation spark a new idea in your life?

AUTHOR CONTACT INFORMATION

Kevin McDonald, Founder and Host of Positive Talk Radio
Website: https://www.positivetalkradio.net/
Email: kevin@kmmedia.pro
Social: https://www.youtube.com/@PositiveTalkRadio
Tags: Host, Founder, Podcast, Positive

June 13

WENDY B KING

Abundance is an inside job.
No one can take that away from you.

THOUGHT

The Key

Leaving home at 17 and losing my firstborn child at 25, I know that abundance is not about material wealth or external success. It is about the richness of our inner world, our connections, our resilience, and our ability to navigate life's challenges. It is not something you get; it is something you develop within your mind and soul. How? Through:

1. Connection

The truth is that we only need one or two people in our lives who genuinely know us and accept us for who we are. Our life is not about 'seeking approval from others.' Develop and treasure those friendships.

2. Accepting and Understanding Life

If we have a preconceived idea of how life 'should' be and it doesn't turn out that way, it can cause heartache and freak us out. We cannot control life. Life's twists and turns are inevitable, but how we respond to them is the key.

3. Handling Rejection

You are not going to be everyone's flavor and vice versa. Imagine this: People are like candy; we don't have to like all the Flavors. Rejection doesn't mean something is wrong with us or them or that they are bad. Rejection is a part of life; it does not define who we are.

QUESTION

What can I do or learn to be better prepared for the life that will allow me to live with abundance with less mental pain, anxiety, and fear?

AUTHOR CONTACT INFORMATION

Wendy B King, Founder of Wendy B King Life Is Beautiful Limited
Website: https://www.wendybkinglifecoaching.com/
Email: wendyking@xtra.co.nz
Social: https://www.facebook.com/WendyBKingLifeCoach/
Tags: Life and Transformation Coach

June 14

KENNY ROCHON

*Tomorrow is my favorite day because
I'll be alive to enjoy it.*

THOUGHT

Tomorrow is my favorite day because we should be thankful for everything that gives us more time to spend with our loved ones, with pets, on video games, watching family movies, putting on clothes, making our bed, and an infinite amount more I can list. My point is that you should be thankful for reading this right now; like an ant and a human, we both have to work hard serving our family, raising other kids, getting in trouble, and being fun.

There is always a way to be thankful in the darkest places, like house fires, family losses, and even passing away yourself. Remember always to say at least; an example is that when your family member passes away in sleep, imagine the army, a heart attack, or being on fire. Although you shouldn't be happy, be grateful that there could've been something worse, always. Basically, in a strange way, life does not happen to you; it happens for you. The pandemic allowed me to become an author, and my books caused me to be happier, more confident, and a little bit more wise.

QUESTION

What is something that could've been worse than something that was already bad?

AUTHOR CONTACT INFORMATION

Kenny Rochon, Owner of AntsOfAmerica
Website: https://www.mylibrary.shop
Email: k3coder@gmail.com
Social: https://www.facebook.com/K3GameChanger
Tags: Speaker, Author, Myrmecologist

June 15
KEN ROCHON, JR.

An abundant mindset on a foundation of integrity fueled by God will give you a journey of impact and service.

THOUGHT

Abundance is one of the most potent mindsets you can have. It allows you to be a great person, a great contributor, a great leader, and a great servant for God and humanity. The abundance journey is filled with opportunities. If you see the gifts, your journey will be more enjoyable.

In writing my 60th book ('My First 60 Years') and witnessing my son publishing 14 books, I am aware that an abundance mindset and faith are needed to empower a quest to believe you can and will make a difference. This book is the perfect message to inspire leaders to create their legacy and leave a mark.

Abundance happens when we live to serve others because we are grateful and believe we have enough. The phenomenon is that we are rewarded with more as we provide more impact and value to others.

When you are committed to living a life of abundance, you will realize that life is about proving to those who believe in you that they are right and proving to those who didn't believe in you that they were wrong.

When you live with this mindset, relationships become unconditional, partnerships become more substantial, and the best news is an Abundance mindset attracts more Abundance and heart-centered leaders.

QUESTION

What are you doing to inspire hope in those who are hopeless and to help those who need a friend and those who are misunderstood?

AUTHOR CONTACT INFORMATION

Ken Rochon Jr., Authority IMPACT Strategist of Perfect Publishing
Website: https://www.perfectpublishing.com
Email: bookdr.smiley@gmail.com
Social: @BookDr.Smiley
Tags: Dad Author Publisher Speaker World Traveller

June 16
JAMES EDINGER

Abundance is sharing family, connection, and life experiences with others.

THOUGHT

Growing up in the late 60s and through the 70s, I only knew my immediate family and friends. We had a TV with a handful of channels, and the nightly news was always on after dinner. A very clear, impactful memory was listening to updates on the Vietnam War. I learned where that country was globally and why our country was there. This fact was my first real exposure to the world and my future experiences.

As I grew up, technology exploded with cable TV, the internet, cell phones, and computers. Travel became easy with destinations worldwide for air and sea travel. As a scientist using this technology, I contacted and collaborated with peers from all over the world. To me, this was the best use of open communication while signaling to me one form of abundance through technology.

It is now possible for anyone to manage, invest, and accumulate wealth using applications on their phone or computers. The combination of information and technology available makes abundance in our lives genuinely achievable no matter how we define it. As we achieve individual wealth, we can share it with others in need. I love the age we are in now and very much look forward to what the future holds.

QUESTION

With so much opportunity and technology at our disposal, what is your current definition of abundance, and how does it look for the future?

AUTHOR CONTACT INFORMATION

James Edinger, Ph.D. Biotech Executive
Website: https://www.365daysofabundancequotes.com
Email: edgeje63@gmail.com
Social: https://linkedin.com/in/james-edinger-68909231
Tags: Biotechnology Executive

June 17

ANDREEA PARC

There are no bad people, only the unconscious - those who are asleep, living in patterns, conditioned to play roles in dreams that are not their own.

THOUGHT

As an Empowerment counselor, I help individuals become aware of their thoughts and feelings, guiding them to see that their actions reflect their level of awareness. We all have both positive and negative tendencies, but when we lack self-awareness, our negative behaviors often take control. When we live "asleep" to our true selves, we react from past wounds and conditioned patterns, sometimes causing harm without even realizing it.

As we "wake up" and grow in awareness, we gain insight into the conditioning that shapes us, seeing how we have been reacting out of pain, unresolved wounds, or unmet needs. This awakening invites us to take ownership of our actions, becoming a bridge to compassion—not only toward others but also toward ourselves. We begin to see that what we once labeled as "bad" behavior was often an unconscious response rooted in unprocessed pain. This understanding marks the beginning of letting go of guilt and shame over past actions and stepping into the power of a deeper, more authentic connection with ourselves and others.

QUESTION

How would it feel to realize that your reaction to a situation was rooted in your pain rather than the actions of others or the event itself?

AUTHOR CONTACT INFORMATION

Andreea Parc, Founder and CEO of PARC Productions Corp
Website: https://www.andreeaparc.com/
Email: andreeaparc@gmail.com
Social: https://www.facebook.com/profile.php?id=100078647104490
Tags: Author, Empowerment Counsel

June 18
CRAIG DARLING

*True abundance is creating purpose,
uplifting others, and sharing success—because when we help
others grow, we all thrive.*

THOUGHT

Craig Darling – Creating Abundance by Lifting Others

I've always believed that true abundance isn't measured by what you have but by what you give and how many people you lift along the way. My journey has been full of twists, challenges, and unexpected turns—from building businesses to moving to a new country to help a community prosper. Yet, through it all, my focus has stayed the same: helping others grow.

Abundance comes when we use our skills and resources to elevate people and businesses around us. It's in connecting, sharing knowledge, and being willing to provide value—whether that's helping small businesses show up on Google, building networks for locals, or supporting friends in tough times.

For me, success is helping more people for free than for a fee. It's about the relationships and moments where giving back brings results beyond dollars and cents. When I'm out meeting business owners, creating solutions, or sharing a moment of joy, that's when I see the power of abundance. Because when we grow together, we truly succeed.

QUESTION

*Do you see abundance as just what you possess or as the
difference you make and the lives you touch?*

AUTHOR CONTACT INFORMATION

Craig Darling, President and CEO of Darling Local, Inc.
Website: https://www.darlinglocal.com
Email: Craig@DarlingLocal.com
Social: https://www.linkedin.com/in/craig-darling-0a35881b/
Tags: Digital Visibility Specialist

June 19

SHANNON MORRISON

Abundance unfolds when clarity and courage unite, inviting the world to respond to our true selves.

THOUGHT

Recognizing that a victim mindset can constrict growth, embracing our authentic selves transforms our paths to abundance. Many are led to believe that doing more leads to abundance; this can lead to burnout and disconnect. Instead, aligning with our authentic selves opens new avenues for wealth and fulfillment.

Let clarity guide you beyond past limitations; it fuels the courage to pursue your unique mission and realize your potential. Seek spaces where you feel seen and cherished, and cultivate an unwavering belief in your journey. With an "I get to" mindset, transform challenges into opportunities. Balance action with flow, shedding inherited constraints to embrace your destiny.

Though juggling roles may feel overwhelming, remember that life is a divine opportunity. Align your strengths with your mission to unlock endless possibilities in your career and relationships. Embrace authenticity, build trust, and let your fears fuel your transformation. By viewing life as a series of learning opportunities, you invite abundance and signal your readiness to embrace it. As each person connects with their truth, they light up the world, creating a brighter, interconnected future for all.

QUESTION

How will embracing clarity and courage today transform your tomorrow?

AUTHOR CONTACT INFORMATION

Shannon Morrison, Founder of MyResilient Wellness
Website: https://www.my-rw.com/
Email: shannon@my-rw.com
Social: https://www.facebook.com/MRWshannonmorrison
Tags: Author, Speaker, Relationship Coach, Generational Healing Expert

June 20
MELODY VACHAL

*When you release the things you hold so tightly,
it allows you to open your hand to receive.*

THOUGHT

As a speaker, author, and caregiving expert, I empower caregivers to rise with resilience and move forward with purpose.

This quote emerges from my journey as a family caregiver – a role I still hold. As caregivers, we are often in a space that is held tightly. We keep a firm grip on our self-expectations and the responsibilities that are an integral part of caregiving. We may also hold guilt, shame, and resentment towards a situation we did not expect or feel prepared to take on.

This tight hold can seem to be an anchor in a stormy sea, coping with challenging situations. In fact, the inability to let go leads to burnout and hinders our ability to provide optimal care. It keeps us stuck in a space of fear and feeling overwhelmed.

When we open our hands, we let go of the belief that we must be perfect and the feeling that all of the responsibility is fully on our shoulders. When we learn to release control, we allow others to support us, discover new opportunities, and find joy in the journey. This release allows us to pause, breathe, and create a space for grace, a space where gratitude can enter, and then, there is an opportunity for growth, acceptance, and unexpected blessings.

QUESTION

What can you release that is holding you back from gratitude and growth?

AUTHOR CONTACT INFORMATION

Melody Vachal, Founder of RISE UP Care and Wellness
Website: https://melodyvachal.com
Email: mvachal@riseupcareandwellness.com
Social: https://www.linkedin.com/in/melody-vachal-ccc-slp-mchwc-638ab7177/
Tags: Speaker, Author, Caregiving Expert and Coach

June 21

MARY VAN ALSTYNE

*Fulfillment comes from a state of being,
not having - it's embracing the divine flow of life and knowing t
hat everything needed is already within.*

THOUGHT

Most of us have heard the phrase: "fill in the blank" as a way of being. How does one 'be' wealth, health, success, or love? In a world focused on doing and having, how do we shift into 'being' something instead of striving to obtain it?

Here is a simple yet profound game that could transform your state of being.

The Gratefully Abundant Game, and here's how it works:

1. Start your day with an intention. "Today, let me notice the abundance that surrounds me."

2. As you experience your day, actively seek out everything freely available to you. Notice things that you usually overlook: the air you breathe, beauty in nature, a smile, a compliment, finding a penny. Have fun! Note everything!

3. Commit to this for 30 days. Out of the blue, you'll feel a profound shift in your heart. That feeling is gratitude, and that is the shift into 'being.'

The universe operates on the law of giving and receiving. Give generously, and be astounded by what returns. If you want more love, give more love. If you want more success, help others succeed. If you want more time, volunteer your time. Giving cultivates a grateful heart, lifting the veil to reveal the abundance that has always surrounded us.

QUESTION

*I challenge you to look at the area of life where you feel scarcity.
Now ask yourself: How can I give instead? Can you play the game of life with your heart wide open and step into true abundance?*

AUTHOR CONTACT INFORMATION

Mary Van Alstyne, Chief Love Officer of Meva Method
Website: https://meva.love
Email: mevamethod@gmail.com
Social: https://instagram.com/maryevanalstyne
Tags: Embodiment and Intimacy Mentor, Spiritual Mentor

June 22
JOSEPH BLAKE, JR

*Financial abundance is built on faith.
Trust the journey, embrace the promises,
and see how belief turns challenges into prosperous opportunities.*

THOUGHT

In personal finance, abundance is connected to faith, offering a powerful perspective on wealth and prosperity. This spiritual approach to money transcends mere numbers, encouraging individuals to view their financial lives with gratitude and generosity. Financial abundance is grounded in faith and the belief that there is enough for everyone. This mindset challenges the scarcity mentality that often dominates discussions about money, suggesting instead that the universe, or a higher power, provides ample resources for all willing to receive them. Recognizing and appreciating the financial blessings in one's life creates a positive environment that can attract even more prosperity. This practice of thankfulness transforms one's relationship with money, shifting the focus from what is lacking to what is already abundant. A generous heart opens the floodgates of abundance.

By sharing resources through charitable donations, helping family and friends, or supporting community initiatives, individuals engage in a cycle of giving and receiving that can lead to unexpected financial blessings. True prosperity encompasses monetary riches and richness in relationships, experiences, and personal growth.

QUESTION

What daily habits can you adopt to shift your mindset from financial scarcity to abundance? How can these habits tangibly improve your financial situation in the next six months?

AUTHOR CONTACT INFORMATION

Dr. Joseph Blake, Jr, Founder and CEO of Actionable Financial Literacy Center
Website: www.actionablefinancialliteracy.com
Email: drjblakejr@actionablefinancialliteracy.com
Social: https://www.facebook.com/ActionableMoney
Tags: Financial Literacy, Faith-Based, Actionable-Money

June 23

BARBARA HAZELDEN

*Abundance is akin to a shapeshifter,
as both entities bring blessings in multiple forms.*

THOUGHT

I've long been aware of the "abundance" concept. However, it took on a special significance on the day I left my last brick-and-mortar full-time job: June 23, 2019. During my decades in the business world, I have had many full- and part-time jobs. "Abundance" always meant having enough money to pay the bills and enjoy a comfortable lifestyle.

However, June 23, 2019, marked my transition out of the conventional workforce and into the gig economy. I left my position as a full-time non-profit store manager and stepped into a full-time freelance writer role. For several years, my writing work had taken a back seat to an increasingly stressful day job.

After taking the plunge, I saw abundance in an entirely new light. First, it meant a constantly flowing stream of work from fast-paying clients. Each assignment would open the door to new writing opportunities, intriguing collaborations, and enough income to satisfy our needs (not always our "wants").

Today, I'm surrounded by natural beauty, and I share my life with a wonderful husband and an exceptional rescue dog. Every day, abundance flows into my life from many sources. And every day, I know this cool, bubbling spring will never run dry.

QUESTION

How can you switch from a scarcity mindset to an abundance mindset?

AUTHOR CONTACT INFORMATION

Barbara Hazelden, Founder of The Verbal Alchemist
Website: https://365daysofabundancequotes.com
Email: hazeldenopportunities@gmail.com
Social: https://www.linkedin.com/in/barbara-hazelden-067aa210/
Tags: Executive Ghostwriter, Freelance Writer

June 24
JENNIE JAMES

Emptiness is the beginning of abundance.

THOUGHT

We learn to want and then need all those things; then, the needs grow, and we must have more. And more until our life is focused on acquisition because more is better.

If Feng Shui is correct, all those things have mental and emotional weight. To continue to add more only adds heaviness and concern to our lives.

When does the fullness cease to bring us joy? Do we become immune to lightness? I learned this while traveling; the bigger and heavier my suitcases were, the more hassle it was to collect everything, and the more it cost me to transport it.

I learned to lighten the load significantly. I only packed what I absolutely needed and only what I loved. It was so freeing. I enjoyed the travel so much more! It taught me that more is not better and that light is so liberating.

I got to feel the joy of lightness and the freedom to take in all of the beautiful experiences. I felt so rich, so filled with the excitement of new places and different lives – things I might have missed if my stuff had created distractions and other concerns to address.

To me, abundance is a trust that I will have what I need and want without worry or avariciousness, a feeling of fullness and joy.

QUESTION

What is enough? If more is never enough, will you ever be satisfied?

AUTHOR CONTACT INFORMATION

Jennie James, Owner of Different Answer
Website: https://www.differentanswer.com/
Email: jennie@differentanswer.com
Social: www.linkedin.com/in/jennie-james-7586962
Tags: Debt Consultant, Speaker

The Art of Connection

June 25

BRENT KESLER

*Every decision is an investment in our business,
personal abundance,
and the legacy of prosperity we create.*

THOUGHT

When I first began my journey, I thought investment was only about money. But over the years, I realized the most valuable investments aren't always measured in dollars. Life is the sum of all our choices, and every decision we make is an investment. Not just in our businesses but in the abundance we cultivate within ourselves.

Every time I chose to push boundaries, embrace innovation, or listen to client feedback, I wasn't just shaping my business's trajectory; I was molding my character, refining my vision, and crafting a legacy.

These personal investments became the cornerstone of my philosophy, creating a twofold effect: one that propelled my business forward and another that enriched my legacy.

The true wealth we create isn't just in profit margins or balance sheets but in the lessons, stories, and values we pass on.

It is these personal investments, made in character, growth, and purpose, that shape a lasting legacy of abundance and prosperity.

QUESTION

How are the choices you make today shaping the abundance and legacy you wish to leave behind?

AUTHOR CONTACT INFORMATION

Brent Kesler, Owner of The Money Multiplier
Website: http://www.themoneymultiplier.com
Email: jamie@themoneymultiplier.com
Social: https://www.facebook.com/themoneymultiplier
Tags: Infinite Banking

June 26

AMBER GOLDEN

For me, connection has always meant having the courage to show up authentically as I am, flaws and all, and creating space for others to do the same.

THOUGHT

For a long time, I didn't feel like I was good enough. I hung back, stayed quiet, and tried not to draw attention to myself. I was the student in the back row with my hoodie pulled tight over my head. I avoided raising my hand and stayed quiet. I felt less than those I felt had it together. As a young adult, I realized how much it was holding me back. I'd spent so much time hiding that I felt invisible.

One day, I asked myself, "What do I have to lose?". Cautiously, I began to speak up. I started telling the truth about my flaws. The first time I shared with an audience about my imperfections, I still wanted to shrink back into my "hoodie." I felt exposed, raw, waiting for the judgment I was sure would come.

Instead, people nodded. Some smiled. I saw recognition in their eyes. In that first public moment of honesty, I noticed something remarkable. The more I shared about my struggles—the more people related to me. They connected because what people are really looking for isn't perfection; it's presence. It's that feeling of being in the room with someone who isn't hiding behind a mask. It creates space for others to be genuine with us in return. In that space, connection thrives.

QUESTION

When was the last time you shared something vulnerable with someone? How did it impact your connection with them?

AUTHOR CONTACT INFORMATION

Amber Golden, Founder, CEO, Golden Leadership Institute
Website: https://www.goldenleadershipinstitute.com
Email: ambergoldenraskin@gmail.com
Social: https://www.linkedin.com/in/amber-golden-b639b417/
Tags: Entrepreneur, Leadership Coach, Speaker, CEO

June 27

REGINA LA FRANCE

*To all people who have fallen victim to abuse as children and never had a voice to speak up.
I hear you, and I am with you because I am you.*

THOUGHT

When I began drafting my book *Shayla*, I had only one sole purpose, and that was to create awareness to keep children safe. As I continued to write about the abuse I suffered as a young girl, I began to feel alive and free of the burden I secretly carried for so many years. The burden was the secret and lack of self-love.

As a result of releasing my secret, I discovered that my inner child was still hurting. I took a serious look at how I had lived my life for the last 45 years. I stood in front of the mirror and told myself that the problems lay within me. It took strength, courage, and belief in my power to overcome depression, anxiety, and self-doubt to achieve the emotional freedom that I now have.

I am on a mission to bring forward an abundance of positive energy and inspiration to those who are still hurting from the trauma they may have suffered as a child. Serving others with love and compassion is my journey.

With positive affirmations and taking baby steps to achieve a healthy self-image and love for self, one will discover the divine power they possess.

It is never a child's fault, and that is why I hear you; I am you.

QUESTION

Are you still hurting from child trauma? I know you can overcome it, but first, you must accept what happened to you and then understand and believe it wasn't your fault. It is never a child's fault.

AUTHOR CONTACT INFORMATION

Regina LaFrance, Author of Shayla
Website: https://www.lafrancemedia.com/
Email: reginalafrance@yahoo.com
Social: https://www.facebook.com/thebookthattellsall
Tags: Author, Survivor, Activist, Speaker, Wife, Friend

June 28
DEIDRE LOPEZ

It's not the fortune we accumulate but the love we share that defines us; every act of kindness creates ripples with the ability to transform lives.

THOUGHT

Fortune and privilege were not words my husband and I would use to describe our younger years. My husband, Alejandro Lopez Hernandez, is an immigrant from Mexico. For him, even a basic stove was a privilege. He started with little means but had an abundance of love for his family and community. The close-knit family unit and camaraderie in his small town nurtured children in a supportive environment.

Although I was born a US citizen, I faced hard times and became homeless, living under a couch in an alley. Yet, even at my lowest, I encountered genuine kindness from people who genuinely cared. Their support helped me begin to stand on my own.

Many see such moments as "hitting bottom." Still, with a shift in perspective, we can appreciate the true abundance we often overlook. While material wealth is overwhelming and what we are often programmed to seek, it doesn't shape or fulfill us. Stripped of possessions, we find space to cherish life's richness through human connection, friendship, and love.

QUESTION

In a society that frequently prioritizes material achievement, what practices do you engage in to cultivate and strengthen your relationships with those around you?

AUTHOR CONTACT INFORMATION

Deidre Lopez, Co-Owner/COO of A3D Services
Website: https://www.a3dservices.com
Email: deidre@a3dservices.com
Social: https://www.facebook.com/profile.php?id=100092251990183
Tags: Janitorial Services

June 29

LARRY LINTON

A diagnosis of Parkinson's disease may not mean the beginning of the end - it could be the start of the most rewarding period of your life.

THOUGHT

Looking back on my 13-year journey with Parkinson's disease, it's not the day of diagnosis that I recall most vividly. It's the day when I finally accepted Parkinson's into my life. That's the day when I started living with it and no longer against it. It's the day that I stopped feeling sorry for myself. It was the day that I realized I still had value.

That day was the start of my journey of self-discovery, my emerging transformed, re-centered, and re-calibrated. I like the person I have become with Parkinson's. I have found my true purpose in life, living it authentically with humility and grace (a sense of humor helps, too).

I would never have believed it had I been told that, with Parkinson's, I would rekindle my love for drumming, that I would run more half-marathons after my diagnosis than before, that I would complete a 500-kilometer bike ride in five days, that my career would still progress to the point of being admitted as a partner at a large, international professional services firm, and that I would even be taking less medication today than at the start of my journey. I have achieved all of that and an abundance more. I have Parkinson's, but it doesn't have all of me.

QUESTION

Would you choose to be diagnosed with a chronic, incurable, progressive illness if you knew that your life after that life-changing event would be more rewarding, meaningful, and fulfilling?

AUTHOR CONTACT INFORMATION

Larry Linton, Founder of Linton Coaching
Website: https://livewellwithPD.com
Email: larry@livewellwithPD.com
Social: https://www.linkedin.com/in/larry-linton-428a70b1/
Tags: LivingWellWithPD, AcceptingPD, LifeAfterDiagnosis

June 30
DANIEL PEDEMONTE

*We're all storytellers and creators.
The stories we tell ourselves, good or bad, are the foundation
of the destiny we're in the process of creating.*

THOUGHT

"Fire is a gift from the Great Spirit," the old woman said to the boy as they sat by the bonfire watching the flames; "It symbolizes His presence here on earth. It is there, but we cannot touch it, yet it touches us with its warmth and light. We have some of that same power, a light that shines within us and dwells in our thoughts, our words, and the stories we tell ourselves. It is through them, through those stories, that we mold that power and give it shape, either constructive or destructive, to create our destiny. Did you know that?"

He didn't, of course. His eyes were opened in amazement, really wanting to understand. The old woman nodded kindly.

The boy spent a while feeding the fire with sticks and branches that caused a delightful dance of sparkles flying towards the already darkening sky. As he watched them merging with the stars above, the old woman added something else:

"That power is bound by an immutable law, though, an irresistible need to remain consistent with those stories we tell ourselves.

Be mindful of that. Create a good story for yourself, offer it to the fire, and let the spiraling sparks carry it along with them, knowing it will find its way back to you."

QUESTION

*We are all storytellers, and we are all creators,
so what kind of story are you going to tell yourself? What kind of destiny are you going to start creating today? Make it a good one.*

AUTHOR CONTACT INFORMATION

Daniel Pedemonte, Owner of Delta Charles Inspirational Writer
Website: https://www.deltacharleswriter.com/
Email: contact@deltacharleswriter.com
Social: https://www.facebook.com/DeltaCharlesWriter/
Tags: Writer, Storyteller, Creative Director, Designer

July 1

JEFFREY MORRIS

Abundance flows when trust is cultivated—acts of integrity, transparency, and connection sow the seeds of opportunity and lasting collaboration.

THOUGHT

To some, abundance is the physical manifestation of wealth or material possessions; however, I want to shift our collective mindsets as you read on. My challenge for you is to consider that true abundance begins with trust. Trust is not merely a passive virtue; it is an active process of choosing integrity, transparency, and authentic connection in every interaction.

Abundance thrives in environments where trust creates fertile ground for collaboration and innovation. Abundance is not merely a collection of material possessions; it includes the richness of meaningful relationships, the fulfillment of purposeful work, the peace of a balanced life, and the joy of personal growth. Abundance is not confined to what we own but is deeply rooted in how we live, contribute, and connect with others.

Trust and abundance coexist, creating a cycle of continuous growth and fulfillment. Trust acts as the seed, and abundance is the harvest that follows. The interconnected cycle reminds us that true abundance is not achieved in isolation but in a community of like-minded, heart-centered communities seeking collective good for all.

QUESTION

How can you actively cultivate trust through integrity, transparency, and authentic connections in your daily interactions to create a foundation for lasting abundance and meaningful collaboration?

AUTHOR CONTACT INFORMATION

Jeffrey Morris, CEO of DreamSmart Behavioral Solutions
Website: https://dreamsmartbehavioralsolutions.com/
Email: jmorris@dreamsmartbehavioralsolutions.com
Social: https://www.linkedin.com/in/jeffreymorris1/
Tags: Coach, Consultant, Speaker, Team Development

July 2
GINNY CORREA-CREAGER

*Abundance Appears After We Fully and Freely
Give to Others, And Then It Comes to Stay*

THOUGHT

Abundance comes to those who willingly provide something needed or wanted—be it service, comfort, help, thoughtfulness, added value, or an unexpected gift. Without offering noteworthy value beyond expectations, rewards are often mediocre. To merit abundance, one must first do something special.

Employees may get automatic raises, but bonuses, perks, and partnerships come from superior effort and producing valued results. In business, abundance often flows from clients based on the exceptional service, products, or support provided. When you deliver uncompromising value, you become "top of mind," leading to repeat business, larger orders, credibility, or even fame.

Abundance isn't limited to business; it extends to personal life—measured in friendships, networks, satisfaction, joy, natural beauty, family pride, or material ownership. Each person's understanding of abundance reflects their unique efforts to achieve it.

Best of all, once abundance is attracted and shared,
it often becomes a lasting presence in life.

QUESTION

What are you knowingly doing to achieve greater abundance for yourself and others? Are you reaching the financial areas as well as the personal and humankind?

AUTHOR CONTACT INFORMATION

Ginny Correa-Creager, (Ret.) of ProVantage Coaching
Website: https://365daysofabundancequotes.com
Email: gibby5708@gmail.com
Social: https://www.linkedin.com/in/ginny-creager-phd-60096344
Tags: Retired Professor, Author, College and Career

July 3
COWBOY JOE MARQUES

The objective of life isn't about trying to get through the ride without getting thrown; it's about how quickly we can get back on after being thrown.

THOUGHT

Life is like riding a wild horse—you can't avoid getting thrown off. As someone who's lived a longer life than most predicted, I've learned that the goal isn't to stay in the saddle the whole time but to see how quickly you can get back up after a fall. In my younger days,

I thought the best riders never hit the dirt, but I was wrong. Life is unpredictable, and no matter how skilled or strong you are, you're going to get thrown. What matters is how you rise after each fall. Getting up after being knocked down builds strength, humility, and resilience. Every fall shapes you, teaches you grit, and reminds you that control is an illusion—what you can control is your response.

The actual failure is staying down. To live fully, you must embrace risks and falls as part of the ride. Life's beauty comes from uncertainty, and with each fall, you grow stronger, braver, and more determined. The mark of a true cowboy is not in avoiding the fall but in how quickly you rise again. From this cowboy's perspective, the essence of life is resilience, riding to the fullest, embracing the inevitability of being thrown, and having the courage to rise again.

QUESTION

What would life be like if you lived your life without the fear of being thrown?

AUTHOR CONTACT INFORMATION

Cowboy Joe Marques, Founder of Cowboy Joe Alliance
Website: https://cowboyjoe.me
Email: joe@cowboyjoe.me
Social: https://www.linkedin.com/in/joe-marques
Tags: Speaker, Author, Cowboy Wisdom, Wealth Formula

July 4
JOHN VERRICO

When our forefathers fought for our Independence, they created a land of opportunity and abundance. The most important is the abundance of freedom.

THOUGHT

While there may be many things for people to find fault with, the United States is still a land of abundance.

We may complain about the healthcare system, but we are luckier than a million people in the world who may not survive the week due to lack of access to medical care.

We can attend a church of our choice without fear of arrest, torture, or death. A privilege three billion people around the globe cannot do.

Some food in our refrigerator, clothes on our backs, and a roof to sleep under make us richer than 75 percent of the world's population.

A little money in the bank or wallet, or even some spare change in our pocket, classifies us among the top eight percent of the world's wealth.

We don't have soldiers storming our neighborhoods, nor fear being imprisoned or tortured for political differences or voicing our opinions. Nearly a billion people in the world do not have such security.

Thanks to our access to education, we can read these pages, while billions cannot read.

Yes, there are still challenges – impoverished neighborhoods, homelessness, and discrimination. Yet, when we realize our abundance, we can turn our energy toward helping those in need.

That is freedom!

QUESTION

How can you reframe your thinking and perspective to appreciate the abundant blessings in your life? How can you share your abundance with others?

AUTHOR CONTACT INFORMATION

John Verrico, Founder, Speaker, Coach of John Verrico - Share Your Fire, LLC
Website: https://www.johnverrico.com/
Email: john@johnverrico.com
Social: https://www.linkedin.com/in/johnverrico/
Tags: Leadership, Positivity, Speaker, Coach, Motivate

July 5
JULIE D'ANN

The feeling of abunDANCE is a feeling that makes your buns wanna dance!

THOUGHT

I've heard it said that gratitude is the frequency that is synonymous with abundance and receiving. For myself, I look at the word "abundance," and I see: a + bun + dance = makes my buns want to dance!

And it's true! When you feel genuinely abundant, you are so overjoyed you feel like dancing! Dancing through life and having fun in this earthly experience is what living a life you truly love is all about. We humans are here to create, to live better lives, and thrive, and generating a constant state of abundance through consistently practicing gratitude is the way to achieve this level of joyful, abundant living.

So, choose an attitude of gratitude and watch how your abundance expands. And remember to continue celebrating! Every little win is amplified through celebrating, which is the way you tell the Universe to bring you more of the same - or even better still!

QUESTION

Every day, you have the choice to do the 'dance of abundance' by cultivating an attitude of gratitude - but will you choose to do it?

AUTHOR CONTACT INFORMATION

Julie D'Ann, Owner, Transformational Illumination Guide of JD Illuminate LLC
Website: https://juliedannauthor.com/
Email: julied@juliedannauthor.com
Social: https://www.facebook.com/profile.php?id=100014005230828
Tags: Speaker, Coach, Author, Transformation, Children

July 6
LABARBARA DHALIWAL

The abundance of a mother's love for her children can never be diminished! It is an unbreakable connection and a lasting presence – even beyond life.

THOUGHT

Mother,

As I look up and my arms reach toward the sky, I feel your loving presence moving and swaying and dancing with the stars. The moon reflects the beauty of our hearts – reaching out, connecting, intertwining. The sun reflects your warmth, bringing comfort and healing the wound that is a gaping hole left by your absence.

I never thought that I would be here without you. Your presence is always there like a backdrop – ready to be the web that catches my many emotions. The butterfly that flits around my head softly speaking encouraging words, the giant moth that opens its wings to enfold me with your loving protection. You whisper in my ear: Be happy; do not worry, dear daughter.

Thank you, Dear Mother, for the abundance of your selfless nurturing and your unconditional love. I will always cherish and live by the gifts you so graciously and lovingly bestowed - to live by faith, to express gratitude for all, to give generously, and to love wholeheartedly. I will pass them on to future generations. I wonder if you know just how much you are loved. Though your physical presence has departed, I rejoice in your remembered smile, your laughter, your hugs and kisses. I love you.

QUESTION

Have you shown your Mother how much she means to you and how important she is in your life? Do it today!

AUTHOR CONTACT INFORMATION

LaBarbara Dhaliwal, Brain Performance Coach of Student of yoga; coach at N/A
Website: https://www.365daysofabundancequotes.com
Email: labarbarad@gmail.com
Social: https://mybook.to/artofconnection5
Tags: Student, Coach, Energy Worker

July 7
BRETT COTTER

Creating with the Infinite - Abundance Multiplies Right Where Our Attention Lies.

THOUGHT

We are constantly creating our reality; thoughts and emotions paint the next moment automatically. Generational fear stains our creations, as 90 percent of our thinking occurs unconsciously. Maybe that's why we see so much stress throughout humanity.

When we were young, stress happened to us; as adults, stress happens through us. So, how can we cleanse the fear from this manifestation machine we call the human being? If we surface the fears from our formative years, we let the pain go, let the tears flow, and finally hear 'yes,' where there was always a 'no.'

Our heart is the birth canal for the abundance in our life. It attracts atoms based on beliefs while our brain delivers the electricity to help manifest the things we see. To paint reality with infinite abundance, we rewire our hearts to stay open and our thoughts to remain clear as we feel gratitude for our deepest desire as if it were already here.

This state changes behavior as the pulse of the universe moves through us. We receive inspiration that turns into action as abundance begins to fill in all around us. It's who we are, who we'll always be, as the amnesia of this world wears off from humanity.

QUESTION

If humanity created an abundance of stress, can we create an abundance of happiness?

AUTHOR CONTACT INFORMATION

Brett Cotter, Founder, Trainer, Retreat Leader, Coach of Stress Is Gone
Website: www.StressIsGone.com
Email: brett@stressisgone.com
Social: https://www.instagram.com/stressisgone/
Tags: Trauma Recovery Expert, Emotional Healing Coach

July 8
JENNIFER FARRAR

Abundance simply means "a lot of."

THOUGHT

A mentor asked me what I wanted. I replied, "Abundance."

She responded, "So you want a lot of bad luck, a lot of horrible things happening to you, a lot of tragedy, a lot of trauma." On and on she went.

"No, that's not what I meant. I want financial abundance, abundant friends, and abundant clients. A life filled with an abundance of joy and ease."

"Knowing that abundance simply means, 'a lot of.' You were being too vague, and your brain and body can misinterpret that, which spells disaster. Your brain sends a signal to your body, specifically your heart, every time you have a thought, every time you utter a word with emotion, and your body believes it. In this state, everything aligns. This state creates powerful frequencies, and you activate the Law of Attraction, which is either for you or against you. You have to be more specific in your thoughts, wants and desires. You have to send out the frequencies of what you want, not what you don't want."

"I get it now! I need to think, speak, and feel exactly the abundance I want in my life to bring it into existence. That is powerful."

QUESTION

What type of abundance are thinking, speaking, and feeling that send signals to your brain and body, telling the Universe to send them to you?

AUTHOR CONTACT INFORMATION

Jennifer Farrar, CEO of Healing Peace Within
Website: https://www.healingpeacewithin.com/
Email: jennifer@healingpeacewithin.com
Social: https://www.facebook.com/healingpeacewithin
Tags: Healer, Speaker, Business Transformation Coach

July 9
TAWNI ACOSTA

*Abundance is created through
living your Life's Purpose*

THOUGHT

Abundance can be easily confused or misunderstood. Many would have a first reaction to it being defined in terms of financial assessments, which we may immediately think of when this word comes up. Yet that can lead to a void that is dismissive of one's fundamental humanity.

Abundance itself could perhaps be phrased as having lived a full life to the greatest extent possible.

Living in congruence with who they are, the time and period in which they came into this world, and how their life has played out. Living in abundance transcends roles, nationalities, social status, cultural definitions, and certainly more.

This diversity approach would entail cultivating an inner richness of character, which in turn is freely expressed in life and the environment. Many of those who may have appeared to live a 'humble life' have indeed lived a life full of richness, fulfillment, legacy, and profound impact for all.

Abundance is the richness of living the life and creating a story that is uniquely yours to claim and actualize.

QUESTION

How can my day create abundance for someone in my life?

AUTHOR CONTACT INFORMATION

Tawni Acosta, Founder and Owner of Empowered Journeys
Website: https://www.empowered-journeys.com
Email: empoweredjourneys21@gmail.com
Social: https://www.linkedin.com/in/tsacosta/
Tags: Life Coach, Speaker, Entrepreneur

July 10
SAM KNICKERBOCKER

Change is inevitable; growth is intentional.

THOUGHT

I believe our highest purpose is to master our Minds, Souls, Paradigms, Bodies, and Realities, creating a life of pure light and love. When these elements align, we live a legacy defined by truth, impact, and intention—a legacy that reflects our greatest potential.

To help others achieve this, I created the S.M.A.R.T. Legacy Formula: Sexy, Massive, Audacious, Remarkable, and Transparent. Applied to the 9 Pillars of Legacy—Haters, Believers, Passion, Faith, Family, Health, Clients, Team, and Country—this formula provides a powerful roadmap for aligning vision with action and creating an enduring impact.

I wasn't born with this clarity. Growing up in a condemned home, I learned the difference between surviving and thriving. This clarity inspired me to develop proven systems that have transformed the lives of my clients, helping them turn fear into confidence, uncover their passions, and create lives of fulfillment.

Your legacy isn't something you leave behind—it's something you live today. With the right mindset and tools, you can build a life of purpose and extraordinary impact. Let's start your journey together—reach out to me today.

QUESTION

Who are you going to decide to be, and whose life will be better as a result?

AUTHOR CONTACT INFORMATION

Sam Knickerbocker, Host of The Fuel Your Legacy Podcast
Website: https://www.samknickerbocker.com
Email: fylinstantly@gmail.com
Social: https://youtube.com/@sam.knickerbocker
Tags: Legacy, Leadership, Speaker, Finance, Podcast

July 11
J. LUMEN

Abundance is a force-field of resilience superpower.

THOUGHT

Incorporating an attitude of abundance allows you to see possibilities and opportunities rather than limitations. This attitude enables you to find potential even in the most challenging situations. Additionally, your confidence in approaching life with optimism and creativity is supported when you embrace an abundant attitude.

Resilience, on the other hand, is the strength and determination to persevere through life's unexpected twists and turns. It's the ability to bounce back when life knocks you down and helps you adapt to change. Resilience acts as a protective shield, your personal force field, that provides you with the courage and tenacity to push through when faced with adversity and emerge stronger on the other side.

By infusing your force-field of resilience with abundance, you unlock a superpower of positively charged strength and capability. This superpower elevates your ability to face ordinary challenges and navigate them with an almost seeming ease and grace, even transforming them into extraordinary opportunities. Utilizing this superpower not only helps you overcome life's hardships but can propel you toward more significant success, both personally and professionally.

QUESTION

Thinking of the daily challenges in your own life, how might activating this superpower allow you to navigate them more positively or optimistically?

AUTHOR CONTACT INFORMATION

J. Lumen, Founder and Creator of The Unknown Bucket List
Website: https://theunknownbucketlist.com
Email: info@theunknownbucketlist.com
Social: https://www.instagram.com/theunknownbucketlist/
Tags: Speaker, Life Transformation and Empowerment Coach

July 12
SUZI FREEMAN

*True abundance is emotional freedom,
the courage to shed what no longer serves us and
embrace what brings us pure joy!*

THOUGHT

Life is a journey of growth, and with growth comes the responsibility to align ourselves with what truly fulfills us. After turning 45, I reassessed my life, the relationships, environments, and energy I invested.

I realized abundance isn't in material possessions but in the emotional freedom to live authentically. Emotional freedom takes courage to release what no longer serves us, whether it's toxic relationships, stagnant environments, or unaligned habits. For me, this meant a 'people detox,' letting go of draining relationships, even close family.

My journey has also yielded many, I mean many, pivots in my business, downsizing my life and prioritizing experiences with my kids, grandkids, and those who uplift me. I have learned that it's never too late to make a change, to take risks, and to believe in yourself.

QUESTION

What would your life look like if you let go of what no longer serves you and embraced what truly brings you joy and purpose?

AUTHOR CONTACT INFORMATION

Suzi Freeman, Founder of Special Teams Mindset Academy
Website: https://www.suzifreeman.com
Email: suzi@suzifreeman.com
Social: https://www.instagram.com/suzifreeman/
Tags: Mindset Coach, Mental Performance Coach

July 13

BECKY ESTBY

*When your heart calls, answer it.
Be your best you by honoring your own heart and
giving of your heart abundantly.*

THOUGHT

I love seeing the light shine in clients when they transition from feeling lost to listening to their hearts and living in their passion. We often dim our own light. We have an abundance of unique talents and strengths, and we do not always have the courage to show the world, or we do not even know how special our unique gift is.

Being your best self is not about arrogance or ego; it is about owning who you were created to be—it is about your purpose. Step into who you are. Free yourself of self-doubt and embrace your uniqueness fully.

You can be your best you by first taking small actions every day to listen to what your heart is telling you and secondly by finding moments to give of your heart abundantly to others through small yet meaningful gestures: a hug, your time, sit with someone in silence, listen, be a mentor, and more. Giving from your heart abundantly and sharing your unique gifts is a two-way gift: a gift to the recipient and a gift for you as you get to choose to show up to be the best person you can be.

QUESTION

*Are you listening to your own heart or holding yourself back?
How will you live to your purpose and share your unique gifts with the world?*

AUTHOR CONTACT INFORMATION

Becky Estby, Owner & CEO of Next Monday
Website: https://next-monday.com
Email: beckyestby@next-monday.com
Social: linkedin.com/company/next-monday
Tags: Facilitator, Coach, Business Consultant, CEO

July 14
CORINA BLAKE

Abundance: God's perspective.

THOUGHT

A parable in the Bible speaks of ten virgins. The ten virgins had carried lamps to go and meet their bridegroom. Five were wise, and five were foolish. The five wise virgins took lamps with extra oil, while the five foolish virgins took their lamps without extra oil. While the virgins waited for the bridegroom to come, they all slept. Then, at midnight, they were called to go and meet the bridegroom. As they went, only the five virgins, who were wise, were able to meet the bridegroom.

"Bridegroom" here in the parable is Opportunity.

The oil is knowledge and understanding.

The Wise were prepared for opportunity. They sought out all the oil needed to be prepared when the opportunity came by.

The Foolish were not prepared for the opportunity. The window of opportunities can be for a brief moment. When you're not prepared for opportunity, then the door will shut, and you've missed it.

Seek to fill your lamp. When you diligently seek the oil of knowledge and understanding, you set yourself for Abundance.

Wise (people) think "Abundance," and Foolish (people) think "Lack."

Always Seek to prepare yourself to receive Abundance.

QUESTION

Who do you want to be? Wise or Foolish.

AUTHOR CONTACT INFORMATION

Corina Blake, Co-Owner of Blakemediallc
Website: http://blakemediallc.com
Email: corablake@gmail.com
Social: https://mybook.to/artofconnection5
Tags: DM

July 15

NAHEED OBERFELD

I'm open to the possibility that...

THOUGHT

Do you know what determines whether you will achieve a goal or not?

We've all experienced the thrill of manifesting something. If it is small or trivial, we may dismiss it as luck. If it is big and momentous, we typically point to the hard work it took to accomplish it. If we determine it was outside of our control, it was serendipity.

In short, we don't believe there is an easy, replicable way that we can put our faith in. What if there is? Your mindset is the key to determining whether you will be successful. Let me explain.

I participated in my first Toastmasters Club competition against a 20-year veteran. There was no way I could win. That's when I reminded myself of something I tell my clients, "we lose twice, first in our head, and second when we play the game." It was time for me to turn my mindset around.

When I doubt that something will happen, instead of suppressing my thoughts or pretending to feel positive, I recite my go-to phrase: I'm open to the possibility that…I could win this competition. This simple phrase creates space between the uncertainty and introduces hopefulness and possibility. It's everything you need to turn your mindset around and change your "luck."

QUESTION

What possibilities are you open to creating this year?

AUTHOR CONTACT INFORMATION

Naheed Oberfeld, Owner of Oberfeld Coaching
Website: www.OberfeldCoaching.com
Email: Naheed@OberfeldCoaching.com
Social: https://www.instagram.com/oberfeld_coaching/
Tags: mindset coach, speaker, EFT/Tapping coach,

July 16
YOUSEF QABAZARD

If you have a roof over your head, a fridge with food, clothes to wear, a person to hug, and a caring community, you have all the riches on earth.

THOUGHT

The moral of the quote is that waking up in a calm, safe place is something we take for granted. Having a bed to sleep on is the most fulfilling feeling you can ever have because out there, someone wishes to have a bed to sleep on. Waking up knowing that there is food in the fridge and not worrying about where food is going to come from is a blessing we must be grateful for every day, knowing that we will have a full stomach before bed because out there, people wish to feel that feeling of a full stomach.

Having a person to hug with love because love is the ultimate law of the universe, and so many of us humans lack that feeling or don't even exchange the feeling with another human being. With a heart full of love within each of us, can you imagine the world we live in, walking past each human and giving a smile? How can that affect a person's day, knowing that there are good people in the world with pure hearts and unconditional love? The question is, why not you? Why not start spreading the smile to people and make them comfortable with their skin? Having a community where everyone gives unconditionally without asking for something in return is a community that must be respected.

QUESTION

The question to ask ourselves: Can we as individuals start spreading the abundance we have within us and share it with the world by doing a small thing to another human by spreading a simple smile?

AUTHOR CONTACT INFORMATION

Yousef Qabazard, Owner of Yousefqabz
Website: https://www.365daysofabundancequotes.com
Email: ykqabazard@gmail.com
Social: https://www.instagram.com/yousefqabz/profilecard/?igsh=eTh2ZGc3ZGo1dzBl
Tags: Influencer

July 17

OPHIR ADAR

*Abundance is not a glass half empty or half full.
Abundance is the glass is always full.*

THOUGHT

I remember growing up with a family that liked to focus on what could go wrong vs what could go right. I spent my childhood in frustration and anxiety. Imagine always focusing on what could go wrong and all the reasons why you should not be bold or fearless.

As I started to transition into an adult and was away from my family, I had an epiphany. What does focusing on the negative aspects of a potential situation do for me? Absolutely nothing except give me reasons to quit, give up, and not even get started. Why not focus on all the reasons why I should be bold and brave and what that would create in my life?

I realized that whatever I feed my mind will result in my approach to life. You can't control your environment as a child. The best news ever is that as an adult, you choose what to feed into your mind, and you choose what you will focus on.

QUESTION

*Each one of us has a dark wolf and a white wolf inside us,
and we determine which one we feed. Which Wolf are you feeding?*

AUTHOR CONTACT INFORMATION

Ophir Adar, C.E.O and Head Coach of Real Momentum
Website: https://www.realmomentum.com
Email: ophir@realmomentum.com
Social: https://www.instagram.com/realmomentumcoaching/
Tags: Businesscoach, Realmomentum

July 18

DANIEL SIMON

Trusting the Creator's perfect timing. I'm unique, made to share joy and abundance with every breath. This trust is for you, too, when you choose it!

THOUGHT

All aspect of our minds shapes reality. The way we think determines how we see and experience life. Proverbs 23:7 reminds us, "For as he thinks in his heart, so is he." If you focus on abundance, joy, and peace, you will see these manifest daily. Doubt and negativity, however, create stress. Your mind cannot distinguish between reality and fiction—what you focus on grows.

Nature shows us abundance effortlessly. The Earth is 70% water, as is the human body. Trees grow toward gravity with roots and against it with branches. A single seed creates a tree with thousands of seeds, illustrating endless potential. Psalm 1:3 says, "He shall be like a tree planted by rivers of water… whatever he does shall prosper."

Science reveals your brain can form new pathways, enabling change and growth. Every breath you take sustains you automatically. By noticing these gifts, you shift from scarcity to gratitude. Even in darkness, stars shine—symbols of abundance, constant yet hidden. Like a tree growing above and below ground, challenges and abundance coexist. Your perspective determines what you experience.

QUESTION

"Where is the abundance here?" Reflect on the roots you're planting. Close your eyes—feel the wind, hear the leaves, and smell the rain. Where and How does nature remind you of life's abundance now?

AUTHOR CONTACT INFORMATION

Daniel Simon, Managing Director of Simon3mgroup.com
Website: http://www.simon3mgroup.com/
Email: dansimon.tmlp@gmail.com
Social: http://www.youtube.com/@AncientWisdomSecrets
Tags: Ambassador of Abundance, IT Managing Director

July 19

TROY HIPOLITO

Stop thinking about negative thoughts; they are more powerful in magnitude than positive thinking for removing the barriers to achieving your goals.

THOUGHT

One thing I am grasping is the power of not constantly thinking about things, people, or situations that have done damage.

Learn to starve it…

The relentless cycle of negative thinking drains your energy. It hinders progress and is an anchor, holding you back from reaching your full potential.

You're not just removing the anchor; you're freeing up precious energy for creativity and problem-solving.

We are not talking about suppressing emotions but mindful redirection.

Acknowledge the negative thought and observe without judgment.

Then, gently steer your attention toward a solution.

Also, it is essential to have a support network, so think about cultivating meaningful relationships. Investing in genuine connections is about building solid and long-term relationships. These can provide emotional, practical, and spiritual support when you need it most.

Celebrate small victories, learn from setbacks, and stay committed to building a life filled with purpose. By starving the negative voice and nurturing durable relationships, you're not just building a better future; you're building a stronger, more resilient "you."

Imagine your success with the best version of yourself.

QUESTION

What could you achieve if you could stop getting in your way and remove at least some of the significant barriers that are preventing you from being great?

AUTHOR CONTACT INFORMATION

Troy Hipolito, Founder of The Troy Agency
Website: https://www.thetroyagency.com
Email: troy@thetroyagency.com
Social: https://www.linkedin.com/in/troyhipolito/
Tags: LinkedIn Influencer, App Developer, Business Coach

July 20
LAURA BALLET

*Contained within the structure of Abundance is
your unique energy-print of brilliance; your creational potential awaits.*

THOUGHT

It is your birthright to gain awareness of the creational energy that resides within the framework of possibilities. Each one of us carries within our consciousness the imprint to unlock a life of brilliance and, thus, engineering a life of Abundance. Here, in this state of higher recognition, we can position ourselves in the "power seat of choice" and become all that is possible. To authorize personal directives over designed abundance aligns with the greatness that is uniquely defined by our intentions.

Thought Energy, intentional collaboration, and compassionate service are Abundance in action. How we personally define abundance and how it is expressed is one of the powers that belongs solely to the human condition. Each interaction is an opportunity to create and exchange acceptance, favor, and lasting value. Awaken to the energy that stirs your senses and ignites a life well experienced.

QUESTION

*Who would you evolve into if, rather than glancing at the power,
you became the power?*

AUTHOR CONTACT INFORMATION

Laura Ballet, Thought Energy Leadership - Founder of The Science of Empowerment
Website: https://thescienceofempowerment.com/
Email: laurabballet@gmail.com
Social: https://www.linkedin.com/in/laura-brennan-ballet-bb426751/
Tags: Author, Thought Energy Speaker, Empowerment Coach

July 21

ELISABETH GARNER

The blessings found in everyday life multiplied by the joy found in each one can create abundance beyond your wildest dreams.

THOUGHT

Merriam-Webster defines abundance as an ample quantity, an abundant amount, affluence, wealth, and a relative degree of plentifulness.

To me, abundance is so much bigger than a collection of tangible things. There were times I was flat broke, but I still had an abundance of love, support, and joy in my life. There were also times when I had my finances in order, but I was surrounded by betrayal, loss, and heartache.

Regardless of what I thought I was 'lacking,' there was always an abundance of something in my life. The choice was then deciding what to do with it.

Everything has a purpose and potential.

While your surroundings can beat you down or encourage you to thrive, there is also your effect on them. What you choose to do with the pieces handed to you, life literally is what you make of it.

Abundance does not inherently equal happiness. Some of the most miserable people in the world have the most possessions, and some of the happiest people in the world don't have a roof over their heads.

Abundance means you have the tools needed to survive and thrive. The trick is knowing and appreciating what you have and then using it to its fullest potential.

QUESTION

What do you feel you have an abundance of in your life?
Is there something more you think you could do with it?
What would your life look like if you shared that abundance?

AUTHOR CONTACT INFORMATION

Elisabeth Garner, Owner of Elisabeth Garner
Website: https://emgarner.net
Email: emgarner22@gmail.com
Social: https://www.instagram.com/booksbyemgarner/
Tags: Author, Editor, Graphic Designer, Cover Designer

July 22
NATALIE MCQUEEN

*Abundance is found in the love and wisdom
we share; we create ripples of legacy that last forever.*

THOUGHT

Abundance isn't measured by wealth; it's measured by the lives we touch. My grandmother, now 105, taught me that lesson in the most beautiful way. She didn't have riches to share, but she gave something far greater—her time, her love, and her wisdom. She taught us to knit, to season a cast iron pan, and to value the stories that shape who we are. Sitting on her backyard swing, she would share tales of her childhood, laughing until her face lit up or making us laugh with her exaggerated expressions as she described moments of bravery or standing up for what was right.

Her life has been a masterclass in giving—giving kindness, strength, and the kind of love that makes everyone feel seen and valued. Even now, people flock to her, not for what she has but for who she is. She embodies abundance in the purest form, proving that a legacy isn't built on what you leave behind but on the love and lessons you give while you're here.

Her life inspires me daily to take the lessons she's poured into me and make my own mark on the world—one story, one act of kindness, and one connection at a time. If I can impact even a fraction of the lives she has, I'll know I've lived abundantly.

QUESTION

*Who from your family tree would you ask to share their abundance of wisdom?
Who would benefit from your abundance of wisdom?*

AUTHOR CONTACT INFORMATION

Natalie McQueen, Founder of Gifts Of Legacy
Website: GiftsOfLegacy.us
Email: GiftsOfLegacy@gmail.com
Social: https://www.linkedin.com/in/nataliejmcqueen
Tags: Legacy Publisher, Author, Speaker, Journal, Legacy

July 23
SHIRLEY TURNER

Like sunshine breaking through night, we can rise from darkness, embrace our potential, and light up the world around us.

THOUGHT

Just as sunrise dispels the night's shadows, we possess an innate ability to overcome challenges and rise above adversity. Embracing our potential means recognizing the wealth of talents, creativity, and resilience within us. By tapping into this inner abundance, we illuminate our paths and inspire those around us. Our growth becomes a beacon of hope, encouraging others to seek their light and contribute to a collective brilliance.

By embracing a mindset of abundance, we shift focus from scarcity to potential. This mindset empowers us to make an impact, give generously, and live passionately. Each step toward enlightenment amplifies positive change in our communities. Our inner abundance fuels our passions, drives ambitions, and helps us overcome obstacles with grace and determination.

An abundant mindset cultivates gratitude, fostering a positive outlook on life. It makes us more resilient, adaptable, and open to love and kindness.

Together, our rays of light converge to create a new dawn of possibilities, a testament to our capacity for growth. Living in the present allows us to connect to our true selves, free from past regrets and future anxieties, granting clarity and strength.

QUESTION

How will you harness the power of living in the present moment to tap into your innate abundance, light up your path, and inspire those around you to contribute to a brighter, collective future?

AUTHOR CONTACT INFORMATION

Shirley Turner, Creator of Prime Life Mastery
Website: https://www.theprimelifemastery.com
Email: turners@vodamail.co.za
Social: https://www.instagram.com/theprimelifemastery/
Tags: life mastery coach

July 24

LINDA MAC DOUGALL

We possess all we need by having a colorful abundance of heart, mind, body, and soul.

THOUGHT

Our senses are made to experience the abundance of life. Our imagination recreates our emotions and how we have colored our experiences. Our world, and we as part of it, are full of a rainbow of possibilities. What do you see when you think of a rainbow?

Colors (1986)

A purple sound comes humming In a yellow dawn's full bloom. Red eyes read the rising.

Of another marbled moon. And the jagged, blinding whiteness That crowned the sightless night. Sleeps above blue heaven. And the rainbow's prism light.

Green life lifts and stretches. Aqua waves anoint the shore. Brown bodies kneel and kiss the earth. Black yields to blue once more.

Close your eyes. Deepen your breathing. Listen carefully for the sounds of nature, either of reality or your favorite imaginary place. Frogs serenading. Birds calling. Leaves dancing in the wind and the aroma of grasses and trees. Or is there the salty scent of the sea and the cries of gulls overhead? Or feel the sun of a desert at dawn and wonder at the endless sky above. See the colors.

The abundance of the natural world and your own imagination can calm and center a distracted mind. Both are with you every day and wherever you travel.

QUESTION

What colors make you feel the most abundance in your life?

AUTHOR CONTACT INFORMATION

Linda Mac Dougall, Owner of Mac Dougall Consulting for Disabilities
Website: https://loveyourlongevity.com
Email: speakerholistic@gmail.com
Social: https://www.linkedin.com/in/linda-mac-dougall-984820/
Tags: Speaker, Senior Health Advocate, Caregiver Trainer

July 25

JANA SHORT

*The secret to abundance? Appreciate the present,
and the future unfolds with greater gifts.*

THOUGHT

The quote, "The secret to abundance? Appreciate the present, and the future unfolds with greater gifts," creates such an emotional response within my soul. I understand that abundance isn't just out of my reach somewhere in the distant future but in the here and now!

When a life-threatening illness forced me to confront my mortality, suddenly, the future I'd been so fixated on seemed irrelevant. It took facing possible death to realize the only thing that truly mattered was the present moment.

This realization triggered a desperation to survive. I started searching for hope and embracing every extra moment I was gifted. I fed my mind abundant thoughts daily, educating myself on what the world had to offer.

As I started learning to live in the present, each day became abundant. Love for life flooded my soul, and opportunities appeared out of nowhere. It was as if, by letting go of my attachment to the future, I'd opened myself to the universe's infinite possibilities.

I understand now that abundance isn't just about survival but more about learning to thrive. Being forced to slow down opened a new world of gifts and opportunities.

The future is uncertain, but each moment is a gift.

QUESTION

*Is it possible that the very thing you've been
dreaming of is already right in front of you?*

AUTHOR CONTACT INFORMATION

Jana Short, Editor-in-Chief of Best Holistic Life Magazine
Website: https://www.bestholisticlife.com/
Email: jana@bestholisticlife.com
Social: https://www.linkedin.com/in/bestholisticlife/
Tags: Best Holistic Life Magazine, Author, Editor

July 26
REBECCA BABCOCK

Life is a hike; No two hikes turn out exactly the same because of the paths you choose.

THOUGHT

Life's journey doesn't have a perfect map to follow. Life is about waking up every day and appreciating what we have in front of us. Recognize the small daily wins as we inch closer to our goals, whether they are personal or professional. Take a moment to look back at how far you have come from various points in your life, finding a sense of accomplishment in all that you have overcome to reach this point. It's about finding our balance and giving ourselves the opportunity to do so. One gift that we often take for granted is the ability to choose. We can choose how we proceed through life. We can choose our goals and how we handle the obstacles in our path.

Remember that you hold the power within yourself to make choices. Regardless of the past, look to your future and the potential abundance it holds. Close your eyes and think, "What do I want my life to look like?" Now, choose your first step to get you started on this path. You are stronger than you think and hold more power within yourself than you ever knew. You woke up today and took a breath; now it's time to make a choice and move forward on your path.

QUESTION

What is one thing you can do today to choose your course?
What could your first step look like?

AUTHOR CONTACT INFORMATION

Rebecca Babcock, COO of Amerind Soul
Website: Amerindsoul.org
Email: rebecca@amerindnation.com
Social: https;//www.linkedin.com/in/Rebecca-babcock-93457630b/
Tags: Personal Growth Mindfulness Inspiration Resilience

July 27

DORIS LUM

Abundance is built on strong, transparent relationships, collaboration, fun, and creating lasting memories together.

THOUGHT

For me, fun and happiness are the "XO sauce" to abundance. Some may think of XO as a sign-off for hugs and love, expressing sincerity, faith, or friendship. But for me, XO sauce is also a secret ingredient I enjoy using in cooking. Aromatic, spicy, sweet, and salty, it carries the richness of dried scallops and brings unique flavor to dishes. In the same way, abundance starts with building strong relationships. Everyone's taste and favorite flavor profile are different, and every relationship is unique. How we engage with others is like choosing ingredients for a dish—are we being honest and transparent? Just as cooking involves blending flavors, relationships require using all our senses. When a relationship is strong and nurtured, it can endure challenges and help create a journey toward abundance.

QUESTION

What is your secret sauce to abundance, and how do you infuse it into your life and connections?

AUTHOR CONTACT INFORMATION

Doris Lum, Blockbot Leader of Connect United Affiliate
Website: https://www.workwithdoris.com
Email: workwithdoris@gmail.com
Social: https://linkedIn.com/in/workwithdoris
Tags: Actor, Business Coach, Blockchain Advocate

July 28
SYLVIA BAFFOUR

The questions you ask yourself shape the path to your potential.

THOUGHT

In the landscape of our minds, questions act as gateways or barricades.

Barricading questions typically begin with "Why," like "Why is this happening to me?" or "Why aren't my ideas being heard?" They restrict our thinking, close off possibilities, and keep us focused on problems, not solutions.

Conversely, gateway questions—often starting with "How" or "What," such as "What can I learn from this challenge?" or "How can I contribute my ideas more effectively?"—open our minds to possibilities and invite abundance. They pivot our focus toward solutions and expand our perspective to include new opportunities.

Consider shifting from a limiting question to an empowering question. This reframing can profoundly influence how we perceive and interact with our world, leading to a richer, more abundant life.

Embrace the practice of asking gateway questions. They not only provide clarity and promote problem-solving but also enhance your emotional intelligence by fostering a mindset of growth and resilience.

QUESTION

Today, what gateway question can you ask to open the door to abundance in your life? How will changing your questions change your outcomes?

AUTHOR CONTACT INFORMATION

Sylvia Baffour, President of Baffour International LLC
Website: https://sylviaspeaks.com
Email: sylvia@sylviaspeaks.com
Social: https://www.linkedin.com/in/sylviabaffour/
Tags: Speaker, Leadership Coach, Emotional Intelligence

July 29
DEBBIE STEAGALL

Creating a lasting impression on the world and those around you involves having a family legacy.

THOUGHT

Creating a meaningful impact involves leaving a lasting impression legacy.

A legacy love letter and business succession involve more than mere words; they represent our identity and illustrate how we express our deepest emotions. By crafting these intergenerational messages, we share invaluable insights from our triumphs and challenges, connecting the past, present, and future to foster lasting relationships. Our aim should be to live selflessly, supporting one another with gratitude and respect. Embracing unity is essential, as visionary leaders who value diverse talents can achieve remarkable success.

Research shows that 67% of Americans leave this world with regrets, often due to inadequate estate plans that create challenges for their loved ones. Journaling and writing legacy love letters are excellent ways to convey our love and appreciation.

Everyone should take the initiative to create a legacy plan. This strategy allows us to live joyfully and abundantly while uplifting and supporting others in all aspects of their lives.

QUESTION

Are you excited to write your Living Legacy Love Letter?
This is a wonderful chance to convey a heartfelt message to future generations!

AUTHOR CONTACT INFORMATION

Debbie Steagall, Founder and CSO, Steagall & Associates
Website: https://debbiesteagall.com
Email: debbiensteagall6@gmail.com
Social: https://www.linkedin.com/in/debbiesteagall
Tags: Transformational Leadership, Coach, Mentor, Speaker

July 30
SARAH CLARK

We build a better world by connecting. Connecting with ourselves, with the world's realities and possibilities, and with others on the same quest.

THOUGHT

As a Higher Ed leader turned leadership coach, I think a lot about how mission-oriented teams can build a better world without burning out in the process. Even in a world of abundant possibility, there are hard limits—the number of hours in a day, the level of knowledge and insight available to make high quality decisions, and the amount of talent and treasure your organization can sustainably expend on a given project.

So, does the fact that the world has limits mean that the Abundance mindset is a lie? Of course not! It just means that you and your team may need to think about abundance in a different way. Your organization can accomplish any goal it sets its collective will to accomplish. However, it cannot accomplish every possible goal at the same time.

Abundant leadership is kind leadership. It's the art of growing humanely, managing effectively, and creating collaboratively. Those three skills enable you to make the decisions that will grow your and your team's confidence, effectiveness, and mutual trust. And that shared confidence, effectiveness, and trust will empower all of you to create the better world you wish to see.

QUESTION

How could your team more effectively, humanely, and collaboratively navigate its abundant opportunities to build a better world?

AUTHOR CONTACT INFORMATION

Sarah Clark, Founder of Kind Leadership Guild
Website: https://kindleadershipguild.com
Email: oklibrarian@gmail.com
Social: https://www.linkedin.com/in/sarah-clark-60283b2/
Tags: Leadership Coach

The Art of Connection

July 31

DANIEL KNIGHT

You are just one connection away from meeting your Golden Connection!

THOUGHT

You're at an event, your friend grabs you by the arm, swings you around, and suddenly you're in front of a complete stranger, and they say, You two have to meet, and just like that... Magic! Little did you know, this connection would turn into stories you tell your friends and family, stories you tell your colleagues, stories you tell on stage—about the successes you experienced together.

What started as an idea sparked by a connector to create Unity between two amazing people that established a relationship and a chain of Joy for people worldwide and for generations to come through intentionality, aligned values, and the consistent pursuit of a shared mission. If it weren't for Abundance, this Golden Connection might have competed to destroy each other.

When we stop fighting and competing to get ahead and recognize there is an Abundance of everything we could ever need, want, or dream of—we can crush the destructive, competitive mindset and establish a world of Unity through collaboration and create a world of more Joy.

QUESTION

Who made an introduction to you that created abundance in your life?

AUTHOR CONTACT INFORMATION

Daniel Knight, Chief Executive of Unicorn Universe
Website: http://www.UnicornUniverse.io
Email: daniel@unicornuniverse.io
Social: https://www.linkedin.com/in/10xunicorn/
Tags: Speaker, Connector, Community Leader, 10xUnicorn

August 1
SHAWNA JAMES

Abundance is a constant, and it reveals its true magic when it flows from a life well-lived.

THOUGHT

As humans, each of us is on a unique journey, one exclusively our own. This life—our life—is unlike any other in its depth and detail. Over my fifty-plus years, I've realized there are some universal truths, a few constants, that we all encounter.

One such truth is our experience of abundance. Abundance is always present—that's how the Universe functions, in constant expansion. Yet, feeling truly abundant is tied to the joy, love, and gratitude we embrace at any moment. The real question is, what abundance are we creating? Are we caught in fear and lack, or are we flowing with love and possibility? What vibration, what magic are we inviting into our lives?

We create more of whatever we resonate with, consciously or not. And I'll admit, I sometimes struggle to amplify higher frequencies over lower ones. Often, we amplify what our environment has imprinted—fear, scarcity, and limitation. But when we awaken to our true power, we can choose to amplify infinite possibilities, shifting from constriction to flow. Let gratitude tune us into the abundance already within reach, shifting our focus from lack to limitless potential.

QUESTION

Feeling abundant yet? Or are you still busy perfecting the art of worrying?

AUTHOR CONTACT INFORMATION

Shawna James, Coaching/Consulting of A Different Normal
Website: https://www.linkedin.com/in/shawnajames/
Email: shawna.naomi.james@gmail.com
Social: https://www.facebook.com/adifferentnormal/
Tags: Empowerment Coach, Leadership Mentor, Strategist

August 2
ERICA CROUCH

Endurance today leads to the blessings of tomorrow.

THOUGHT

Strive to finish something today that will set you up for a better tomorrow. Abundance rarely has a short runway and requires a ton of energy alongside determination, persistence, and hard work. Sometimes, it feels like it will never pay off, and then we let frustration sideline us.

That's when an enduring mindset focused on "succeed or learn, but never quit" will kick in for those willing to go the extra mile. Plus, there's a tremendous incentive to keep going: Your future you.

Can you let yourself down? Imagine going 30 years into the future and seeing yourself. Go ahead, close your eyes, and see the future. You could see a tired person opening a third-floor apartment door asking, 'Why did I…' or a person parking their shiny toy in a three-car garage saying, 'I'm so glad I…" Penetrating pain, the exhaustion of hard work, and the blood, sweat, and tears of persistent effort are a willing price for those seeking the blessings of tomorrow.

QUESTION

What will you finish today that will bring the tomorrow version of you?

AUTHOR CONTACT INFORMATION

Erica Crouch, Owner of Phoenix Online Notary
Website: https://PhoenixOnlineNotary.business.site
Email: phoenixonlinenotary@gmail.com
Social: https://mybook.to/artofconnection5
Tags: notary, apostille services, Arizona

August 3
JENNIFER MILLER

Find the beauty or create it yourself.

THOUGHT

Keys to Abundance.

An abundance of health, wealth, family, friends, love, and time to enjoy all of these has everything to do with gratitude, worthiness, and knowing oneself.

Gratitude is an action, a state of being, and a frequency. Count your blessings, find the good, and be genuinely grateful for all that is. Taking stock of what you already have allows you to be clear about what you really need. Daily gratitude lists anchor this energy, allowing you to align your frequency with Abundance.

Worthiness: an action, a state of being, a frequency.

Do you genuinely love and believe in yourself? Do you think yourself deserving of abundance? What are the root causes of feeling unworthy of abundance? Dive deep and heal any blocks to worthiness.

Know Thyself: an action, a state of being, a frequency.

My job as a Life Activation Practitioner in the Lineage of King Solomon is to remind you that you are a divine eternal being. The process of remembering this includes healing all forms of trauma, removing labels, masks, programming, negative mindsets, behaviors, thought patterns, and anything that stops us from remembering who we indeed are. To Know Thyself = Abundant in all areas of life.

QUESTION

What actions will you take today to Know Yourself?

AUTHOR CONTACT INFORMATION

Jennifer Miller, Owner of Magick Hour Studios
Website: www.magickhourstudios.com
Email: Jennifer@magickhourstudios.com
Social: www.instagram.com/ynnej
Tags: Empowerment, Photographer

August 4
CAROLINE BIESALSKI

An Inspired Choice Today creates the change leading to your success story tomorrow.

THOUGHT

Success isn't the result of a single event but the outcome of a series of inspired choices made daily. Each decision we make today can shape our tomorrow, steering us closer to our goals or further away from them. When we make conscious, inspired choices, we set the stage for meaningful change, which ultimately leads to lasting success.

But it's not just about success in terms of wealth or career. It's about cultivating a life of abundance, where personal fulfillment, growth, and connection with others all play vital roles. By making choices aligned with our values and passions, we invite abundance into every aspect of our lives, from our relationships to our well-being.

True success is built on the foundation of consistent, inspired actions. It's the small, daily decisions—choosing growth over fear, opportunity over procrastination—that open doors. Today's choice is the chance to rewrite your story, foster genuine connection, and step into a life rich with abundance and purpose. Make the choice today, and watch how tomorrow unfolds.

QUESTION

How will you use today's choice to invite abundance and connect with what truly matters to you?

AUTHOR CONTACT INFORMATION

Caroline Biesalski, Inspired Choice Coach, Writer & Podcast Host of Reflection8 Inc.
Website: https://www.inspiredchoice.today
Email: book@inspiredchoice.today
Social: https://www.linkedin.com/in/biesalski
Tags: Coaching, Podcasting, Speaking, Training, Writing

August 5
LEANN COAKLEY

*True richness comes not from the belongings
we own but from the cherished moments we experience
and the connections we foster.*

THOUGHT

I believe that true abundance isn't measured by the material things we accumulate but by the memories we create and the relationships we build. It's in the laughter we share with friends, the acts of kindness we extend, and the gratitude we feel in our hearts. Every day that we wake up is a gift, a chance to experience life anew, while someone else may not have that opportunity.

We should be mindful of those who struggle to achieve or perceive abundance and allow their plight to influence how we embrace each day with an open heart. We can uncover the wealthiest treasures, those that touch our souls and bring genuine happiness. We can share those blessings with those less fortunate and embrace the feeling of altruism. This perspective helps me stay grounded and focused on what truly matters in life.

QUESTION

How might your life change if you started each day by acknowledging the gift of waking up and focusing on the connections and moments that truly enrich your life?

AUTHOR CONTACT INFORMATION

Leann Coakley, Entrepreneur of Revolution Financial Management
Website: https://agents.worldfinancialgroup.com/Leann-Coakley-94SRI
Email: coakley.leann@gmail.com
Social: https://www.linkedin.com/in/leanncoakley3
Tags: Financial Markets, Best Selling Author, Non-Profit

August 6
DAVID KNEPP

Live an inner-directed life, giving, doing, loving, serving, all from your abundance!

THOUGHT

Although it has been decades since I attended Life University, I will always live and give based on the school's guiding principle: "We have a Lasting Purpose: To live an inner-directed life, to give, to do, to love, to serve, out of your abundance." Life University believes that a willingness and desire to serve your community and your fellow man are just as important as academic pursuits.

This attitude stems from the recognition that each individual has been given certain gifts, and as a citizen in the world community, it is your duty to give, to do, to love, and to serve out of your abundance. Start every morning recognizing the abundance your gifts bring into your life; find a way to share that reality with the less fortunate, and embrace gratitude as the blessing it is as you follow your teachings.

QUESTION

How will you share your abundance with others today?

AUTHOR CONTACT INFORMATION

David Knepp, Owner of San Diego Chiropractic Group
Website: https://www.sdchirogroup.com
Email: robert@networktogether.net
Social: https://www.linkedin.com/in/david-knepp-aa749a9/
Tags: Chiropractor

August 7
LYDIA G. FOUGÈRES

*It isn't logical that world leaders have convinced
the human race that it takes wars to bring back peace.*

THOUGHT

Every day, I wake up grateful that I live in a place of peace where deer eat from my hand and I can walk in the woods without fear.
I was raised in an area where racism did not exist.
As a child, I woke up every morning looking at the lake in front of our house and was brought up with pure thoughts.
My upbringing is proof that our surroundings shape our actions. I did not have any hate inside me, nor was I told not to share my thoughts by adults.
I was respected by those in my neighborhood as well as anywhere in the town.
I never had the feeling of either being superior or inferior. Everyone was equal.
Religion was practiced in every way. It was just normal. We learned several languages.
There was no cultural shock since it was part of being in the community to accept one another's differences with love.
There was no such thing as whites, natives, Muslims, Portuguese, Greeks, Italians, or Mexicans, for we shared recipes and learned one another's customs.
If the entire planet were like where I come from, there would only be peace, for war and hatred are learned.
Sharing is part of human nature. We are one consciousness.
Eventually, we will learn cohabitation just like I did.

QUESTION

What do you think the world would be like if all places would be like my native town?

AUTHOR CONTACT INFORMATION

Reverend Lydia G. Fougères, Founder of Holy & Holy
Website: http://lydiafougeres.com
Email: Greatdivinemother@gmail.com
Social: http://instagram/@divadivinemother_
Tags: Reverend, M.MSc., Author, R.N., Chakra Healer

August 8
ANDY TANNER

The most successful wealth plans I've seen are, in no small part—escape plans.

THOUGHT

Deep within every soul lies the desire to be free—to spend our time as we wish, with whom we wish. But the typical plans we're given were never designed to deliver true freedom. The school system is built to create a workforce, while government programs offer only limited support. And 401(k) plans? They enrich Wall Street, offering vague hopes instead of clear paths to freedom, trapping many in the rat race for far longer than they planned.

An actual escape plan offers not just financial freedom. Money isn't the only obstacle—education, discipline, and mindset are just as important. We need to become investors in our futures, not just participants in a flawed system. It's about breaking free from the limitations that hold us back, not just following advice but transforming ourselves.

That's why the best wealth plans are escape plans-- or battle plans. Your wealth blueprint should lead to emancipation from the system and a personal victory over the self.

An escape plan is worth working for. It's worth a little effort every day because it leads to actual, lasting freedom.

QUESTION

Do you want to fight for your freedom?

AUTHOR CONTACT INFORMATION

Andy Tanner, Founder of Cash Flow Academy
Website: https://thecashflowacademy.com/
Email: andy@thecashflowacademy.com
Social: https://www.youtube.com/@AndyTannerTraining
Tags: Financial Education, Investing, Wealth Building

August 9
MARY GAUL

*Abundance flows through the connections we cultivate.
Every shared success celebrated amplifies our growth and joy.*

THOUGHT

The quote above captures my belief in how interconnected success and abundance are with the relationships we cultivate. As a business coach for solopreneurs, I frequently witness how overwhelming it can feel to carry the weight of everything alone. No business thrives in isolation. When we intentionally build connections—whether through networking, collaboration, or supporting another small business—opportunities for abundance multiply.

In my book, Vitamin C3 for Business, I emphasize that success is built on Connection, Contribution, and Celebration. By focusing on connections, we create a foundation of abundance that enriches our lives and those around us. Connection isn't just about expanding your numbers or making sales; it's about fostering genuine relationships where trust, encouragement, and shared knowledge fuel growth for all.

Abundance isn't just financial; it's also found in satisfaction, fulfillment, and joy. When we celebrate and share our challenges and successes, we amplify growth by tapping into the collective wisdom of our community. Together, we create something far more powerful than what we could achieve alone. That, to me, is true abundance.

QUESTION

What small step could you take today to cultivate deeper connections in your business and community, support your abundance, AND contribute to the growth and joy of those around you?

AUTHOR CONTACT INFORMATION

Mary Gaul, Business FOCUS Coach of Success Magnified
Website: https://www.successmagnified.com
Email: mary@successmagnified.com
Social: https://www.linkedin.com/in/marygaulcoach/
Tags: Business Coach, Speaker, Author

The Art of Connection

August 10
TRICIA LIVERMORE

Intentional Abundance is a Practiced Mindset

THOUGHT

When I reflect on my life, I notice times when I felt abundant and other times when I did not. The difference between those two feelings was what I had imagined about my life prior to those situations. I went to college to make the most money in the shortest time, so I chose accounting. After some time, I realized the job had provided me with financial abundance, which is what I imagined, but it did not provide me with a sense of fulfillment because that was not my goal.

After my corporate career and marriage ended, I imagined having abundant peace, well-being, conscious community, and self-love. I spent time healing myself physically, mentally, emotionally, and spiritually and feeling into the abundance of my intentions. I now live in a state of incredible peace.

In this next phase of my life, I've decided I don't want to work hard to receive financial wealth. I intend to do what I love by being exactly who I am and easily attracting financial wealth from various sources. This practiced mindset helps me feel successful no matter what I'm doing, as I trust in the evidence of the abundance I have received when I set purposeful intentions.

QUESTION

What intentional practice have you chosen for abundance in your life?

AUTHOR CONTACT INFORMATION

Tricia Livermore, Founder & Coach of Soul Business Advisor
Website: https://www.soulbusinessadvisor.com
Email: tdlivermore@gmail.com
Social: https://www.linkedin.com/in/tricia-livermore
Tags: Heart-Centered Coach

August 11
SANET VAN BREDA

*"If your WHY is big enough, you will do anything;
you will do everything!" Dancing to My African Drumbeat.*

THOUGHT

In life, we often take two steps forward and one step back, echoing the heartbeat of our journey. When I live in gratitude, it feels like I'm walking on cloud nine. When I witness abundance in my life, I send God an air kiss in thanks, and more blessings unfold.

My African drumbeats harmonize with sunlight, guiding me toward a fantastic future. One of my favorite quotes is, "If your why is big enough, you will do anything." This realization became my turning point. I chose to live, not just exist, transforming my lifestyle through mindfulness, gratitude, and self-compassion.

I named my company "Self Love Ignites Me," despite my husband's doubts. The name spells slim, and I've lost 165 pounds. In Afrikaans, "slim" means wisdom, and I'm using mindfulness daily. I embrace my self-love, keeping my word and taking action. I am the luckiest person when I hear, "Everything you touch turns to gold," I accept it for myself and everyone I've touched.

If time, money, and fear were no obstacles, what bold step would you take today to live your dream life? Who must you become to make that vision a reality as you move to the rhythm of your drumbeat?

QUESTION

What intentional practice have you chosen for abundance in your life?

AUTHOR CONTACT INFORMATION

Sanet Van Breda, Founder of Self Love Ignites Me
Website: https://selflove4me.com/
Email: slim@selflove4me.com
Social: https://www.linkedin.com/in/sanet-van-breda/
Tags: Media Enterprise

August 12

NAHEED OBERFELD

I see evidence of my alignment with my manifestation.

THOUGHT

What do you do when you don't accomplish a long-cherished goal? Try harder? Push further? Blame yourself or the situation?

There are only two reasons you don't accomplish your goals, and none of them involve a personal shortcoming or more complex work.

1. It is because you are pursuing a goal that is not your true heart's desire.

2. Or, you have convinced yourself that you won't be able to achieve your true heart's desire

My client Bailey was stuck in her job. She was a senior manager with years of experience but wasn't being hired for the higher-level positions she desired. Bailey didn't believe in the value of her skills and strengths. She judged the worthiness of the position not on her strengths but rather on her weaknesses. Furthermore, the results from her job search reinforced her limiting beliefs. She didn't think she was qualified and, therefore, didn't get the position, which was further proof that she wasn't qualified.

When Bailey stopped fighting for her goal, she was guided to take inspired action, which opened the right doors for her. She chose to be in mental, emotional, and spiritual alignment with her goal. No stress or struggle is required!

QUESTION

What goal are you willing to get into alignment with and allow inspired action to bring into your life?

AUTHOR CONTACT INFORMATION

Naheed Oberfeld, Owner of Oberfeld Coaching
Website: www.OberfeldCoaching.com
Email: Naheed@OberfeldCoaching.com
Social: https://www.instagram.com/oberfeld_coaching/
Tags: Mindset Coach, Speaker, EFT/Tapping coach,

August 13
KRISTIN HANNUM

*Abundance isn't chased; it's a state we embrace.
Your journey today creates the richness of tomorrow and the joy of now.*

THOUGHT

This quote embodies the wisdom that my mom, Susanne Uerling Osberg, instilled in me—always to have a vision and something to look forward to. It highlights that abundance is not merely an external acquisition but a mindset we choose to embrace. By fostering gratitude and positivity, we open ourselves to experience the fullness of life in the present. This shift in perspective helps us see the abundance of opportunities, connections, and possibilities around us.

Moreover, the quote affirms the significance of having a future vision to shape our present reality. By envisioning a future brimming with abundance and positivity, we allow this vision to guide our current actions, thoughts, and emotions. This forward-thinking approach helps us experience the present more richly. By imagining a prosperous future, we encourage ourselves to take purposeful actions and adopt attitudes that align with that vision, thereby enhancing our present experiences.

Ultimately, it's about aligning our present mindset with the abundant life we envision, enabling our future aspirations to infuse our present moments with purpose and fulfillment.

QUESTION

Do you have a vision for your future, and how can you bring the feeling of achieving that vision into your present experience to nurture an abundant mindset?

AUTHOR CONTACT INFORMATION

Kristin Hannum, Sr. Partner Success Manager of Thryv
Website: https://emp.thryv.com/site/kristinhannum
Email: osbergkristin@yahoo.com
Social: https://www.linkedin.com/in/kristin-hannum-8915259a/
Tags: SAAS, Small Business Software, Digital Marketer

August 14

SUSAN FLERCHINGER

Soar with faith, and abundance will follow.

THOUGHT

Abundance is the divine overflow of blessings and grace that permeates our lives. It is God's unending provision, manifesting in material wealth, spiritual fulfillment, emotional well-being, and meaningful connections. Abundance is not something outside of us to earn or pursue; it is a state of being. When we practice this state of being, wealth, health, joyful relationships, and amazing opportunities show up.

Apply the soar process (from FormedToSoar.com) to embrace this divine abundance:

* Surrender: Let go of fears and doubts. Trust in God's plan and timing.
* Open: Open your heart to opportunities and blessings. Choose to be abundant.
* Ask: Communicate your wants and needs to God with faith. Ask for His help and call upon angels for guidance.
* Receive: Accept God's abundance with gratitude and grace. Celebrate and share your blessings, becoming a channel of His love.

To cultivate an abundant mindset, practice daily gratitude and affirmations. Serve others joyfully, network with positive individuals, maintain a healthy lifestyle, declutter your space, and visualize abundance in all areas—finances, relationships, health, and personal growth. Choose to be abundant through God's love now.

QUESTION

What legacy do you want to leave? What do you need to surrender today to open your heart more fully to God's abundance? What if you embraced the SOAR process and recognized abundance as a state of being?

AUTHOR CONTACT INFORMATION

Susan Flerchinger, VIbrant Energy Engineer @ Formed To Soar
Website: https://FormedToSoar.com
Email: susansenergy@gmail.com
Social: https://www.linkedin.com/in/susanflerchinger/
Tags: Energy, Healer, Angels, Retreat, Faith, Speaker

August 15
MARY E. KNIPPEL

Sharing your Transformational Soul Story offers Hope to others.

THOUGHT

Your transformational Soul Story is one that changed the trajectory of your life and set you on your true path. Webster's Dictionary defines transformation as a noun: a dramatic change.

Here's the thing: Your Transformational Soul Story is the wisdom you've learned from a life lesson laid on your heart and living in your soul. More importantly, sharing that wisdom offers hope for the world. It demonstrates another way of thinking and offers options about life situations.

No one else on this earth has lived in your skin and had the experiences you have had. You are the only one who knows that Ah Ha moment when you decided to make a change. And only you know the significance of that change. That story gave you the courage to make a different choice. That story has gotten you to where you are right now. That is the transformational soul story that taught you the skills you have today.

That's the message of hope people need to hear.

I believe we have many transformational Soul Stories. One of mine depicts the integral role writing played in my breast cancer journey and healing process. I encourage readers to write their own stories.

QUESTION

What is one life experience that has changed the trajectory of your life?

AUTHOR CONTACT INFORMATION

Mary E. Knippel, Soul Story Mentor of Your Writing Mentor
Website: https://maryeknippel.com
Email: mary@yourwritingmentor.com
Social: https://www.facebook.com/maryeknippel
Tags: author, writing coach, publisher, editor, retreats

The Art of Connection

August 16

RACHAEL HUDSON

The mind is limitlessly spacious and limitlessly powerful.

THOUGHT

How does the same 'uneducated' mind paint something as beautiful as La Scapigliata, develop an accurate theory on anatomy, and conceptually invent the helicopter? Da Vinci allowed his limitlessly spacious mind to explore and imagine the possibility of ideas and applied his limitlessly powerful mind to bring these concepts into form.

I'm not suggesting we must each be exquisite artists, groundbreaking anatomists, or innovative engineers. Few of us are polymaths like Da Vinci. I am saying we can always conceive and do better for ourselves by staying in the intention and discovery of what we can do as opposed to limiting ourselves in deciding what we can't do.

Changing requires the symbiotic alchemy of imagining that something can happen and then applying our will to make it happen.

We begin to imagine something different, innovate and expand into its possibility, plot the actions and adaptations required to grow, and then implement these so it is actualized. Whether or not what we conceive for ourselves is even plausible, the only way it ever has a chance to become probable is to use the limitless power of our mind through intention, determination, focus, and action.

Grow, my love.

QUESTION

What have you decided about yourself that cuts you off from the potential treasure within you yet to be discovered?

AUTHOR CONTACT INFORMATION

Rachael Hudson, Founder of Rachael Hudson Coaching
Website: https://rachaelhudson.com
Email: rah@rachaelhudson.com
Social: https://www.linkedin.com/in/rachael-hudson-b399a214/
Tags: Empowerment and Mindset Coach, Change Agent, Speaker

August 17
RADAVIE RIOM

Think about what is the Greatest Abundance!

THOUGHT

How can we get beyond the mindset of fear and anxiety when triggered by our circumstances? Or when we see that the world around us is in chaos? The greatest abundance is to expose the inner peace that is always present, albeit veiled, in the midst of life's challenging situations. How can we unveil inner peace?

Inner peace is not revealed by masking our feelings with substances, manipulating our thoughts, or getting lost in distractions. Attempting to change our thoughts or mask emotions will provide temporary relief. Inner peace is revealed as the stillness, the Light of Awareness, that rests silently as the witnessing presence amidst the changing and challenging tides of everyday life.

Awareness is prior to the mind-made world of fear and conflict. It is that which witnesses and peacefully embraces the mind with all its machinations, from the serene to the tumultuous. To abide as Awareness is to not place oneself in conflict with what is happening within you or around you. Instead, it is to say, "Yes!" Saying "Yes!" opens our hearts to feel the abundance of peace that is always present 'underneath' the agitation. Then, let any action we take flow from peace rather than from fear.

QUESTION

Can you take a moment? Rest is the witnessing presence of thoughts, sensations, or emotions as they come and go; allow them all. Rest as Awareness with no agenda for a moment. Be aware of being aware.

AUTHOR CONTACT INFORMATION

Radavie R., Author and Messenger, Serving Inner Peace
Website: https://www.radavie.net
Email: radavie01@gmail.com
Social: https://www.linkedin.com/in/radavie-riom-35b48511/
Tags: Author, Messenger, Compassion, Inner Peace Guide

August 18
CHING FONG SIN

*Every pain comes with a blessing in disguise,
an opportunity to learn and grow.*

THOUGHT

Pain in life is inevitable. Everyone wants to avoid pain, yet pain in this world is abundant. No one has a perfect life. Everyone has/has had pain, no matter how successful, wealthy, intelligent, or perfect they seem. If one has never experienced pain, do they know what joy is? Could a pain-free life be the most significant pain in life?

My most immense pain in life is the miscarriage I had 13 years ago. I was still in great pain and tears a few days ago when I thought about my baby, whom I never met. Time didn't heal as I did not face my pain. Now, I understand that my baby has completed their journey on this earth, and it's time for my baby and me to move on. The baby I never met has taught me unconditional love and not to take things for granted. I also learned to be more patient with my kids and cherish the family time we have together. I know one day, we will be apart too. I will forever love my baby even though I never felt their warmth in my arms. I know my baby is happy as heaven has no pain.

After every storm, there is a rainbow. After every pain, there is joy and wisdom. I embrace the pain. I cherish the moment, learn, and heal.

QUESTION

What's your blessing in disguise?

AUTHOR CONTACT INFORMATION

Ching Fong Sin, Founder of Ching Fong Sin
Website: https://www.365daysofabundancequotes.com
Email: coach.ching88@gmail.com
Social: www.linkedin.com/in/ching-fong-sin
Tags: Life Coach, Healing, Transformation, True Self

August 19

JACLYN ZOCCOLI

My life is so full of abundance that it overflows.
I am in wonder at how this happens. I am "wonder. . .full."

THOUGHT

So often, I meander through life, creating a routine I count on and inattentive to my path. The way appears clear; the weeds are challenges. As long as they are overcome (the weeds picked), then I merely walk.

So much is taken for granted as I maintain that routine. I assume that the pattern will always be there. Then, when a "weed" (a challenge) appears, I at once question. And perhaps for the first time I see the routine, see the disruption, and then see how good it was without the challenge.

This Awareness need not wait for an interruption, a challenge, or a weed to be present. Consider what your day would look like if you were to see abundance daily. . .

I commit to doing that every moment I possibly can. I begin my day, before my feet hit the ground, in Awareness of my abundance. I end my day before I nod off, recollecting the same. And whenever I take an hourly break, I look around and notice how blessed I am.

What does this do? Since we can only think of one thing at a time, and if that thought is in an Awareness of our abundance, how can anything else exist? I am only here on borrowed time. My Creator calculates each moment. Abundance Awareness rules my life.

QUESTION

When can you insert a moment of Awareness into your day?
Make it one of Abundance and see how your life changes.

AUTHOR CONTACT INFORMATION

Jaclyn Zoccoli, LinkedIn Strategist & Global Impact Concierge of Network Builders Arizona

Website: http://JaclynZoccoli.com

Email: JacqueZoccoli88@gmail.com

Social: http://LinkedIn.com/in/Jaclyn-Zoccoli

Tags: LinkedIn Strategist, Global Impact Concierge

August 20
AUDREY KERGER

Life. Breath. Thought. Sight. Smell. Taste. Touch. A Spark of All That Is. YOU, Source/God/Goddess/Divine Spark, You Are Abundance!

THOUGHT

Why do we so often connect abundance to the material things of our human world? When we know, deep in our soul, that true Abundance is none of that. It is Mama Gaia; it is the plant, animal, and mineral kingdoms. It is the stars and planets in the sky above. It is the breath that we breathe each moment that we are here. You/We are the abundance that truly is the gift to this world: our heartbeat, our thoughts, our senses, our lives. Abundance is the sounds that we hear; it is the frequencies that create All That Is.

This knowing is the true abundance that we all have, that we all are, and that is all around us at all times. It is the lessons that we learn and the choices that we make to either thank them for our growth or blame them and stay in lack consciousness. Abundance is seeing beyond the tangible and embracing the spiritual essence that connects all things. It is a reminder that we are whole and complete, no matter our circumstances, as we embody a spark of the divine abundance that flows through all creation.

QUESTION

What is abundance to you? Is it material things or the lessons you've learned through this life? Do you remember what your true abundance is?

AUTHOR CONTACT INFORMATION

Audrey Kerger, Founder, CEO of Haus of Life & Co.
Website: https://hausoflife.com
Email: admin@hausoflife.com
Social: https://www.linkedin.com/in/audrey-kerger
Tags: Holistic Healthcare, Consultant, Spiritual Healer

August 21
THERESE JOHNSON

*Your presence is the "greatest gift" you
can give and receive in abundance.*

THOUGHT

Living in the moment is truly living an abundant life.
It is when our soul is in sanctity with the present that true creativity happens.
Living moment to moment is the most cherished blessing of abundance!

Truly living in the moment requires methods that entail digital detox
by limiting screen time and prioritizing real-world interactions
with mindfulness and gratitude practices.

Being present allows you to connect deeply with others.
Being present is a skill that takes practice.

When you're fully engaged in the present, you open yourself up to
a world of possibilities and opportunities. Stay in the moment, be mindful,
and cherish each eventful moment as an intentional gift for yourself.
Unlock your full potential and experience a more abundant
and fulfilling life by learning to live in the moment.

QUESTION

*How can you stay in the moment to create abundance in your life on a daily basis,
moment to moment?*

AUTHOR CONTACT INFORMATION

Therese Johnson, Owner of The Ideal Placement Inc.DBA Senior Care Of Sacramento
Website: www.SeniorCareOfSacramento.com
Email: caregiving@seniorcareofsacramento.com
Social: www.linkedin.com/in/therese-johnson-7b107544/
Tags: Senior Care Placement Agency

August 22

MARY J ROBINSON

*Plant the SEED - Nourish the STEM - Watch it BLOOM!
And, of course, there's always room to FLOURISH!*

THOUGHT

It fascinates me how a tiny seed grows into something much more complex, like a watermelon, a tomato, or even a tree. For the seedling to survive and thrive, it must be planted in a suitable environment, free of weeds and pests. This concept can be applied to human growth and development.

There was a period of my life filled with work-related quarrels and constant overexertion that depleted my spirit and re-exposed subconscious feelings of inadequacy. I was so focused on proving myself to others that I had forgotten to nurture my true strengths. Eventually, my health took a dramatic turn. I was diagnosed with CANcer, which forced me to reflect on my current situation. I realized that I was not happy - something needed to change.

Sometimes, weeds refuse to leave, and there's no other solution than to spray them with poison. CANcer was brutal, but my roots held firm with the help of a stem cell transplant. Returning to the support of true friends and family helped my plant to survive through even the worst conditions. Now, I know never to let weeds hold me back. A life of abundance can be achieved by surrounding yourself with like-minded people who challenge and support your pursuits.

QUESTION

*Challenging experiences are generally followed by spiritual growth.
What weeds can you prune from your life in pursuit of abundance?*

AUTHOR CONTACT INFORMATION

Mary J Robinson, Owner of Kaleidoscope Energy, LLC
Website: https://kaleidoscopeenergy.com
Email: kaleidoscopenergy@gmail.com
Social: https://www.facebook.com/KaleidoscopEnergy
Tags: Author, Speaker, Teacher, Healing Touch, Reiki

August 23
WESLEY SWAINSTON

The impact of volunteering for the community you are a part of will go beyond the time given. It transforms lives and creates lifetime connections.

THOUGHT

As a professional dog trainer, I am passionate about volunteering in shelters. My journey began in high school when I volunteered in a classroom for children with intellectual and developmental disabilities (IDD). There, I met one of my best friends, who has autism.

This experience inspired me to start a club called Best Buddies, helping kids with IDD form meaningful friendships. After high school, I became an avid runner, completing marathons and ultramarathons, and I got my first dog, which sparked my interest in dog training.

Before joining the USMC, I knew dog training was my future. While serving, I volunteered at my local shelter, training dogs and sharing their stories with my 500,000 followers on social media. This effort led to a tenfold increase in adoptions. Recognizing that many people couldn't volunteer to train shelter dogs, I launched a movement called Running With Shelter Dogs, inspiring trainers and runners to engage with local shelters. This initiative encouraged more trainers to volunteer and motivated runners to join, fostering a greater community of support for shelter animals. We all have unique ways to give back to the communities we love, so go volunteer!

QUESTION

What experiences have inspired you to give back to your community, and how can we motivate more people to volunteer and support the communities they are a part of?

AUTHOR CONTACT INFORMATION

Wesley Swainston, Owner of forthedogs
Website: https://alwaysforthedogs.com
Email: wesley.forthedogs@gmail.com
Social: https://linktr.ee/FORTHEDOGS_
Tags: forthedogs

August 24
GREG GODDARD

*If people understood that happiness is a skill,
something we can practice and teach our brains to do on command,
the world would change forever.*

THOUGHT

Meditation is a scary word to a lot of people, but to me, it simply means taking time to practice who I want to be. A few minutes of thinking about the people I love and why I love them changes something in me. A few minutes of remembering the things that make me a beautiful human being changes something in me. A few minutes of appreciating the many wonderful things in my life and this world, changes something in me. All these changes stack on top of each other and add up to a huge difference in who I am and how I feel each day of my life.

For many years, I did the opposite. I practiced fear, regret, and a feeling that I wasn't enough. I felt these things thousands of times as I went about my life. Just as with learning to play the piano or throw a ball, before long, my brain had learned how to create these emotions in me effortlessly. They became my default state. These emotions were what I felt when I woke up in the morning because that is how I had trained my body to feel. Then, I started to practice love, peace, gratitude, and worth, and my default changed. My life changed. Few things will change your life more than practicing positive emotions and making happiness a skill.

QUESTION

What would it cost you to spend ten minutes a day practicing emotions such as love, worth, and gratitude? And how would it affect your life if you started feeling these things every single day?

AUTHOR CONTACT INFORMATION

Greg Goddard, Founder of Happier You
Website: https://happieryouapp.com
Email: gregbgoddard@gmail.com
Social: https://www.instagram.com/happieryouapp/
Tags: Meditation Trainer, App Creator, Entrepreneur

August 25
TANNER SEEHAUSEN

To build, you must first destroy.

THOUGHT

To truly grow, we often need to dismantle our old thinking, much like tearing down an outdated structure to build something new. This process involves understanding the limitations of our established beliefs and embracing the discomfort of change.

Old thinking consists of the beliefs and assumptions formed through early experiences. These mental frameworks can confine us, limiting creativity and adaptability. For instance, rigid ideas about success can stifle innovation and prevent us from embracing risk.

The path to rising above our limitations involves the necessary destruction of old thinking. By engaging in self-reflection and embracing change, we create a foundation for innovation and authenticity. This ongoing journey not only enhances our own lives but can inspire those around us to pursue their growth as well.

QUESTION

Why do we look at destruction as a bad thing? It may be good, but could it be better?

AUTHOR CONTACT INFORMATION

Tanner Seehausen, CEO of Wrap Your Tip, LLC
Website: https://wrapyourtip.com
Email: wrapyourtip@gmail.com
Social: https://www.instagram.com/tipwrap/
Tags: Wound Care Inventor, Healthcare Entrepreneur

August 26
SHERRY ANSHARA

*"What I say makes my day, and
what I say can make or break someone else's day!"*

THOUGHT

Words exchange energy, thoughts, ideas, and connections; the difference is how words are spoken and shared with each other, including words spoken to our Selves! For example, at thirty, sharing with my mother and sister that I was going to learn how to fly an airplane… they said to me, "How can you fly a plane? You are a "girl and too old"? Oh my God, what an oxymoron!!!

No judgment of them by me! wow! This example is the difference between a supportive inquiry and a criticism of not being able to do something based on another person's idea of you! When it is really about their own inner limitations from their Belief Systems, Duality's B.S. It's not an inquiry, for sure!

So, I bought one! They said, "How did you buy a plane?" What!!! It's the same as buying a car or a home…so much down, and every month you get a bill. If you don't pay for it, they take it! I loved flying! Remember, do what your heart and intuition guide you to do, and your life will be filled with extraordinary doings leading to a feeling of abundance!

QUESTION

Do you know how powerful or depowering your words are from your inside out?

AUTHOR CONTACT INFORMATION

Sherry Anshara, Founder of Anshara Institute
Website: https://ansharainstitute.org/
Email: sherry@ansharainstitute.org
Social: https://www.facebook.com/AnsharaInstituteofAccelerateHealing
Tags: Medical Intuitive, Speaker, Author

August 27
NICOLA SMITH

*Hold the vision; trust the timing.
The course is already set.*

THOUGHT

In my own life, I've come to understand that abundance often takes time to manifest. It doesn't always happen as an instant shift but as a steady turn, like an immense ship slowly changing course. When I create a vision for my future—whether it's financial abundance or a more profound sense of fulfillment—I remind myself that the wheels have already been set in motion, even if my present reality doesn't fully reflect it yet.

There are moments when it feels like things have slowed down or even stalled. But just like a ship doesn't rush into a turn, I've learned not to rush the process. Instead, I hold the vision and trust in the unfolding. The key for me is to feel the abundance as though it's already here. I'm not waiting for it to arrive—it's already happening.

There are moments when I catch myself thinking, "This feels like my vision," as I notice small things that already carry the same feeling of abundance I've envisioned. By focusing on the wealth in my daily life—the richness of connection, growth, and opportunities—I align with the future I'm creating. The course is set, and I trust that abundance is finding its way to me, unfolding in its perfect timing.

QUESTION

What part of your life already feels aligned with your vision, and how can you keep that feeling close as the rest unfolds?

AUTHOR CONTACT INFORMATION

Nicola Smith, Founder of The Next Level 'training for the mind'
Website: https://thenextlevel.co.nz
Email: nicola@thenextlevel.co.nz
Social: https://www.linkedin.com/in/executive-coach-mindset
Tags: Mindset, Coach, High Performance, Speaker

The Art of Connection

August 28

RABEA KATHARINA STENGER

*Don't let anyone tell you something about you
that they don't know about themselves.
They can't know who you are, for they don't know who they are.*

THOUGHT

Have you ever felt like you are living "undercover" because you are so different from most of the people around you? You wish you could be yourself, but you are afraid they wouldn't understand or approve? Is there a voice inside of you bursting with passion, waiting to be expressed to the world?

During the past 15 years on my journey of becoming a conscious leader, I have discovered that the more you follow that quiet voice, the louder it becomes, and the better the ideas it brings you! It's like the voice wants to make sure it is heard and acted upon before it gives you the gold. You are spirit, and spirit is always for fuller expansion and expression. The world will reward you abundantly if you act in harmony with this fundamental law of creation.

My mission is to support millions of individuals in living the lives of their dreams because everyone deserves to live in abundance. My big why is to guide others in discovering their why - to accompany you on your way to closing the gap between who you were meant to be and who you are on the outside. Be brave enough to bring more of you to the table in a world that will do anything to distract you from who you were meant to be.

QUESTION

What do you want to be remembered for?

AUTHOR CONTACT INFORMATION

Rabea Katharina Stenger, Owner of RK Group - making the invisible visible
Website: https://www.rabea-katharina-stenger.de/en
Email: rabea.k.stenger@web.de
Social: https://www.instagram.com/rabea.katharina/profilecard/?igsh=MW5pYW42eWl1dHh5eg==
Tags: Artist, Success Advisor, Well-being Coach

August 29
CLIFFORD STARKS

True strength is firm yet flexible.

THOUGHT

I came up with this quote as a service to others because the depth of this lesson has positioned me to influence so many along the way. It is my hope that, as a leader, you focus on influencing others to reach new levels of potential while equally influencing yourself along the way.

Creating true strength through being both firm and flexible.

Strength isn't just about being unbreakable or standing rigidly in the face of challenges; it's about the ability to hold onto your core principles while remaining adaptable to change.

The firm aspect of strength embodies the unwavering commitment to our values, the resilience to keep pushing forward, and the courage to stay true to our path.

Yet, one of the greatest lessons I learned is that flexibility is equally crucial—it's the capacity to pivot when necessary, to listen, learn, and evolve without losing sight of our ultimate goals. For high-achieving entrepreneurs and business owners, mastering this flow is vital to sustainable success.

I hope this reflection serves as a reminder that true strength lies in the ability to be both steadfast and adaptable, empowering you to lead with both conviction and compassion.

QUESTION

What can you practice today with the intention of powerfully influencing your tribe?

AUTHOR CONTACT INFORMATION

Clifford Starks, Owner of Starks Enterprises
Website: https://thefightersformula.com
Email: cliffordstarks1@gmail.com
Social: https://www.linkedin.com/in/clifford-starks/
Tags: Speaker, Thought Leader, Coach, Hall of Famer

August 30
ALTHEA SAMUELS

Upgrading your mindset is like updating your software; an outdated mindset can't support the changes you need to level up in life.

THOUGHT

The insights we gain throughout life should guide our decisions to upgrade our mindset continuously. The way we think can impact our choices, from the people we associate with to the goals we set for ourselves. Our thoughts are the foundation of all we achieve or fail to achieve. So, when we choose to upgrade our thinking, we're choosing to open doors to new possibilities and align our actions with our purpose.

Reflecting on this, I remember when I upgraded my cell phone. It might seem minimal, but at that moment, I realized my old phone wasn't compatible with the apps and tools I needed. I had to let go of the past version to make room for what would serve me better in the present. Likewise, upgrading our mindset requires us to let go of outdated beliefs, habits, and fears. Just as a new phone can enable us to communicate and create in ways we couldn't before, a refreshed mindset allows us to tackle life's challenges and seize opportunities with renewed energy and focus. To upgrade our mindset, we must actively replace old ways of thinking with new ones. This choice includes adopting better habits and pursuing new ones. It means prioritizing the things that truly matter to us.

QUESTION

Consider your current mindset. What beliefs or habits do you feel may be outdated? If you had the opportunity to make a change in how you view or approach life, what would you focus on upgrading?

AUTHOR CONTACT INFORMATION

Althea Samuels, Owner of LeadSamuels
Website: www.leadsamuels.com
Email: nataanderson8@hotmail.com
Social: https://www.facebook.com/profile.php?id=61564310373180&sk=friends_likes
Tags: Online Digital Marketing Coach, Career Coach, Adult Educator

August 31
KARA ATKINSON

The "how" is the story we will tell afterward;
it was never meant to be used to look forward.

THOUGHT

So many people search for the "how" in life without considering that "how" is something that is actually revealed throughout life. We can make our plans, but God determines our steps. You only know how when you look back. God is walking with us, and our job is not to figure out the "how" but to keep our minds focused on the result we wish to manifest. The life we wish to live, then let God give us our story.

The journey will test your patience, faith, and perseverance, but every challenge is preparation for the blessing ahead. Trust that every delay, detour, and disappointment is part of a greater plan. When you surrender control, you open yourself to possibilities far beyond what you could have imagined. Your story isn't random; it is divinely orchestrated. Stay steadfast in your vision, and remember that the "how" isn't your burden to carry. Your only duty is to believe, take inspired action, and stay aligned with purpose. The "how" will be revealed when you need it most.

QUESTION

What results are you focused on manifesting now, and can you see "how" it is unfolding already?

AUTHOR CONTACT INFORMATION

Kara Atkinson, Founder and Managing Director of Liquid Gold Capital
Website: www.liquidgoldcapital.com
Email: invest@liquidgoldk.com
Social: https://www.linkedin.com/in/karaatkinson
Tags: International Financer, Private Money Expert

September 1

PAT YOUNG

I am grateful for all the Abundance that has already been given in the past, as well as the time yet to come.

THOUGHT

UNIVERSAL ABUNDANCE

Come, bathe with Us In the infinite waters of Universal abundance.
We join you in the comfort of these calming waters.
Cup your hands and drink in these healing droplets
Allow them to wash all ills from your Sweet Being.
Come, splash the clear, soothing liquid over you.
Stand with us, arms outstretched,
Beneath the ceaseless cascade of great abundance.
It offers Unlimited wealth:
The wealth of unending love, of all-available goods,
Of heart-warming laughter, of fulfilling friendship.
The wealth of jobs well done, of family's strong ties,
Of unquestioning faith, of purposes fulfilled.
The wealth of lessons quickly learned, of lives being touched,
Of holy encounters, of soothing silence.
The wealth of closeness with Peace within,
And of quietness and meditation.
Step out of these waters and know that we are truly blessed
With Universal abundance as our own.
These waters have enhanced our drab, everyday life,
And elevated us to be abundant beyond comparison.
This directive assures us that as we walk through our lives
We are capable of Having all...Within the all.

QUESTION

Gratitude is the basis of Joy. Can you imagine all things coming to you easily and effortlessly from unforeseen sources?

AUTHOR CONTACT INFORMATION

Pat Young, Ph.D. Founder, Transpersonal Psychologist of A Place of Peace
Website: https://www.365daysofabundancequotes.com
Email: pyoung4099@aol.com
Social: https://mybook.to/artofconnection5
Tags: Psychologist, Counselor, Speaker, Class Director

September 2

IRA ROSEN

The most powerful thing in the universe is mind clarity. Once we discover what we want, we need to commit to excellence and whatever it takes.

THOUGHT

Over the centuries, people have asked one question: What is my most significant power?

It's not power over others. Power over others is weakness disguised as strength.

Your most significant power is more extraordinary; it's your power to choose. The choices we make consciously and unconsciously affect our daily lives, relationships, and health.

Choose not to live in fear; fear shuts us down and overwhelms us. Fear robs us of confidence and peace of mind. Is fear renting space in your head? Evict it.

Replace fear with gratitude. Reflect on what you have to be grateful for and how little you need for a fulfilling life.

Eliminate negative self-talk. Choose to be kinder to yourself. Choose to nourish your mind and soul daily with positive thoughts, healthy food, and an attitude of gratitude.

Create a daily routine that makes you feel fabulous. We need this like oxygen. Choose to laugh. Laughter is like taking a five-minute vacation. Choose to look for the best in others.

Choose to celebrate your wins every day, big or small. Our lives are the sum of the choices we make. Choose gratitude, love, and happiness, and always remember that your most significant power is your power to choose.

QUESTION

Today, what will you choose?

AUTHOR CONTACT INFORMATION

Ira Rosen, Co-Founder of Mojo Global
Website: https://mojoglobal.com
Email: ira@mojoglobal.com
Social: https://www.linkedin.com/in/ira-rosen/
Tags: Globally Recognized Motivational Speaker

September 3
KYLAH WAITS

Encouraging young people to do acts of service and kindness will bring about an abundance of joy and love into our world for generations to come.

THOUGHT

Love and happiness are the most abundantly rewarding components of life. At fifteen years old, I am a high school freshman. Being involved in countless activities, such as giving back to my community, non-profit service, and helping out, are very important to me. Even though giving is fulfilling, the most crucial part or lesson to me is teaching younger students and kids that giving to others is more valuable than earning money.

Teaching youth about giving back is essential because kindness goes a long way and changes our world into a better place. I was accepted into the National Junior Honor Society, which includes helping in numerous community services and events. Lots of services and activities come along, and sometimes, these things can get boring when I am doing them by myself.

Working together with friends is more fun and easier than doing things alone. I plan to continue with service in the future because even though I don't get paid, it's still rewarding to make other people happy. In the end, true happiness isn't bought with money; it comes from being of aid to others and experiencing their joy and happiness from your service.

QUESTION

What young people in your life could you encourage to become involved in doing acts of service in their schools, church, community, or families and who do you think this would impact the most?

AUTHOR CONTACT INFORMATION

Kylah Waits, Social Media Director of Starlit Grace
Website: https://www.nurtureourworld.net
Email: kylaughs2much0@gmail.com
Social: https://www.instagram.com/_starlitgrace/
Tags: Custom-made jewelry and rosaries

September 4
LAURA PIEL

Acknowledgment gives voice and viability to another.

THOUGHT

Have you ever had the experience of not being acknowledged – even just your physical presence: Greeting someone who looked past you, approaching a group of people, and being ignored?

Of course, this can happen without intention. Earbuds, for example. Or people so caught up in their thoughts and interactions that they don't see, hear, or acknowledge you.

The root words combined 550 years ago to make the word Acknowledge include Recognize, Discover, and Reveal. Acknowledging, then, is more than seeing. It is seeing that you learned and saying what you learned.

Acknowledgment can be quiet and still – a nod, a glance.

Acknowledgment can be physical – a hug, a touch to the shoulder, applause.

Acknowledgment can be verbal – giving voice to the contribution of the other.

Acknowledgment can be respectful – offering one point of view and recognizing someone else's.

Acknowledgment can express thanks – recognizing the contribution another makes.

Acknowledgment is powerful. It is a vehicle to connect. It lets others know they are seen and understood.

When you acknowledge someone, you give them both a personal building block and a blessing for their well-being.

QUESTION

Who will you acknowledge today?

AUTHOR CONTACT INFORMATION

Laura Piel, President of Renaissance Personnel Group
Website: http://www.renaissancepersonnel.com
Email: Laura@jobsinarizona.com
Social: https://www.linkedin.com/in/laurapiel
Tags: Executive Search, Temporary Staffing

September 5
ANNIE DECKERT

Ditch food stress & scale drama!
Adulting = freedom (even if you burn dinner).

THOUGHT

Growing up, I struggled with body image and feeling comfortable in my skin. Despite achieving professional success, I couldn't find sustainability for my weight and relationship with food. I tried every fad diet imaginable, but the cycle of yo-yo dieting left me feeling defeated.

In 2020, I decided to stop letting the scale define my worth and learn about nutrition. I learned to fuel my body correctly, ditch the "all-or-nothing" mentality, and started making minor changes. This shift changed my life, and I knew I wanted to help others.

I became a certified nutrition coach and found my passion in helping people heal their relationship with food and change their bodies for good. My tailored approach goes beyond weight loss; it helps individuals develop a healthy lifestyle, improve their metabolism, and heal their relationship with food.

There's no greater satisfaction than helping others experience the joy of living a healthy, fulfilling life. I believe in you, and I'm here to support you on your journey.

QUESTION

Do you let the number on the scale dictate your mood?
Do you experience food "guilt" and find yourself always committing to "starting Monday"? Are you ready to positively change your life for good?

AUTHOR CONTACT INFORMATION

Annie Deckert, CEO, Founder of All Day Coach
Website: www.allday.coach
Email: annie@alldaycos.com
Social: www.instagram.com/alldaycoach
Tags: Nutrition Coach, Health and Wellness Coach

September 6

CRYSTAL D. TURNER-MOFFATT

*Your birthright of abundance is in your DNA.
Unlocking your unique access code will lead you to a life of abundance and success!*

THOUGHT

In a conversation with a wise elder, I was asked what I wanted in life. I said abundance in all areas of life: My Spirit, mind, health, marriage, family, business, community, and the world. They asked me, "Crystal, would you say oceans are abundant in the world? I said knowingly yes, of course. What about people? I said, "Yes, of course, knowing there are billions of people." What about money in all its forms? I said, "Yes, money is in abundance."

They responded next and said something so profound. "Crystal, there is abundance all around you. In all forms, you have abundance; what you do not have is access." They said, "With access to the abundance in the universe, you will be known, sought after, and in demand!" That encounter changed my life and mindset from one of lack to one of abundance. I now appreciate my core DNA and accomplished self.

I am present to the glass as half-full as opposed to half-empty, with an optimistic outlook and a fulfilled life. I don't have to do anything else in life; it is what I get to do by divine choice. To unlock your unique abundance and your birthright, access your unique divine gifts that are born out of what's in your core DNA and follow your purpose.

QUESTION

Is your DNA coded for abundance? What purpose is driving you toward an abundant future? What is available to you through accessing the power stored within your unique DNA, unlocking your abundance?

AUTHOR CONTACT INFORMATION

Crystal D. Turner-Moffatt, CEO CDT EHS Consulting LLC.
Website: https://www.safetydiva.org
Email: crystaldturner@cdtehsconsultingllc.com
Social: Crystal D. Turner-Moffatt's Blinq Card
Tags: Speaker, Coach, Safety SME, Consultant, Advocate

September 7

UCHENNA FAUMUINA-EZE

*Abundance isn't something to chase;
it's something to uncover and share.*

THOUGHT

Growing up as a military brat, I often didn't get all I desired. We moved regularly, and I had to leave behind sentimental possessions. Nonetheless, my parents consistently reminded me that I had more than enough. They taught me that true abundance is found within ourselves rather than in material possessions. I lost my father when he was 35, but what he instilled in me and our family will last forever.

The secret to abundance is realizing that we have all we really need already. It's about realizing that our relationships, talents, and knowledge are worth more than anything we could buy. Realizing this allows us to share our innate richness with others and experience profound fulfillment, giving our lives significance as well as direction. Trusting in what we already have inside and letting it shine is the genuine source of wealth—an inner treasure that can never be taken away.

QUESTION

How can you find the special things you already have inside you? What are some ways you can share your strengths with others?

AUTHOR CONTACT INFORMATION

Uchenna Faumuina-Eze Founder -CEO of We Speak Media
Website: https://wespeakmedia.org/
Email: wespeakdaily247@gmail.com
Social: https://www.linkedin.com/in/uchenna-faumuina-eze-ms-mat-43529815/
Tags: Speaker, WeSpeakMedia, Afakasi, Mental Health

September 8
TINA KOOPERSMITH

Dis-ease is not a sign that our bodies are broken but rather a nudge from our bodies to push us to live more in alignment with our true nature.

THOUGHT

Reality exists in perception. While we see ourselves as physical matter, Einstein's $E=MC^2$ reminds us that matter is simply energy vibrating at a slower frequency. Our eyes perceive this energy as a physical form, but when we tune in, our ears, hearts, and minds sense the energetic vibrations that define us.

What's more, our bodies are ecosystems: a symbiosis of the trillions of microbiome cells that outnumber and cohabitate with our human cells. Dis-ease in the body, then, might be the language of this complex ecosystem—a way for the microbiome to communicate with the human brain. It often begins as a whisper, a subtle gut instinct nudging us to change, evolve, and realign our thoughts, emotions, and habits so we can fulfill the needs of our human as well as the microbial and energetic communities within us.

Reconceptualizing dis-ease as a nudge rather than a flaw and reimagining ourselves as beings of energy, interconnected with everything on this planet invites us to explore new ways of being—ways that honor the symbiotic relationship between humans, our microbiome, and the world we inhabit. What if we began living not just for human desires but for the joy and balance of all?

QUESTION

What if we could, in this present moment, remember ourselves home? Truly, we are the entire universe, embodied in human form.

AUTHOR CONTACT INFORMATION

Tina Koopersmith, Founder and Medical Director of West Coast Women's Reproductive Center

Website: https://womensreproduction.com

Email: drtinacoaches@gmail.com

Social: https://www.linkedin.com/in/tina-koopersmith-13585823/

Tags: Transformation Coach, Speaker, Author, Physician

The Art of Connection

September 9

DANIEL PEDEMONTE

*We're all storytellers and creators.
The stories we tell ourselves, good or bad, are the foundation
of the destiny we're in the process of creating.*

THOUGHT

"Fire is a gift from the Great Spirit," the old woman said to the boy as they sat by the bonfire watching the flames; "it symbolizes His presence here on earth. It is there, but we cannot touch it, yet it touches us with its warmth and light. We have some of that same power, a light that shines within us and dwells in our thoughts, our words, and the stories we tell ourselves. It is through them, through those stories, that we mold that power and give it shape, either constructive or destructive, to create our destiny. Did you know that?"

He didn't, of course. His eyes were opened in amazement, really wanting to understand. The old woman nodded kindly.

The boy spent a while feeding the fire with sticks and branches that caused a delightful dance of sparkles flying towards the already darkening sky. As he watched them merging with the stars above, the old woman added something else:

"That power is bound by an immutable law, though, an irresistible need to remain consistent with those stories we tell ourselves.

Be mindful of that. Create a good story for yourself, offer it to the fire, and let the spiraling sparks carry it along with them, knowing it will find its way back to you."

QUESTION

*We are all storytellers, and we are all creators, so what kind of
story are you going to tell yourself? What kind of destiny are you going to start
creating today? Make it a good one.*

AUTHOR CONTACT INFORMATION

Daniel Pedemonte Owner, Author, Writer of Delta Charles Inspirational Writer
Website: http://www.deltacharleswriter.com
Email: contact@deltacharleswriter.com
Social: https://www.facebook.com/DeltaCharlesWriter/
Tags: Writer, Storyteller, Creative Director, Designer

September 10
MAURICE MONTOYA

Think abundantly; don't allow limited thinking to change your mindset, as those who think abundantly have a better chance to attract a lot more.

THOUGHT

When we think abundantly, some may interpret it initially as monetary wealth or materialism. In this context, it would make sense to explore other possibilities and a way for us to imagine the possibilities of opening new doors through a new way of thinking through abundance.

Abundance could be a way to attract anything you set your mind to, for those who think any less will most likely experience the least desired result. While this can be rather philosophical and help explain positive thinking in this regard, the meaning perhaps could be from that well-known saying, "What we put out there is what we get back," in layman's terms.

When thinking about how one can be abundant in a role or circumstance, especially when one is lacking something to make it all happen, abundance could be represented in a situation that is full of new ideas, aspirations, goals, or even gratitude; in other words, whatever comes to mind. I believe that once we allow ourselves to think abundantly, there will be a better outcome by simply focusing and thinking about what is crucial for us to accomplish.

Allowing ourselves to think abundantly could change the way we think to make it all possible.

QUESTION

In what ways can this message help overcome daily challenges? How can you share your abundance with others? What areas can you improve when thinking through abundance? How relevant is this to you?

AUTHOR CONTACT INFORMATION

Maurice Montoya, President, CEO and Founder of Kreo Solutions
Website: https://kreo.co
Email: maurice.montoya@kreo.co
Social: https://www.linkedin.com/in/maurice-montoya
Tags: Entrepreneur, Author, Advisor, IT Professional

September 11

MARIS SEGAL

We're All Connected As Humans First & The Bottom Line Begins with Relationships - How We Choose to Relate Daily Determines What We Create Daily!

THOUGHT

The 9/11 terrorist attack is etched on the hearts and minds of the world, especially those who lost loved ones and friends. This tragic "choice" of terrorism changed life in a moment and connected humanity in unprecedented ways.

That day, I arrived at my midtown NY office, suitcase and backpack in hand, ready for a 2-week vacation with friends. My client joined our weekly call apologetically late to say a plane "hit" the tower next to hers. Together, we watched the live news: Two World Trade Center towers crumbled, and people jumped to their deaths. It seemed like a horror movie. I had just been at the WTC the day prior!

Thousands of New Yorkers filled the streets, bonded in eerie silence. I felt gratitude for living and profound sadness, thinking of lost generations: pregnant mothers who would later explain to their children who their fathers were. In those hours crossing Manhattan, I made new friends.

I chose to turn my vacation into volunteerism and my backpack into hope. I was blessed to serve the recovery and healing efforts. Through collective anger and mourning of the loss of life rose heart-centered action – uniting strangers who chose to be in service to and with each other.

QUESTION

What choices and committed actions are you taking today to connect and relate in a way that builds confident relationships and collaboration with your team at home and work?

AUTHOR CONTACT INFORMATION

Maris Segal, CEO and Founder of Segal Leadership Global
Website: www.SegalLeadershipGlobal.com
Email: msegal@segalleadershipglobal.com
Social: https://www.instagram.com/_the_rfactor/
Tags: TEDx Speaker, Relational Leadership Coach, Author

September 12
ROBERT THORNTON

*Abundance must be found in
the heart before it has meaning.*

THOUGHT

We spend our entire lives looking in all of the wrong places for abundance; it is within us all of the time. God gave us abundance through our creation, and we can only ruin it or throw it away from that point on. Regardless of what Creator you believe in, you have value by simply "being."

Oh, sure, we live and die through comparison, anchoring our self-worth on a pecking order we can never hope to control or conquer. Does it genuinely matter if we have more than our neighbor, our peers, or that pesky bully from high school? I seem to remember being taught that "You can't take it with you" is central to the issue of abundance, alongside, "If you got it, life can seem better, but it is always more complex." So, before you waste more time chasing "things," look inside your heart and take a good measure of yourself, the people around you, and the relationships you embrace. I'll bet you will find more abundance than you can spend in your lifetime.

QUESTION

Have you thought about how much abundance your closest friends and associates bring to your life? Shouldn't you?

AUTHOR CONTACT INFORMATION

Robert Thornton, IT Director of Fighters for Hope
Website: https://www.fightersforhope.org
Email: robert82382@gmail.com
Social: https://www.facebook.com/robert.thornton.58/
Tags: IT, Advocate for Suicide Prevention, Photographer

September 13

CHAR MCCREADIE

*This day, this life - it's a gift.
That is why it's called The Present.*

THOUGHT

Thoughts and conversations on the topic of abundance many times center around material things, such as financial wealth, property, vehicles, and so on. In today's world, it is very easy to get caught up in that energy and the associated emotions/thoughts.

I have been just as guilty as any myself. While, many times, my physical and emotional body wants to play in this sandbox, I have learned to stop, take as many deep breaths as necessary, and then step forward. Two life-threatening events and their associated heavenly experiences were the perfect impetus for this new thought process and change of perspective on life and abundance.

Abundance - You and I are that. Everything needed to experience abundant life is already present. Imagine the most beautifully exquisite gift ever seen. All of the glitter radiating, the flowing ribbon that comes to the peak of a bow on top of the gift, the vibrant colors, the crisp edges of the wrapping, pristine on every corner ... see its full beauty in your mind's eye. that, my friend, is how The Creator gave you The Gift of Life and exactly why it's called The Present. Abundantly flowing daily in the presence with others.

QUESTION

*"What intention will you set to keep the abundant
gift of life front and center for you daily?"*

AUTHOR CONTACT INFORMATION

Char McCreadie, Owner and Founder of Fly Far With Char
Website: https://www.FlyFarWithChar.com
Email: char@flyfarwithchar.com
Social: https://www.facebook.com/charmccreadie
Tags: Speaker, Travel, Wellness, Coach, Digital Marketer

September 14
MATTIE MURREY

A book isn't just words on a page – it's your legacy, a story that will live on long after you've written the final chapter.

THOUGHT

Friends don't let friends write bad books. Our mission at My Own Ghostwriter is to write excellent books because we believe that skillfully sharing our stories with others is one of the most powerful ways to make a lasting impact. If you want to be seen as a leader and a trusted source of knowledge, write a book.

That's because a book has the incredible potential to inspire readers, build connections, and remind people they are not alone. It's an opportunity to invite others to learn from you and see the world from a new perspective.

Know that every book begins with a single idea. Start by jotting down your ideas, and those ideas will naturally begin to form chapters. Soon, those chapters will form an outline, and then you will be ready to begin writing. Don't worry about perfection; focus on getting your story out, one idea at a time. Embrace the process, trust yourself, and take that first step—your book is waiting to be written.

Writing a book is about more than just the end result—it's about the journey and the legacy you leave behind. At My Own Ghostwriter, we're here to help and offer done-for-you, done-with-you, and DIY programs. Let's work together to write an excellent book!

QUESTION

If you could write a book that would inspire or impact your world, what would you write about?

AUTHOR CONTACT INFORMATION

Mattie Murrey, Owner/Founder of My Own Ghostwriter
Website: www.myownghostwriter.com
Email: mattiemurrey.tegels@gmail.com
Social: https://www.linkedin.com/in/myownghostwriter/
Tags: Ghostwriter, Book Coach, Creator, Editor, Speaker

September 15

RIZAH VALDEZ

The definition and manifestation of abundance in one's life depends on the perspective of the one defining it.

THOUGHT

Abundance is accessible everywhere. Wherever you look, there's an abundance of good as well as not-so-good. It's how you see and where you look. It is not limited to what each person has or what one lacks. And though it fulfills needs, it is not confined to money matters alone. Valuable virtues like love, joy, and peace of mind are as essential to have in abundance as their monetary counterpart.

Abundance is unique to everyone. Different individuals differ in their views, mindsets, and choices. Each choice is directly proportional to the input and the output. Each of us chooses what we value, what we work on, and so forth. It is best to focus on working toward your desired outcome. You are accountable for everything you have in abundance, so take a conscious note of what you already have. Decide what you want to keep and let go of the non-essentials.

QUESTION

How do you define abundance?

AUTHOR CONTACT INFORMATION

Rizah Divah A. Valdez, CEO, Founder of Winning Tandem LLC
Website: https://www.winningtandem.com/
Email: winningtandem@gmail.com
Social: https://www.facebook.com/profile.php?id=61551912626526
Tags: Winning, Tandem, Legacy, Abundance, Growth Mindset

September 16
AYDEN VANWIE-HAMERIA

*Abundance isn't what you store;
it's about what you offer.*

THOUGHT

When I say, 'Abundance isn't about what you store; it's about what you offer,' I'm reflecting on a lesson I've learned over the past year about what true richness really means. People often connect abundance with accumulating more—whether it's money, possessions, or achievements. But I've discovered that genuine abundance isn't about what we have; it's about what we share with others. It's found in the time, kindness, and appreciation we give to the world around us.

The more I give, the more fulfilled I feel, even though I'm not receiving anything material in return. Offering help, support, or simply kindness costs me nothing, but it adds immeasurable value to my life. I've realized that abundance multiplies when we pay it forward. True richness isn't about collecting things or wealth—it's about being generous with what we already have and sharing it with those around us. That's what natural abundance is all about.

QUESTION

*What Abundance have you been storing in your life
that you are willing to share with others?*

AUTHOR CONTACT INFORMATION

Ayden VanWie-Hameria, Student
Website: https://365daysofabundancequotes.com
Email: gibby5708@gmail.com
Social: https://mybook.to/artofconnection5
Tags: Student, Speaker, Baseball Player

September 17

STUART GETHNER

The quotation that I have submitted is my own and not from anyone else or any other source.

THOUGHT

Thought....A few months ago, I went to a department store to buy a scarf for my wife. The lady behind the counter didn't notice me at first. When I called her attention, she reluctantly came over, making me feel like I was inconveniencing her. I asked for advice on the scarves, and though she was honest, she wasn't very friendly. After choosing a scarf, she helped me check out and said, "Thank you, have a nice day," without much enthusiasm. As I left, the manager asked if everything was okay. When I asked why, she explained, "The lady's mother passed away last week, and she's working extra shifts to help pay for the funeral."

It is impossible to know the whole story, or perhaps the backstory, of everyone we interact with daily. Unless they are willing to share, perhaps we give them an abundance of our grace to uplift them.

QUESTION

Should another person's challenges and attitude affect your day?

AUTHOR CONTACT INFORMATION

Stuart Gethner, CEO of Gethner Education & Consulting
Website: https://stuartgethner.com/
Email: stuart@stuartgethner.com
Social: https://www.linkedin.com/in/stuartgethner/
Tags: Real Estate Investing, Create Wealth, Wealth

September 18
KIMBERLY LECHNICK

*Abundance flows where gratitude and love meet,
reminding us that everything we need is already within reach.*

THOUGHT

Our yearly family tradition took us back to the heart of downtown Chicago, where we opened the holiday with shopping and dining at the iconic Walnut Room. As we weaved in and out of stores, laughter flowed easily between us. Besides the joy, part of our tradition was giving back. We'd made it a mission to share our blessings with those we met along the way because giving felt like the truest spirit of the season.

At one point, while trying to keep warm and make it to our next stop, something unexplainable happened. Without hesitation, I entered a market and bought a sub sandwich, some fresh fruit, and a tall bottle of cold water. It felt instinctual, a calling I couldn't ignore. As I handed it to a stranger while smiling, his face awoke with surprise and hope, as if in disbelief. "Is this really for me?" I said, "Of course. We wanted to bless you today."

He shared that he had been there for two weeks, all alone, without notice. My heart sank as I thought, "Imagine two weeks of feeling invisible." As he shared, he asked if I could touch his hand, as if needing the reassurance of human connection. Never assume abundance is universal, and remember this tale when you see those in need.

That experience left an imprint on my heart, a reminder that kindness isn't about grand gestures—it's about being present, being willing to connect, and letting love and gratitude guide us. The holidays can be a whirlwind, but that day, we were reminded that sometimes the most meaningful moments are the ones we didn't plan, the ones that call us to step outside ourselves and simply care.

QUESTION

When thinking of this story, will you remember that kindness isn't about grand gestures, that kindness is being the human connection and sharing your abundance unconditionally?

AUTHOR CONTACT INFORMATION

Kimberly Lechnick, Relationship Coach at Intentional Pathways by Design
Website: https://intentionalpathwaysbydesign.com
Email: klechnickk@gmail.com
Social: https://linktr.ee/kimberlylechnick
Tags: Empowerment, Relationship Coach

The Art of Connection

September 19

LEONARD DECARMINE

The man who learns to embrace abundance will live a full life of experiences, relationships, and personal growth.

THOUGHT

What if genuine abundance isn't about what you own but how you live? Consider the man who sees abundance in all things and does all he can to maximize his life experience.

He fills his hours not just doing what he already knows but also learning new hobbies, reading new books, and traveling to new places. Each adventure adds another layer to his life, filled with new experiences and knowledge.

He forgoes the usual networking for personal gain and instead invests in relationships rooted in authenticity and genuineness. He spends time with his family and lifts those in his circle, supporting and challenging them to improve. He serves his community by offering help and finds joy and a sense of belonging that fills a different kind of tank that money can't buy.

A man of abundance never settles for what he already knows how to do; he always looks for ways to do it better with an open mind. He continually challenges himself to move beyond his limits to evolve and grow. Such a man cannot just exist; he must thrive.

A man who learns to embrace abundance demonstrates that life is much more than things; it is a way of thinking and living that results in a more meaningful and fulfilling life.

QUESTION

What is one small change you can make today to start living a more abundant life?

AUTHOR CONTACT INFORMATION

Leonard DeCarmine, Founder & CEO of The Mindful Man Method of The Mindful Man Method

Website: https://www.mindfulmanmethod.com

Email: len@mindfulmanmethod.com

Social: https://www.mindfulmanmethod.com/connect

Tags: Men's Coach, Facilitator, Author, Speaker

September 20
FERNANDO SANCHEZ

Adjust and pivot to the changes around us, no matter the circumstances. Be willing to change our attitudes to embrace the growth that comes from it.

THOUGHT

Take the example of a Coyote or Jackrabbit- they have learned to adjust and pivot to the changing circumstances of their environment.

As we learn and move forward in life, we can realize that there's no comfort in the growth zone and no growth in the comfort zone. So, never give up and never surrender to moving forward.

Do it with a positive attitude and ask, "What can I learn?" Smile the whole while, especially when it's hard!

QUESTION

How can we adjust to changes in our lives, relationships & businesses?

AUTHOR CONTACT INFORMATION

Fernando Sanchez, Founder of Color Pros/Nu-Clear
Website: https://www.365daysofabundancequotes.com
Email: kolorprosink@gmail.com
Social: https://mybook.to/artofconnection5
Tags: Business Owner, Leader, Innovator, Instructor

September 21

ANNETTE DERNICK

Every kind word contributes to the well-being and peace of us all, just as every plastic bag saved contributes to the well-being of our planet.

THOUGHT

Peace evolves when we stop fighting. This line was a sentence that I wrote on one of my drawings during the time I spent in some clinics where I found out that my burnout was related to the traumatic experiences of my parents during wartime.

Working in and with different companies and organizations, I have experienced situations that were not very peaceful.

Where does peace start?

It starts within me. How do I treat me? Am I my best critic? How do I start my day? With a grumpy face that stares at me in the mirror? Or do I greet myself with a broad smile and look eagerly forward to my day?

The good thing is I can always change my thoughts every second if I want to. The only person who can do this is me.

Peace starts with my thoughts. It doesn't mean neglecting conflicts, as they can lead to a new level of understanding and cooperation when we resolve them positively and constructively.

So much is possible with thoughts of appreciation and peace!

It is so easy to bring more peace into this world. I can start with myself at any time. This choice has a positive effect on my surroundings, including the companies and organizations in which we work, as well as on our environment.

QUESTION

What do you contribute to peace every day? Within you? In your surroundings? For the environment? Peace starts with me and then continues on the outside, in my surroundings, my environment.

AUTHOR CONTACT INFORMATION

Annette Dernick, Owner of Love & Peace in Companies
Website: www.dernick.eu
Email: info@dernick.eu
Social: https://www.linkedin.com/in/AnnetteDernick
Tags: Speaker, Coach, Author

September 22
MYRA MURPHY

Today is my calling; tomorrow is its reflection; abundance is embedded within it.

THOUGHT

Yesterday, the sticky notes on my fridge written to myself months ago, renewed my strength for a new day. Owning its truth of abundance allowed me to move forward.

An executive. A lover of nature and art. A mother. A woman of Faith. Through many facets of myself, I face the opportunity to orchestrate my presence in today-each thought, word, and action. I see today, the present, as a vast array of individuals, thoughts, actions, reactions, and choices melting together to create the next moment, minute, hour, and day, writing history and molding tomorrow. How I conduct today, inward and outward, has a direct effect on my tomorrow.

Who I choose to be today is not intended to restrict myself but instead to compose with intention each moment with its emotions, strengths, weaknesses, growth, and sometimes setbacks. All this combined creates true life, contentment, and wholeness of all so graciously given. It has a direct effect on how I treat myself and others, its impact or the lack thereof on our present and future, be it an environment, a culture, a people, a faith, or all the combined to create a fulfilling and abundant space on earth.

Today, I choose lasting wholeness and abundance.

QUESTION

What version of tomorrow are you orchestrating today? What truth is allowing you to choose the abundance within and around you?

AUTHOR CONTACT INFORMATION

Myra Murphy, Author
Website: https://myradawn.com
Email: myradawn1@yahoo.com
Social: https://www.linkedin.com/in/myra-murphy-552945a/
Tags: Executive, Christian, Author, Survivor

September 23

DEBORAH KYM

With each exhale, release doubt; with each inhale, allow for infinite possibility, and you will know that abundance is who you genuinely are!

THOUGHT

I have learned that the most potent measure of where we are along our Abundance Path is expressed in the way we breathe. If we are not consistently exhaling and inhaling like the ebb and flow of the ocean, we are not fulfilling our potential. Each exhale has the potential of letting go of what is blocking our fulfillment.

With each inhale, we have the potential to amplify our magnificent light. When we shift from fear to infinite possibility, we let go of the thoughts spinning in our reptilian brain, which keep us running from the proverbial saber-toothed tiger, and align our mind-body-spirit to harness the potential power of a thousand suns. We no longer focus on scarcity, which teaches our bodies to fight, take flight, freeze, or feign in the prison of hopelessness. We trust the universe, without a doubt, and go wherever our inner GPS calls us to be. Wherever that is, it will inevitably lead us, and those we are here to serve, to our true potential and guide us to fulfill our destiny.

QUESTION

If we believed at our core that we were an infinite light source sent here for the purpose of connecting others to their abundance frequency and, therefore, connect to our own, what would that change?

AUTHOR CONTACT INFORMATION

Deborah Kym, Founder of The Deborah Kym Studio
Website: https://AmplifyYourMagnificence.com
Email: TheDeborahKymStudio@gmail.com
Social: https://instagram.com/thedeborahkymstudio
Tags: Performance Coach, Speaker, Director, Author

September 24
NATHALIE BOTROS

*Infuse your life with abundance,
and watch your happiness multiply!*

THOUGHT

When you center your life around abundance, you're making a conscious decision to focus on the positive, on growth, and on the endless possibilities that surround you. This choice isn't just about material wealth; it's about creating your perfect "Happiness Cocktail." It also means recognizing the richness of your relationships, investing in the opportunities that knock on your door, and enjoying every day of your life.

Shifting your mindset to abundance will naturally attract more of it into your life. Because the energy you put out - whether it's through your thoughts, actions, or words - has a powerful impact on what you receive. When you genuinely believe that there is more than enough for everyone, you start to see opportunities where others see obstacles.

You begin to experience growth in areas where you once felt stuck. Roll up your sleeves and start mixing your happiness cocktail by making abundance your foundation, and watch as it continues to grow, flourish, and enrich every aspect of your life.

QUESTION

What if focusing on abundance was the shortcut to living your best, most joyful life and creating the perfect Happiness Cocktail?

AUTHOR CONTACT INFORMATION

Nathalie Botros, Founder of The Bon-Vivant girl
Website: https://www.thebon-vivantgirl.com/
Email: nat@thebon-vivantgirl.com
Social: https://www.instagram.com/thebon_vivantgirl/
Tags: Psychotherapist, Author, Speaker, Mindset Coach

The Art of Connection

September 25

NICO STRINGFELLOW

Some Will, Some Won't. So What, Someone's Waiting!

THOUGHT

This quote is more than a mantra—it's a mindset. In business, rejection isn't failure; it's a filter. Every "no" clears the path for the right "yes." Imagine this: someone, somewhere, is yearning for the solution only you can provide. They're silently waiting, hoping for the moment your message crosses their path. Will you let "no" stop you from reaching them?

The truth is, every time you hear "no," you're one step closer to the person who's ready to say "yes." Hold the unshakeable belief that your voice matters, your work has purpose, and your mission is meaningful. Let rejection motivate you, not derail you. Keep going because someone out there is counting on you to show up. So push forward. Speak louder. Share unapologetically. Because your program, your product, and your passion could be the very answer they've been waiting for.

QUESTION

What will you be thanking yourself for six months from today?

AUTHOR CONTACT INFORMATION

Dr. Nico Stringfellow, CEO of The Architect Academy
Website: https://www.thearchitectacademy.com
Email: DrNico@TheArchitectAcademy.com
Social: https://www.facebook.com/nico.stringfellow
Tags: Speaker, Life and Business Coach, Author, Trainer

September 26
SATIE NARAIN-SIMON

It's All About Love.

THOUGHT

"It's All About Love" is a term loosely used; however, I genuinely believe that love is the key to everything, contributing to making our world a better place. The journey begins within. By loving ourselves, by truly loving the "I" that resides in the silence within is love. Loving ourselves exactly the way we are, with all our imperfections. We were all born with this inherent grace, but somehow, along life's journey, it got displaced for many of us at some point in time.

To get there, one must develop habits, using tools such as spiritual practice, practicing gratitude, laughter, the mirror technique, and kindness.
Tools must be used diligently and consistently. The result is accessing our superpowers of self-confidence, self-esteem, and strength, and no desire for external validation, thus resulting in loving the "I."

When one loves self, then we have the capacity to extend love to others: the animals, the trees, and our planet, thus contributing to making our world a better place.

QUESTION

Are you in Love with "I"?

AUTHOR CONTACT INFORMATION

Satie Narain-Simon, Founder of SNS - Powered by Love
Website: www.itsallaboutlove.ca
Email: satiesimon@gmail.com
Social: https://www.linkedin.com/in/satie-narain-simon-20ab5a135
Tags: Speaker, Coach, Retreats, Tax Auditor

September 27

KATHI HALL

*One needs only to invest in others
to realize true Abundance.*

THOUGHT

I sit, fingers poised on the keyboard, struggling to begin. Seeking inspiration, I reference the definition: "To have more than you need." Closing my eyes, I search for the memory, but my mind is blank. I didn't expect that.

Feeling disturbed, I searched through my childhood to a time when I was free to dream, unhindered by reality. But time brought awareness and disappointment as I watched others with more, bigger, and better things. My childhood dreams were set aside as I weathered the reality of life and loss.

I dig deeper still, certain there's more, and I find it. One by one, familiar faces drift into view, a gentle overlay to those memories…my parents, my sisters, my sweet children, my Love. The echo of laughter brings relief and hope. Friends, colleagues, and clients appear, reminding me that joy comes with walking beside them. Each one has touched my heart, and I, theirs.

So, you see, Abundance was always there…in the cumulative effort of investing in others, as pebbles dropped in water, the ripples expanding gently to infinity. The richness of relationships brings connection, love, and joy. There's no scarcity in that – I've always had more than enough.

QUESTION

How would your life be different if you invested fully in your relationships?

AUTHOR CONTACT INFORMATION

Kathi Hall, MA, LMFT Owner/Licensed Marriage and Family Therapist of Hope for the Journey Counseling
Website: www.hope4thejourney.com
Email: kathihall@hope4thejourney.com
Social: https://www.linkedin.com/in/kathi-hall/
Tags: Licensed Marriage and Family Therapist, Author

September 28
DOUG GIESLER

Mindsets are static; life moves!

THOUGHT

Mindsets limit, Unlimit the limit. The time is now; now is how! Make room for more than you want; don't limit reality with mind "sets."

Habitual wanting is a desire projecting as a mindset in the future with a lack of orientation. The mind "projector" is captivated in time. It is misusing faith by believing in lack, now! That is a belief in "have not"; it is self-defeating. Wanting≠Having.

Wanting is a future mind "set". It produces more lack, so you get less of what you want. Stop wanting; start having; use faith properly!

True faith believes. Actualize belief! Imagine the future illusion being true already. Feel, taste, touch, play, enjoy, amplify, and add emotion to the experience. Make it believable; leave no doubt. Don't project it in the future mindscape; plant it in the past as if it were true now! Swap desire for satisfaction; visualize "having"! Anchor it with massive emotional appreciation to prove to the mind that it is already true with feeling. Sense the belief!

Live in now! We can't "project" futures if we are present. Master presence; it neutralizes the wanting state. By appreciating what we have, time/lack limits are removed, allowing life to expand now. Now is how!

QUESTION

How does your faith relate to wanting, having, abundance, "time," and belief, and how does that affect your next "NOW"?

AUTHOR CONTACT INFORMATION

Doug Giesler, CEO of Giesler Systems LLC
Website: www.UNlimityourlimit.com
Email: Douggiesler@gmail.com
Social: www.linkedin.com/in/doug-giesler
Tags: Author, Realtor, Personal Coach, Day Trader

September 29

DEBRA LEE MURROW

Abundance is a state of mind!

THOUGHT

Abundance is far more than material wealth; it's a transformative mindset that begins in the heart. As Jesus declared, 'Heaven and earth shall pass away, but my words shall not pass away.' This eternal truth reminds us that true abundance flows from aligning our faith with our words and actions.

As artists must first believe in their creativity to unlock their potential, our mindset shapes our reality. I witness this transformation in my art classes when students declare with conviction: 'I am an artist, and I am creative!' This simple yet powerful affirmation opens doors to breakthrough moments.

My abundance journey began when I was spiritually empty, searching for purpose. As I discovered my calling, my perspective shifted from scarcity to plenty. I learned to anchor myself in the present rather than drown in unfulfilled dreams. In practicing gratitude for life's smallest gifts, I began to recognize abundance all around me.

Pv 3:9-10 offers a timeless principle: when we honor God with our first fruits, our barns overflow with plenty. True abundance isn't about accumulating more; it's about recognizing the fullness present in our lives when we align our hearts with divine purpose.

QUESTION

Where are you experiencing abundance in your life, and where do you need a mental shift?

AUTHOR CONTACT INFORMATION

Debra Lee Murrow, Founder Artist of COLORME Art Spa
Website: https://www.COLORMEArtSpa.com
Email: colormedebralee@gmail.com
Social: https://www.facebook.com/COLORMEArtSpa
Tags: Speaker, Artist, Graphic Recorder, Live Art

September 30

GABRIELLA KIPP

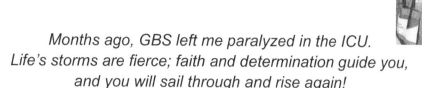

*Months ago, GBS left me paralyzed in the ICU.
Life's storms are fierce; faith and determination guide you,
and you will sail through and rise again!*

THOUGHT

Abundance is found in love, support, and faith, sustaining us through life's trials. This belief became clear in my journey to serve others in the medical field. I was confident this was God's purpose for me, then life took a turn. I contracted Guillain-Barré, a disorder that left me completely paralyzed, unable to move, speak, or breathe. Months in ICU on a ventilator shattered my dreams of a medical career.

Yet, in this trial, I found abundant blessings. The outpouring of prayers from loved ones and strangers wraps me in a sense of comfort, hope, and assurance that this experience has a divine purpose. Reliance on medical staff has given me a new perspective, experiencing firsthand the frustrations of patients who cannot advocate for themselves. This insight altered my opinions of care and deepened my empathy! My physical abilities have changed, but my purpose remains. A profound way we can serve is through lessons we learn in our struggles. I have found an abundance of love, spiritual growth, and clarity, showing me that God's grace is unwavering. My abilities have changed, but my story isn't over; it's evolving- to inspire others with the power of love, faith, and resilience.

QUESTION

When life's trials leave you feeling like you've lost everything, how might your struggles equip you to serve others in new and meaningful ways?

AUTHOR CONTACT INFORMATION

Gabriella Kipp, Advisor of Nurture Our World
Website: https://www.nurtureourworld.net
Email: chriskippntc@gmail.com
Social: https://www.facebook.com/NurtureOurWorld.net
Tags: Nurture Our World

October 1

GINA MATTESON

*True strength isn't in never falling.
It's in rising, growing, and reconnecting with purpose every time you do.*

THOUGHT

Abundance isn't about what we possess—it's about how fully we engage with life. It's the courage to transform our most challenging moments into stepping stones for growth, the grace to thrive amidst uncertainty, and the vision to see beauty in brokenness.

True abundance emerges when we dare to stand tall in adversity, recognizing that even the most shattered pieces can be reimagined and rebuilt into something extraordinary.

As the Founder and CEO of GemTek Recruiting, I've spent more than 20 years helping businesses and individuals unlock their potential by forging meaningful connections. This work has taught me a profound truth: abundance is never a solo pursuit. It is rooted in relationships, shared purpose, and a willingness to uplift others. It's about creating a life that resonates far beyond ourselves.

These lessons inspired *A Thousand Masks*, a deeply personal exploration of shedding societal expectations to uncover your true essence. Through this International Best Selling book, I invite readers to embrace authenticity, resilience, and purpose—to see that abundance isn't found in what we chase, but in who we become through the journey.

Abundance begins within, waiting for us to claim it and share it. Are you ready to embrace it?

QUESTION

If abundance is already within you, what are you waiting for to live fully: permission, the perfect moment, or the courage to finally let the world see you?

AUTHOR CONTACT INFORMATION

Gina Matteson, Founder and CEO of GemTek Recruiting
Website: www.gemtek.company
Email: gina@gemtek.company
Social: https://www.linkedin.com/in/ginamatteson/
Tags: Recruiting, Leadership, Author, Speaker, Entrepreneur

October 2
BUDDY THORNTON

*Abundance is many things,
but it must be a mindset first!*

THOUGHT

Is abundance an accumulation exercise regardless of what you are accumulating? Many people believe they are in a race to die with the most distinctive home, most extensive bank account, or other sign of tangible success. I'm not one of those people. Not even close.

Abundance is a mindset about who is in your corner when you need to call in a chip or two. Abundance is knowing that family is there when you arrive at the emergency room, lacking a clue about how you might look in two days. Abundance is working hard to gain enough of the education necessary to achieve your ends. But think, even those are second-level abundance ideologies.

Life is bursting with abundance when you receive a hug from someone you uplifted out of the goodness of your heart, absent any other reason. I always ask how much is enough, then divert my efforts into making sure others aren't falling through the cracks of our broken society.

When was the last time you did something, and the only reward was a meaningful hug? Add those up over your lifetime, and you will find my portrayal of abundance. And, if I'm correct, your mindset will be balanced. Blessings.

QUESTION

*Can we ignore those with nothing while enjoying material things,
knowing we could be someone's abundance angel by doing very little?*

AUTHOR CONTACT INFORMATION

Buddy Thornton, Founder of Path2Knowing Academy
Website: Path2Knowing.academy
Email: buddypscapro@gmail.com
Social: www.linkedin.com/in/buddycthornton
Tags: Educator, Speaker, Author, Prosocial Advocate

October 3
COLLEEN STRUBE

Warp speed your way to abundance:
Connect… Develop… Succeed…!

THOUGHT

Connect - The universe has an abundance of opportunities for all of us to connect with each other. Start connecting while you're simply living your life. The key is to be open-minded and genuinely interested in the people you meet. Approach each interaction as an opportunity to learn something new or make a meaningful connection. You never know where a chance meeting might lead or what doors it could open in your professional or personal life.

Develop - As someone who has attended thousands of networking events over the last 25 years, I have found that it is about making a connection and building and nurturing the relationship that follows. Have an attitude of abundance and gratitude. What can you do to support them?

Succeed – As they say, the Fortune is in the Follow-Up. However, it's my experience that more people put it on the back burner. I realized if you want to succeed, you need to Fall in Love with Follow-up. For my clients, I leverage the power of community. Bringing together supportive professionals and valuable resources, I create an environment where everyone involved can thrive, thereby finding our fortune/abundance in the Follow-Up while having fun doing it.

QUESTION

How will you nurture your existing and new connections to create abundance for them and yourself? Need some ideas, let's connect!

AUTHOR CONTACT INFORMATION

Colleen Strube, Founder of Connect Develop Succeed LLC
Website: https://www.connectdevelopsucceed.com/
Email: Colleen@colleenstrube.com
Social: https://www.linkedin.com/in/colleenstrube/
Tags: Speaker, Connector, Follow-Up Fortune Finder

October 4
ROBERT ENZMANN

Let's set sail for the stars - it is pointless to wait.

THOUGHT

The construction and launch of starship fleets can be accomplished without major technological breakthroughs, at surprisingly affordable cost, in a relatively short time, and with many beneficial consequences for all people on the Earth, as well as for those who open up the cornucopia of interstellar space.

This statement is a plea to open a new frontier for humankind. We need the space, the freedom, the new lands, the possibility of adventure, and the resources. It's time to see space as the threshold of a vast new frontier - the ultimate endeavor for humanity - and what will come of them and after them. It is the solution and likely the next evolution of the human race.

It would be absurd cruelty if humanity waited for centuries before voyaging to rich new worlds with resources waiting unused, like the two-thousand-year Dark Ages in Europe. Let's go to the stars in our generation.

QUESTION
What are we waiting for?

AUTHOR CONTACT INFORMATION

Robert Enzmann, Astrophysicist, Author, and Geologist of FREA, Inc.
Website: https://enzmannarchive.org/
Email: Jay@enzmannarchive.org
Social: https://www.facebook.com/starshipsnow
Tags: Starships, Astrophysicist, Author

October 5

OPHIR ADAR

Feed Your White Wolf!

THOUGHT

We all have a dark wolf and a white wolf inside us, fighting to take control. Your white wolf is love, abundance, collaboration, joy, and everything else that leads to an abundance mindset. Your dark wolf is Ego, hate, jealousy, and scarcity. When you realize that you are the creator of your existence, excitement, and anticipation, you will focus on engaging with your higher self. Our higher self is surrounded by light and only sees the white wolf.

QUESTION

What are you willing to do to feed your white wolf?

AUTHOR CONTACT INFORMATION

Ophir Adar, CEO and Head Coach of Real Momentum
Website: https://www.realmomentum.com
Email: Ophir@realmomentum.com
Social: https://www.instagram.com/realmomentumcoaching/
Tags: Businesscoach, Realmomentum

October 6
MAYRA HAWKINS

*Abundance is everywhere; it is not invisible;
we just have to be willing to see it.*

THOUGHT

Our thoughts can create limitations and scarcity in our lives. When we decide to notice the abundance that exists all around us, our perception will change. Imagine the sand on the beach, the stars in the sky, the fish in the sea, or the water in the ocean. Look at the moonlight and the sunlight; their brilliance is limitless.

On this day, we celebrate coaches nationwide. Coaching is a gift of abundance and infinite possibilities. It can help us achieve our goals, overcome self-doubt, and realize our true potential. It can help us process our fears and dissolve our anxieties so we can move forward to a place of love and acceptance. It can restore our faith and our hope for the future. It can help us create new habits and help us embrace accountability. It can allow us to discover our strengths and unleash our potential. It can also show us how to release our paradigms and shift our mindset.

Becoming a coach has given me the opportunity to share my knowledge and my pearls of wisdom, transform my life, and abundantly bless the lives of others. It is the gift that keeps giving.

QUESTION

What area of your life would you like to transform and create abundance today?

AUTHOR CONTACT INFORMATION

Mayra Hawkins, Owner, Certified Life Coach of The Leap To Transformation LLC
Website: https://www.theleaptotransformation.com
Email: mayra@theleaptotransformation.com
Social: https://www.facebook.com/theleaptotransformation
Tags: theleaptotransformation

October 7
MELISSA GERACIMOS

Sometimes, you just have to let things unfold.

THOUGHT
More Than I Asked For? Did I wish for this?

It was a first date. I was matched on a dating app to a chatty guy with a flair for the written word. The telling sounds funny. A well-written man walks into a cheese shop for a first date...

And the date was great. It is the kind of evening full of chatter and laughter that goes on and on until the chairs are placed on top of their tables and the floors mopped.

Will he call me? Will he text me? Should I call him? How long should I wait?

And then- there it was, three days later, the joyful ping of a text saying 'good morning.'

That was the start of a grand adventure of chatter and laughter as we learned about each other, closing more restaurants and exploring physical and emotional worlds while opening our hearts.

No rush to the altar; we took our time. And we learned, we grew, and we fell in love.

And we married and blended our happy families before our treasured friends.

Today is our anniversary.

Was it more than I asked for? Did I wish for this?

It is more than I could have ever asked for. And yes, I did wish for this.

Oh, yes.

QUESTION
When did you last take the time to let something unfold?

AUTHOR CONTACT INFORMATION

Melissa Geracimos, Thinker
Website: https://www.365daysofabundancequotes.com
Email: myv0p11@gmail.com
Social: https://mybook.to/artofconnection5
Tags: Thinker

October 8
J. ROBERT SANTANA

To experience lack and be gratefully content is the byproduct of abundance in life!

THOUGHT

Abundance can be a two-edged sword. If you try to capture it, you will be overwhelmed; it becomes counterproductive and even destructive in a person's life. I believe that when you experience abundance, it not only fills you, it overflows so that you can share it with others. We don't need much to be fulfilled, but somewhere along the line, some people get caught striving for more, and even when the goal is reached, it's never enough. I am not saying that having goals and ambitions is wrong; however, when there is no meaningful satisfaction and contentment, you can miss out on the experience of abundance. People can pursue utter happiness and never reach it because they have no Joy.

I have lived with a lack in my life, and I have learned that this experience has prepared me to recognize abundance. I believe that abundance is an attribute of Love. I realized that defining and determining how deep your cup of needs is will determine how much love is necessary to experience an overflow of abundance that is beyond comprehension. I thoroughly appreciated abundance and love when I embraced my relationship with Christ! I am whole, contented, and lacking nothing in this world!

QUESTION

Is your cup of life half empty or half full? What will it take to go from half empty to half full? What will it take to go from half full to full? Remember that abundance has no half-measures!

AUTHOR CONTACT INFORMATION

J. Robert Santana, Owner of The Wellness Benefit Group Inc.
Website: https://www.thewellnessbenefitgroup.com/
Email: rsantana@thewellnessbenefitgroup.com
Social: www.linkedin.com/in/ j-robert-santana-ab20017
Tags: Entrepreneur, Speaker, Travel, EE Benefits

DIANA HOOKER

Discover your greatness through your biggest mistakes.

THOUGHT

I locked myself in the bathroom to escape the rage on the other side. With my heart pounding and my hands and legs trembling, I leaned against the vanity for support. My reflection showed my eyes were wide, my face was streaked with tears, and my neck was covered in red marks, evidence of the violence I had just endured. I yelled at myself, "Diana, you've made the biggest mistake that almost cost you your life! Now what!?"

Then I heard the front door slam shut and the sound of a car engine rev and fade as he drove away. I slipped out of my safe refuge, packed all my belongings, and left, never to return.

After healing, I realized this fateful error was based on my fear and insecurity that I would never find another person to love me. I settled for a person who was fighting their selfish demons and could not love, respect, or honor anyone.

I discovered that I was designed for something greater than this adversity. I found the belief that I was worthy of love as much as I loved, respect as much as I respected, and honor as much as I honored. And on October 9, 2024, I celebrated 31 years of marriage with the person who has been my greatest blessing after my biggest mistake.

QUESTION

The difference between a good mistake and a bad mistake is how quickly you learn and move forward. What is your biggest mistake? What were you able to learn? How were you able to move forward?

AUTHOR CONTACT INFORMATION

Diana Hooker, CEO of The Living Your Greatness Company
Website: http://livingyourgreatness.net/
Email: Diana@LivingYourGreatness.net
Social: https://www.linkedin.com/in/diana-hooker-04517594/
Tags: Speaker, Author, Coach

October 10
DANA SCHON

Leaning into loving yourself through soul work will create recycled energy that you will be able to share abundantly with others.

THOUGHT

God made us to be great, not average, and not ordinary. God created you in his likeness. He wants you to feel abundance. He wants you to share abundance with others, and he wants you to live abundantly. Living out your purpose is how you show up as the best version of yourself. Realizing that your life is directly related to how you share your love with others can be heart-opening.

We often shelter our hearts from the world's hurt, keeping our goodness to ourselves. A practice of soul care can be the catalyst for the change you may need in your life. Showing a positive mindset and strategically showing kindness and love to yourself will strengthen your foundations. Your soul needs time to feel the energy circling through your body, filling up those empty pockets that need a little love.

The most significant aspect of cultivating energy for yourself is that it can be shared with others, empowering them as well. This recycled energy has so much purpose and is the basis for your soul work. When we practice living with an open heart, it is then that we can live abundantly. Creating a balance-filled life and practicing soul care will show up throughout your life and directly affect those close to you.

QUESTION

How will you step into your greatest purpose while taking care of yourself at the soul level and still impacting others?

AUTHOR CONTACT INFORMATION

Dana Schon, Author and Founder of Mama Schon Care Packages
Website: https://www.mamaschon.com
Email: hello@mamaschon.com
Social: https://www.instagram.com/mamaschon/
Tags: Author, Speaker, Curator Mama Schon Care Package

October 11

GEORGETTE COMBS

A life of abundance does not come from material things but from God, gratitude, and love.

THOUGHT

I've noticed that sometimes I feel the least abundant when things are going well and more abundant when I've had many difficulties to face. I've wondered why this is. Upon reflection, these are some of the things I see. Most prominent to me, though, is seeing the good in each day and being grateful for what I have.

Things I Know About Living a Life of Abundance
Do good to others. Small or big.
See the good in people. Encourage them.
Give your time and talents to worthy causes. Use what you have to help.
See the good in every situation, even if it's getting to the other side of it.
Do what you know is the right thing to do.
Hold onto your peace. Be kind. Do not give in to pride or anger.
You don't know what may be going on with someone.
Express your appreciation for people.
Thank the cashier or the delivery person; encourage the produce guy in the grocery store.
Be thankful every day for all things. Don't take your blessings for granted.
Love others. Tell or show them. Smile at people.
Love yourself. Be compassionate towards yourself as you would a friend.
Love God. Know that He is on your side. He loves you. He knows you.
He hasn't forgotten you. He has a good plan for you.

QUESTION

What practices do you have to live a life of abundance?

AUTHOR CONTACT INFORMATION

Georgette Combs, Owner and Founder: Growth & Clarity Coaching
Website: https://www.365daysofabundancequotes.com
Email: gacombs08@gmail.com
Social: https://mybook.to/artofconnection5
Tags: Coach, Growth Coach, Future Speaker, Trainer

October 12
JEFF MARCONETTE JR.

*It's not the happy people that are grateful;
it is the grateful people that are happy.*

THOUGHT

We all want to find happiness; we search our entire lives for things that create happiness, but we're looking in the wrong place.

There are things that most of us are grateful for, like our friends, family, house, clean water and electricity…but I have learned that there are even more that we don't often consider.

Before my car accident on January 7th, 2002, I had lots of abilities; in fact, I played almost every sport. After that day, I could no longer walk, talk, or even breathe on my own or perform any of the other everyday activities. I lay in the hospital in a coma for 2.5 months. After being one of the lucky ones and coming out of the coma, all those abilities were still missing. After 22+ years of arduous work, I can finally do those everyday abilities again.

I am thankful for my life; in fact, the first thing I do every morning is post on Facebook, "I am so thankful to be given today, and I will make it a great day!"

I have learned that if you have gratitude for everything, happiness will grow out of that! It's all about looking at the abundance you have instead of looking at what you are lacking.

QUESTION

Human nature is to focus more on the negative; what if you focus on the positive?

AUTHOR CONTACT INFORMATION

Jeff Marconette Jr., CEO, Owner, and Founder of Jeff Marconette Jr.
Website: https://www.jeffmarconettejr.com/
Email: inspiredbyjeff@yahoo.com
Social: https://www.facebook.com/jefijr
Tags: Speaker, Author, TV host

October 13

TAMMY DEMIRZA LAWING

True abundance is born from the courage to confront our deepest fears, unravel our subconscious beliefs, and transform pain into power.

THOUGHT

In everyone's life, pivotal days define the essence of our being, and we either dig in, embrace the predicaments we create, and make real changes, or we check out and detach from life. I was in that space in 2012 when I realized that the man I had entrusted with everything that I owned had stolen every penny and was a sociopath, and I… was homeless.

Whatever has happened in your life does not identify you either. It is only a symptom of something hidden in your subconscious from a story you framed around an experience, which becomes a belief. You are in a spiritual curriculum and everything; everyone is your servant by being the catalyst for your growth through your current experiences to help you choose differently. Pain is one of our biggest gifts and can be turned into abundance when we choose to walk through it.

You are not a victim of your current life; you are a victor who chose to experience this very thing to overcome it. It's what I help thousands of people with because I, too, had to overcome my reality and embrace abundance by becoming a conscious alchemist. Finding out what is hidden in your subconscious is the gateway to that freedom. Ready to experience true abundance?

QUESTION

What pivotal experience in your life has shaped a belief that might be blocking you from abundance, and are you ready to uncover and transform it into a source of empowerment?

AUTHOR CONTACT INFORMATION

Tammy DeMirza Lawing, Transformation Leader of Tammy De Mirza, LLC
Website: https://www.tammydemirza.com
Email: tammydemirza.com
Social: https://www.linkedin.com/in/tammydemirza/
Tags: Speaker, Author, Intuitive, Transformation Leader

October 14
KEN ASHBY

Expectations without agreement create premeditated resentment.

THOUGHT

I want to share with you a word and a powerful "secret" that affects our relationships, both personal and professional. It's something that is never overlooked in successful business deals. However, too often, it is completely overlooked in our personal and professional relationships.

The word is "Expectations!"

When expectations are not openly communicated or agreed upon, they can lead to misunderstandings, frustrations, and even bitterness. Think about it. Have you ever been disappointed or upset because someone didn't meet your unspoken expectations?

It happens to all of us, doesn't it? We set ourselves up for disappointment when we assume others can read our minds and know what we want or expect of them. You can count on this; most people are not mind readers. They can't possibly know what we expect from them unless we express it clearly.

So, here's the secret: "Expectations without agreement create premeditated resentment."

That's why we need to emphasize the importance of agreement. When we make our expectations explicit and gain agreement from others, we create a shared understanding. It sets the stage for open communication, collaboration, and a fulfilling relationship.

QUESTION

Are the expectations in your relationships aligned and in agreement?

AUTHOR CONTACT INFORMATION

Ken Ashby, COO and Presenter of Segal Leadership Global LLC
Website: www.SegalLeadershipGlobal.com
Email: kashby@segalleadershipglobal.com
Social: https://www.instagram.com/_the_rfactor/
Tags: Speaker, Singer, Songwriter, Author, Coach, Trainer

October 15

SUZANNE LAFLAMME

Abundance is not about the material things you have; it's about the quality of the beautiful things that are in your life.

THOUGHT

Abundance is not defined by the material possessions we have but rather by our experiences and the moments that shape our lives. True abundance comes from the joy of relationships, the love we share, and the memories we create. It can be found in the laughter of loved ones, the beauty of nature, and the satisfaction that accompanies personal growth.

When we shift our focus to the beautiful moments and connections in our lives, we begin to understand the true meaning of abundance. It is about cherishing simple joys and experiencing the sense of fulfillment that arises from living a life filled with meaning, purpose, and gratitude.

In my view, abundance is a state of mind and a way to celebrate the wonderful treasures that make life rich and rewarding. Let's celebrate those treasures together!

QUESTION

What are some of the beautiful, non-material things in your life that make you feel genuinely abundant?

AUTHOR CONTACT INFORMATION

Suzanne LaFlamme, Founder of Suzanne LaFlamme Consulting
Website: https://www.365daysofabundancequotes.com
Email: slaflamme1@gmail.com
Social: https://www.linkedin.com/in/suzanne-laflamme/
Tags: Social Media Marketer

October 16
MISHIANAND MACK

Abundance is only as calm and peaceful as you build it.

THOUGHT

Affluence
Bountifulness
Ultimately Usurping
Numberless
Dynamical
Ample
Nourishing
Copiousness
Extra

Adhering to the laws and regulations established in the Bible, we can build wealth and abundance. For the unseen is more realistic than the seen. Everything seen is just a factual of the unseen. Examine your abundance because it knows no bounds.

To realize the potential of abundance, one must comprehend its significance. Establishing a business process and acting with consistent core principles of abundance is essential for long-term success. Your business success results from aligning operations with your abundance beliefs. The best operations are simply balancing morality and sound business practices. It allows us to understand the true origin of what is around us, allowing for continuous progress and improvement.

Because the universe is complex and multidimensional, life is essential. In both realities, the truth about existence must be sought. Wealth can either give you life or death, so we must stand firm in its aftermath. The battle to achieve or preserve affluence can bring about either happiness or suffering. Having too much of something is bad for you, so watch out for abundance.

QUESTION

How are you going to obtain or maintain your abundance?

AUTHOR CONTACT INFORMATION

Mishianand Mack, Owner of My Divas Style LLC
Website: https://www.365daysofabundancequotes.com
Email: mydivasstyle@gmail.com
Social: https://mybook.to/artofconnection5
Tags: Hair Stylist, Notary Public, Entrepreneur

October 17

MICHELLE MRAS

Change is an emotional journey. Change is uncomfortable.
It forces you to evaluate who you truly are.
The beauty is in the possibilities.

THOUGHT

I developed this quote as a reminder to not give up on myself. In 2014, I was involved in an automobile accident, which left me in a pseudo-catatonic state. For two years, I was utterly trapped in my mind.

Once the therapies were able to evaluate the brain damage, we learned I was suffering from a multifaceted traumatic brain injury (TBI): frontal lobe, over my left ear, back of my head, and the two hemispheres of my brain had detached. This quote keeps me pushing to be the best version of myself at each healing stage. I am still recovering from my TBI. I make great strides in my recovery with seemingly more significant setbacks.

I do get scared, but I promised myself to do my best every day regardless of how small the accomplishment. I learned to forgive myself often. I am proud of the unapologetic woman I am. Throughout my years as a coach, professional speaker, and author, I have witnessed my quote proven true hundreds of times. From my TBI recovery and the many other health obstacles I've endured, I am living proof. The most fulfilling aspect of my quote is to see it manifest in the lives of others. I've had fans of my work share their change stories and how they are so proud of the person they have become.

QUESTION

Evaluate and realize you're in control of how you react to change.
Choose to show up and address the challenge as the best version of you.
Are you prepared to embrace the beauty in your possibilities?

AUTHOR CONTACT INFORMATION

Dr. Michelle Mras, CEO of Mras Incorporated
Website: https://www.MichelleMras.com
Email: me@michellemras.com
Social: https://YouTube.com/MichelleMras
Tags: MichelleMras, Unapologeticallyyou, MentalShift

October 18
LAURA LEE KENNY

Health is the Cornerstone of Abundance.

THOUGHT

As a former CFP, I spent years helping people build financial abundance. Yet, when my health began to falter, I realized abundance means little if your body isn't well enough to enjoy it. Struggling with fatigue, weight gain, and health challenges, I knew I needed a change—and not just for my bank account but for my body and spirit.

My research led me to alkalize the body, and Essante Organics Products resonated with me and my holistic approach. I learned that when the body is too acidic, it creates an environment where disease, fat cells, and even cancer can thrive. By adopting an alkaline-focused lifestyle, I started nourishing my body with natural, toxin-free foods and supplements. This shift not only supported my health but also helped me shed excess weight—something I had battled for years.

Today, I feel lighter, more energetic, and truly alive. The same principles I used to create financial health—focus, discipline, and choosing the right tools—have guided me to reclaim my physical well-being.

True abundance isn't found in numbers or possessions. It begins with a healthy body, and by prioritizing my health, I've unlocked a richer, more fulfilling life than I ever imagined.

QUESTION

If your body is the foundation of your life's abundance, what steps are you taking today to ensure it thrives?

AUTHOR CONTACT INFORMATION

Laura Lee Kenny, CEO of Blue Diamond Club LLC
Website: https://www.essanteorganics.com/LauraLeeWins
Email: support@LauraLeeKenny.net
Social: https://www.linkedin.com/in/lauraleekenny/
Tags: Speaker, Author. Money Mindset Mentor, Podcaster

October 19
CHRIS NAUGLE

Abundance is everywhere. Wealth flows when you offer solutions that enrich others' lives.

THOUGHT

Everyone experiences money challenges, whether it's not having enough or struggling with excess. This experience is where the opportunity to create transformation begins. People may struggle with car payments, mortgages, tuition, or taxes, but when you can provide a solution, you unlock the potential for both personal and financial growth. By showing confidence in your ability to help them solve their problem, you position yourself as a valuable resource. In return, people are eager to compensate you.

When you focus on solving others' challenges, you simultaneously address your own financial needs. For example, if you need funding for a real estate project and someone you know needs extra income to cover a car payment and has untapped home equity, you can help them use that equity to earn interest while securing the funds you need. Their burden is lifted, and your project moves forward, creating abundance for both.

Abundance is everywhere. Wealth flows when you offer transformative solutions that enrich others' lives. Lead with service, and watch how the flow of prosperity works in your favor.

QUESTION

What abundance can you create by transforming your current financial challenge into an opportunity?

AUTHOR CONTACT INFORMATION

Chris Nuagle, Owner and Founder of the Money School and Private Money Club
Website: https://www.chrisnaugle.com
Email: chris@flipoutacademy.com
Social: https://www.youtube.com/c/thechrisnaugle
Tags: Speaker, Author, Money Expert

October 20
NATHAN KELLER

Remember that happiness will never come from an abundance of possessions but through sharing your time and resources with others.

THOUGHT

Lasting abundance starts with the desire to bless and serve others. Most spend the majority of their time focusing on paying the bills, getting to work on time, and just surviving. And those things are not bad in and of themselves. They are necessary. But, if they are the focus, we tend to drift toward operating in scarcity, the opposite of abundance.

What if your focus was helping and serving others, giving of your time and resources, or changing someone else's life? The most fun you'll ever have with money is giving it away. My life and business changed when I realized this shift in thinking. If I'm focused on giving to others (time, money, resources) and their success, then paying my bills and surviving will happen along the way to becoming generous and creating abundance. If your thinking shifts, there is no limit to the lives you can change when focusing on blessing and elevating others!

QUESTION

If you had time & money in abundance, who would you bless or serve? How would the world be different if everyone saw abundance as what they could give to others rather than what they could keep for themselves?

AUTHOR CONTACT INFORMATION

Nathan Keller, Financial Advisor at Keller Financial Associates
Website: http://www.primerica.com/nkeller
Email: nkeller@primerica.com
Social: https://www.linkedin.com/in/nathan-keller-98283330/
Tags: Financial Advisor

October 21

LAUREN MILLER

*Dreamers fill their Bucket Lists;
Courageous souls empty them.*

THOUGHT

We all have choices in life regarding how we spend our time. As we age and have fewer commitments vying for our time as work and family obligations decrease, the change allows us more time to fill our lives with meaningful participation.

I never imagined that I could have accomplished what I have in life. While working through low points or emptiness, there was always something inside that relentlessly pushed me onward. In some childhood photos, I noticed I was pouting, obviously not getting my way in some manner.

This innate stubbornness has been a driving force that has challenged me throughout my life. Through small, courageous steps or the ability to rationalize obstacles, I learned to live filled with abundance. Abundance of accumulating tangibles leads to emptiness, but mine comes from the desire to learn, serve, and challenge myself. Filling my bucket list with new experiences or cultivating personal relationships provides me the opportunity to explore, expand my comfort zone, and create an exhilarating life. Natural curiosity is a blessing, and lifelong learning fills my soul. Living daily with abundant gratitude allows me to continue playing this game of life without regrets.

QUESTION

How do you want to fill your days with abundant living?

AUTHOR CONTACT INFORMATION

Lauren Miller, Owner/Operator of Sonoran Senior Placement
Website: https://www.sonoranseniorplacement.com
Email: sonoranplacement@gmail.com
Social: https://www.facebook.com/p/Sonoran-Senior-Placement-LLC-100057452168840/
Tags: Certified Senior Advisor, Dementia Practitioner

October 22
DIANA RINGER

*I have all the time I need to accomplish what
I have been "called" to do in my life and all the things
I "need" to get done in the meantime.*

THOUGHT

A thousand-mile journey starts with a single step, and an impossible dream starts with closing your eyes. The accumulative effect of small intentional actions, taken consistently over time, can crush impossible obstacles.

What is your life's purpose or calling? If nothing springs to mind, it's okay. Start with openness and curiosity. Do you know people in life who live their purpose? Ask them for a coffee and a chat. It might spark something in you; it will reveal itself when the time is right. Think of an ice sculpture revealing itself chip by icy chip.

Don't worry that you've missed the boat; you haven't. Life has a miraculous way of collapsing timeframes and placing you precisely at the time and place to fulfill your life's purpose. It may seem so random and fantastical; it seems unbelievable even to you. And you're the one who lived it!

If your core disbelief centers around you've aged out, consider some of the legends of the creative arts and business spend the majority of their lives before embarking on their calling. Harry Bernstein lived in obscurity but finally achieved fame at age 96 for his 2007 memoir, "The Invisible Wall: A Love Story That Broke Barriers."

QUESTION

What would your life look/feel like if you invested your time with purpose and intention? Taking your time back is the first step in getting your life back. What is one small step you can take today?

AUTHOR CONTACT INFORMATION

Diana Ringer, Coach of Diana Ringer
Website: https://dianaringer.beekonnected.com
Email: dianaringer@icloud.com
Social: https://www.linkedin.com/in/dianaringer/
Tags: Speaker, Author, Coach, Consultant

October 23

ALEX VITILLO

Abundance is what happens in your life and business when you have no luck, but apply the Four Cs: Clarity- Courage- Confidence - Consistency.

THOUGHT

Often, you may find yourself asking for Abundance while waiting for external circumstances to change. Maybe the economy isn't expansive enough, personal timing feels off, or you find yourself distracted by obstacles blocking your path.

But here's the thing: you are a powerful co-creator of your destiny.

Abundance is not only something you have; it's a reflection of who you are. It's an energy, a mindset that influences every aspect of your life and business.

Here's my tip to fast forward the experience of abundance:
Focus on the four Cs and make them your growth compass.

Clarity: Get crystal clear on what you truly want. Take time to reflect, connect with your soul, and make a decision you'll stick to with unwavering commitment. Courage: Dare to stand out. Be willing to think and act differently. You can outperform by non-confirming. Confidence: Believe in yourself and the value you bring. Confidence is everything. It fuels your actions and helps you stay resilient.

Consistency: Commit daily. Progress takes time—after all, Rome wasn't built in a day.
The Four Cs build on each other day after day. Embody the four Cs; you will align with the Abundance that's already waiting for you.

QUESTION

In the name of Abundance, are you willing to keep your eyes on the prize, stay focused when the going gets tough, and sacrifice short-term rewards for the long-lasting satisfaction you desire?

AUTHOR CONTACT INFORMATION

Alex Vitillo Leading Shamanic Priestess Of Wealth & Wellbeing of BreathingHeart Consultancy
Website: www.breathingheart.co.uk
Email: alex@breathingheart.co.uk
Social: https://www.instagram.com/breathingheartcoaching/
https://www.linkedin.com/in/alex-vitillo-gabay/
Tags: Speaker, Writer, Business and Money Coach

October 24

JOANNE ANGEL BARRYCOLON

To Live Abundantly is to train your mind, body, emotions, and spirit to be healthy.

THOUGHT

Training the mind, body, emotions, and spirit is the gateway to abundance.

When you have a healthy mind, you're capable of problem-solving and decision-making and quickly transforming most feelings into joy.

A healthy body allows you the ability to move with ease while having the freedom to live independently. Conversely, thinking or embracing negative energy creates barriers to your transformation or freedom.

Permitting yourself to feel your feelings opens up the ability for your emotions to flow.

You are a spiritual being having multitudes of human experiences; know that abundance is one of those experiences. Embracing abundance, therefore, requires both training and a capable conduit for spiritual change.

Just For today, in every way, know I am holding space for you and shining light on you.

QUESTION

What would it look like for you to train your mind, body, emotions, and spirit to live an abundant life?

AUTHOR CONTACT INFORMATION

Rev Joanne Angel BarryColon, Founder of Wholistic Fitness NY of Wholistic Fitness NY
Website: www.wholisticfitnessny.com
Email: healingwithin76@gmail.com
Social: https://www.youtube.com/@WholisticFitnessNY
Tags: Wholistic Integrative Teacher, Medical Astrologer

October 25

LANA STEVENSON

*True abundance is not measured by what we gather
but by what we give cheerfully and joyfully with compassion
and empathy and the joy we find therein.*

THOUGHT

True abundance is not about accumulating wealth or material things. Still, it is instead an outward expression of generosity, compassion, and empathy. It shifts the focus from gathering possessions to giving freely and joyfully.

When we offer our time, kindness, or resources to others, we create a more profound sense of fulfillment and open the flow of abundance in our lives. This perspective challenges the common belief that abundance is tied to what we own, suggesting instead that it is defined by the joy and connection we create through acts of giving. The Hebrew word "Natan," meaning "to give," can be read forward and backward in Hebrew & English. This duality reflects this reciprocal nature, as giving also brings rewards back to the giver.

By being fully present and appreciating the richness of each moment, we realize that abundance is already available to us. Ultimately, the most meaningful forms of abundance—such as love, joy, and peace—are intangible. These grow when shared, making true abundance something accessible to everyone, regardless of material circumstances.

QUESTION

How do you personally define abundance? Is it tied to material things or acts of generosity and kindness? How does giving impact your sense of joy, fulfillment, and connection with others, regardless of wealth?

AUTHOR CONTACT INFORMATION

Lana Stevenson Founder/Owner of Resilience Shift Health, Wellness & Fitness
Website: https://www.resilienceshifthealth.com
Email: resilienceshifthealth@gmail.com
Social: https://linkedin.com/in/lana-stevenson-a707b228
Tags: Medical Exercise Specialist, Cancer, Wellness, BFR,

October 26
SHERLYN HALLORAN

It's not about all the "stuff" you have been blessed with or acquired. It's about the people with whom God has graced your life.

THOUGHT

Growing up in a suburb, I was unaware we were in a class of families with barely enough. We wore uniforms to school and hand-me-down clothes from our cousins or what mom and gramma made for us to wear. The sense of lack came when it came time to go to college.

I asked my mom to buy some clothes for school and was told you have what's in your closet. I let her know that that would not work anymore. She handed me $100, with which I proceeded to purchase three pairs of jeans and a package of white T-shirts. The remaining money went into the car's gas tank.

I tie-died the T-shirts. It took years of gathering clothes to fill the gap of what I thought was a lack, only to find out I had a plethora of such. I learned that it wasn't abundance but a situation of too much "stuff" with no more room.

Cleanout took a long time. What I did learn in the process was that I did not need what I had acquired. I found that the people who had been put in my life were who filled the gap, and it overflowed into the reality of where true abundance lies. I am so blessed for the abundance of people in my life God has graced me with.

QUESTION

Where is your focus on the "stuff" in your life or the people who fill you up?

AUTHOR CONTACT INFORMATION

Sherlyn Halloran, Owner of Secure Future Finance
Website: https://www.365daysofabundancequotes.com
Email: shalloran01@gmail.com
Social: www.linkedin.com/in/freedomwithlivingbenefits
Tags: Entrepreneur, Financial Services, Pilot, Educator

October 27

LESLEY KLEIN

All is Well in My Peaceful and Prosperous World!

THOUGHT

Abundance is having more than what you need when you need it. It's more than just money. The Universe is providing for abundance. It is the acknowledgment of an abundant universe, and it happens only if you look at the world through the eyes of abundance. You can't see prosperity around you if you focus on scarcity. What you look for, you will find. And the more you focus on it, the bigger it gets.

An abundance mindset is required to attract manifestations of wealth into your life. It's a belief, a "knowing," that you are provided for because you are a spark of Source. A trust that when you ask, it is given.

Recently, my faith in abundance was tested when a client was late paying me. Instead of freaking out, I chose to send the person and situation love energetically and say the Ho'oponono prayer (I'm sorry. Please forgive. Thank you. I love you.) Then I followed up with "Thank You's" as I spotted evidence of Abundance all around me.

So, I trusted in the Abundance of Source, visualizing the highest and best resolution. It turned out my client's delay was due to a hacked computer. Still, the payment arrived only one day late, confirming that my proactive response made a difference!

QUESTION

Do you use affirmations? Have you tried the Ho'oponono prayer? What is your go-to affirmation or mantra when triggered by a scarcity incident?

AUTHOR CONTACT INFORMATION

Lesley Klein, Host and Executive Producer of Good-Vibes.TV
Website: https://www.good-vibes.tv
Email: lesley@Good-Vibes.TV
Social: https://www.youtube.com/@raiseyourvibeandthrive
Tags: Content Creator

October 28
RO GONZALEZ

Overcoming today's struggles opens doors to an abundance of wisdom and opportunities.

THOUGHT

As a Marine Corps Veteran, overcoming and reinventing oneself is a mission of learning who you are as an individual and leader in the community. If faced with the struggles I overcame and conquered, many would have given up. Try learning through trials and tribulations; sometimes, you must look in the mirror and seek change. It starts with the positive mindset of being challenged daily. What is today's agenda; how can I make tomorrow better, and how do I create impact moving forward?

Veterans are a different breed, and many struggle because they are taught to overcome anything, but that isn't always needed. Often, they need a helping hand or a hand up to get through what they face. It helps when another veteran is the helping hand. I never set out to help Veterans daily; it evolved after navigating the system and getting myself back on my feet. However, the reward and satisfaction of helping another veteran or active-duty member is the best feeling in the world. In short, having experienced what some of these Veterans have endured, it speaks volumes when one of their own is willing to take the time to ask the right questions and have empathy for them, having once been there.

QUESTION

What have you done to give back to your community with the experience or knowledge that you have gained through a setback, whether in a business or personal situation?

AUTHOR CONTACT INFORMATION

Ro Gonzalez, Founder/ Executive Director of Valors Veteran Community AZ
Website: https://vvcazvets.org/
Email: rogee3azusmc@gmail.com
Social: https://www.linkedin.com/in/ro-gonzalez-7616b7b3/
Tags: Veteran, Advocate, Speaker, Connector, Community

October 29
KARLA GARJAKA

*The more you recognize your blessings,
the more the universe expands them—only in
sharing do they genuinely flourish.*

THOUGHT

Abundance isn't about acquiring more; it's about realizing the gifts within us. Each person carries unique strengths—creativity, kindness, resilience—that can transform our lives and others' when embraced.

While recognition is important, gratitude is what turns acknowledgment into abundance. Without thankfulness, our potential remains untapped. Gratitude deepens our connection to our gifts, shifting our mindset from mere recognition to genuine appreciation.

Abundance should not be hoarded. Like a flowing river, it expands through sharing. Holding back out of fear stifles growth, but giving freely creates a cycle of generosity that invites even more blessings. When we share creativity or kindness, we inspire and enrich both ourselves and those around us.

The universe responds to the energy we project; the more grateful we are, the more our gifts flourish. True abundance is realized when we uplift others. By acknowledging what's within us and using our gifts to serve, we embrace a mindset of abundance, freeing us from fear and scarcity. Gratitude transforms recognition into action, revealing that true abundance is already within reach.

QUESTION

What talents or blessings have you overlooked or taken for granted, and how can you begin to use them more consciously to benefit others? How can you shift your mindset from one of scarcity to one of abundance?

AUTHOR CONTACT INFORMATION

Karla Garjaka, Owner/Founder of Globally Brighter
Website: karlagarjaka.com
Email: karla.garjaka@gmail.com
Social: https://www.linkedin.com/in/karla-garjaka/
Tags: Nutritional Psychology, Educator, Speaker, Author

October 30
HEATHER ORLANDO

True abundance flows when we accept life as it is—and as it isn't. By embracing reality without resistance, we open ourselves to all life has to offer.

THOUGHT

Abundance is an open, flowing state of mind and heart, w
here fulfillment isn't bound to possessions or circumstances but emerges from acceptance and presence. It's a deep sense of completeness that comes when we stop resisting what life presents, embracing both its beauty and imperfections. In this space of openness, abundance is limitless, manifesting in forms beyond material wealth—in relationships, experiences, and personal growth.

When we open our hearts and minds to the potential limitless abundance offers us, we can also bind what abundance enters out lives with the gratitude bound to what we enjoy every day. In short, the abundance we have should give us internal peace, even as we strive to embrace the joyful abundance of existence in this world, and share that abundance unconditionally.

QUESTION

"How might your experience of abundance shift if you fully accepted life as it is—and as it isn't?"

AUTHOR CONTACT INFORMATION

Heather Orlando, Real Estate Professionals of EXP Realty
Website: https://heatherorlando.asaphomes.com/
Email: heatherkristeneorlando@gmail.com
Social: https://www.facebook.com/heather.s.orlando/
Tags: Heather Orlando Your AZ Realtor

October 31

SUEZEE FINLEY

*Appreciation Is The Mother Of Abundance
When You Count Your Blessings, The Number Becomes Infinite.*

THOUGHT

Some people are so blessed it seems the sun is always shining on them, while others appear to be veiled in dark clouds. The world portrays itself as unfair at times, but is it really?

Let me let you in on a little secret...If you want abundance, count your blessings, not other people's! Focus on what you have, not what you don't have.

When I was a little kid, I loved Halloween (and still do). I loved being in costume, the sound my feet made crunching through the leaves as I swung my Jack-o'lantern bucket back and forth, Oh, and the wind, I loved the feel of the wind and the look of the leaves swirling around me and my bat wings as I pretended I could fly. The smiles I got from the neighborhood moms were worth more to me than all the candy in the world. But for one of my little friends, Halloween was stressful and disappointing because It was about "scoring" the most candy, and he was so busy looking at what others got and who scared more people with their costumes that he never enjoyed himself and was miserable every year!

I didn't know it then, but there was a lesson in my friend's behavior, and it was this... appreciation is the mother of abundance!

QUESTION

How would you explain abundance to a child? Looking back on your life, what were you abundant in that you didn't understand enough to appreciate? Do you feel abundant now? Why or Why not?

AUTHOR CONTACT INFORMATION

SueZee Finley, Founder of Acoustic Therapeutix
Website: https://acoustictherapeutix.com/
Email: SueZeeQuest@Gmail.com
Social: https://www.linkedin.com/in/suezeefinley/
Tags: Storytelling, Speaker Training, Improv, Retreats, Fun

November 1
SUEZEE FINLEY

My Idea Of Abundance Is Nuts...
Pistachios That Is!

THOUGHT

Growing up, my idea of abundance was nuts, Pistachios in particular! I'll never forget my 12-year-old self sitting on the front stoop with my "bestie," Laura. We would sit there for hours talking as we cracked off the bright red shells of our pistachio nuts until our fingers, lips, and tongues were dyed to match! (Back then, they dyed them red, but I have no idea why!) Each freed nut came with a dream.
We spoke about future spouses, careers, and exotic travels.

Nut after nut, smile after smile, and laugh after laugh until dark and the jar was empty. Laura told me she wanted to be rich - have a million-dollar home and millions in the bank.

Looking into the empty jar, I told Laura my idea of being rich was always having enough money to keep a jar of pistachios on the kitchen table (Back then, they were a whopping $5.00 a pound!) She giggled and called me a nut!

Looking back, it wasn't the nuts I wanted in abundance but the dreams I shared with my friend. My true definition of abundance was, and still is, an infinite supply of dreams and someone to share them with! To this day, I always keep a jar of pistachios on the kitchen table and am an abundant dreamer!

QUESTION

When you were a kid, what were you abundant in? Who do you want to share your abundance with? How would feeling abundant change your life?

AUTHOR CONTACT INFORMATION

SueZee Finley, Founder of Happiness Now Network
Website: https://acoustictherapeutix.com/
Email: SueZeeQuest@Gmail.com
Social: https://www.facebook.com/SueZ.Finley
Tags: Improv, Workshops, Laughter Yoga, Energy Medicine, Joy

November 2
ANDREW PAUL SKOOG

Money, power, hope for a brighter future – all this is secondary. Live fully each day and find something that brings you joy, no matter how small.

THOUGHT

You don't get a second chance to live your life. When I was younger, I was chasing the dream—money, lifestyle, having it all. Every sales call, business deal, and goal felt like progress, but in reality, I was running away from what truly mattered. I was so focused on what I thought was important that I missed out on the life happening in front of me. I wish I had taken the time to smell the roses along the way.

Money, power, and the promise of a bright future are essential, but they're secondary to living and enjoying the present moment. Now, I make a conscious effort to find joy in every day. Life is happening now, not just in the future. I can't change the past, but I've learned not to live with regret. Instead, I focus on shaping the future, staying present and grounded, being intentional, finding joy, and living each day. I discovered that when I started living the way I wanted, everything started showing up, including financial, personal, happiness, fulfillment, and joy. I now live a life of abundance, and it shows up without me forcing it; it is a natural flow. I can show you the way if you're open to considering small shifts in how you think, act, and show up.

QUESTION

Am I chasing external success at the expense of what truly matters in my life, or am I taking time to enjoy the present and live intentionally?

AUTHOR CONTACT INFORMATION

Andrew Paul Skoog, CEO/Speaker/Influence of Andrew Paul
Website: https://andrewpaulskoog.com
Email: AP@andrewpaulskoog.com
Social: https://www.linkedin.com/in/andrewskoog/
Tags: Men's Business Coach

November 3
WENDY SELLERS

*Empower others; inspire growth.
Every person has the power to make a difference!*

THOUGHT

This truth lies at the heart of meaningful connections. No matter your role—whether you're in leadership, a colleague, or a community member—you have the power to make a difference through your words and actions.

Empowering others isn't about grand gestures. Often, it's as simple as acknowledging someone's efforts. But don't just be kind—be specific. Imagine saying, "Thank you for your advice today; it gave me a new perspective," or "You're making a real difference here; I appreciate your detailed approach." These small, genuine affirmations can have an immense impact, reminding people of their value.

Inspiring growth through constructive feedback is equally robust. It's not just about correcting mistakes; it's about recognizing that mistakes are necessary for learning. You might say, "I made a similar mistake once and learned a valuable lesson. I even took a class to build the skills I needed." This progress shows that it's okay to ask for help or seek training to grow.

When we uplift each other, we all thrive. Remember, your words and actions have the power to make a difference. Make them intentional.

QUESTION

Knowing that every person, including you, has the power to make a difference, how will you empower someone today and inspire their growth?

AUTHOR CONTACT INFORMATION

Wendy Sellers, Founder of The HR Lady
Website: https://thehrlady.com/
Email: wendy@thehrlady.com
Social: https://www.linkedin.com/in/wendythehrlady/
Tags: HR Consultant

November 4

HANK LONGO

The secret to life is to believe in yourself, pursue your passion, and never quit believing in making your dreams come true and SOAR!

THOUGHT

The secret of life is to do what you love and are passionate about. In order to do that, you have to believe in yourself and not let other people prevent you from your mission of making your dream come true and being the best you can be. And to make your dreams come true, you can never give up until you do.

The day your dream quits becoming a reality is the day you give up on it. It doesn't get any better in life when you can wake up in the morning and spend your day doing what you love to do. In order to make that happen, you have to be passionate about what you are doing because it is the passion that gives you the strength to make it through all the obstacles and challenges you encounter on your journey of making your dreams come true.

Everyone is blessed with a special gift whether they know it or not; I call it your "Incredibleism." When you discover what that is and pursue developing your special gift, it is what life is all about: living the dream of developing the talents you were born with and making your dreams come true.

QUESTION

To wake up each day doing what you love to do, your "Incredibleism," takes a lot of passion and discipline, not to give up, and to keep making your dream a reality. What dream have you made a reality?

AUTHOR CONTACT INFORMATION

Hank Longo, Executive Director of SOAR Education
Website: https://soareducation.com
Email: hank@soareducation.com
Social: https://facebook.com/soareducation
Tags: Educator, Speaker, Emcee, TV Host, Author

November 5
NIURKA CASTANEDA

*An idea sparked by curiosity is
the compass that lights the way to a
life of abundance that can't be measured.*

THOUGHT

In today's world, which is increasingly being dominated by advances in artificial intelligence and robotics, the irreplaceable power of human curiosity shines brighter than ever. It sparks ideas that act as a compass, guiding us toward a life of abundance.

Throughout history, great minds like Leonardo da Vinci, Michelangelo, Albert Einstein, Nikola Tesla, Hedy Lamarr, Steve Jobs, and many others have shown that curiosity drives innovation and exploration. Our innate desire to question and understand the unknown pushes us beyond the limits of our imagination, leading to discoveries that enrich our lives in ways machines cannot.

True abundance isn't found in material wealth but in the experiences, knowledge, and fulfillment gained from pursuing our curiosity. This pursuit doesn't guarantee a clear path to success, but it does guide us to explore, innovate, and connect with others in meaningful ways.

As we navigate a world increasingly shaped by technology, it's essential to remember that curiosity is the spark that lights the way to a life rich in purpose and discovery. It leads us into realms of infinite possibilities and human connection, where true abundance lies.

QUESTION

How does curiosity enrich life beyond material wealth and redefine abundance?

AUTHOR CONTACT INFORMATION

Niurka Castaneda, Founder CEO of Amor Umbrella Media & Film Co.
Website: https://www.amorumbrella.com
Email: niurkabooks@gmail.com
Social: https://www.linkedin.com/in/niurkacastaneda/
Tags: Speaker, Filmmaker, Media Producer

November 6

JULIE JONES

*Time may be finite, yet love
and abundance are vast in possibilities.*

THOUGHT

For most of my life, I have witnessed the idea that time is finite, personally and professionally. As a police officer, death notifications to loved ones were the most challenging part of my job. In my personal life, my mom passed away at the age of 59, my dad passed 17 hours after a pancreatic cancer diagnosis, and my soulmate, Mike Jones, transitioned just 171 days after a life-altering diagnosis of metastasized colon cancer. He was 57 years young.

The one takeaway in all this is the abundance of love and memories I hold deep in my heart. Time may be short, yet the possibilities for love, kindness, generosity, and abundance run deep and expansive. It is a choice we are given every day. How you spend your finite time is only a choice you can make. Mike and I chose laughter, love, compassion, and making each day the very best. Mike lives on in love and his abundant, giving nature through me, his family, and our memories.

May this remind you to invest in what truly matters most. Every second spent waiting is a second lost forever. Life doesn't wait for you to be ready. Stop Waiting, Start Living.

QUESTION

During the time we have been given, how can we intentionally align our daily actions to maximize the impact of love and abundance?

AUTHOR CONTACT INFORMATION

Julie Jones, Breakthrough Coach of The Adventures of Julie Jones
Website: https://www.juliejones.biz/
Email: theadventuresofjuliejones@gmail.com
Social: https://www.linkedin.com/in/julie-jones-4152425/
Tags: Speaker, Breakthrough Coach, Intuitive

November 7
ART BLANCHFORD

Life is not some splendid monument to be built but an unfolding adventure to be experienced.

THOUGHT

I was an executive officer in a big public company, making seven figures, with a good marriage and three kids. I was slowly working myself to death without knowing it. One of the many nights I woke up in fear at three o'clock in the morning, this quote came to mind. I jumped up and wrote it down. I realized I was utterly on the wrong track.

Everything I was doing was building my life like it was a monument. I was building this remarkable career, not because I loved it but because I thought I needed to. To be enough, to be loved, to be ok. I was building a great family, not in service to my wife and kids, but so that I could have a beautiful family monument.

It was all wrong. I realized this in a silent retreat at a monastery and through working on the 12 Steps of Recovery in Workaholics Anonymous. So I actively worked on becoming nobody, from somebody. I promoted and grew the people around me and worked myself out of my job intentionally.

I started to see my wife and children as themselves, not part of my life, and started serving them that way. I let go and let God. Now, my life is a marvelous unfolding adventure. I am living my dream life every day, every moment, right now.

QUESTION

How do you see life? Are you building a monument? For whom? What would it be like to let it unfold instead?

AUTHOR CONTACT INFORMATION

Art Blanchford, Founder and General Manager of Pinnacle Leadership
Website: www.artblanchoford.com
Email: art@artblanchford.com
Social: https://www.linkedin.com/in/art-blanchford-7790135/
Tags: Speaker, Podcast Host, Transition Coach

November 8

NANCY ITOKAZU

Aligning with your heart and your true self is living in your light and serving at your best.

THOUGHT

I genuinely believe that an abundant person has inner peace and a deeper understanding of themselves. For more than 20 years of self-discovery, learning, and asking some sacred questions like "Why am I here?" "What is my purpose in life?" While going through so many challenges, life has taught me resilience and how to bounce back even stronger every time, finding inner peace even through the darkest moments in my life. Without those experiences, I wouldn't be helping people overcome anxiety and depression today.

For me, finding that inner peace is so important to keep that balance and not allow the outside circumstances to define who I am. To do so, we must learn how to align with our heart's deepest desires and purpose while staying true to ourselves. It is finding the divine light given upon our birth and what we carry through our lives. That light is not only to enlighten our path but to share it with others, those who are searching for their light. Being abundant in your heart means being able to share those gifts with the world so that more and more people can truly find their light and we can all serve humanity at our best.

Be a blessing, and you will be blessed.

QUESTION

What can you do to align with your heart and divine light today?

AUTHOR CONTACT INFORMATION

Nancy Itokazu, CEO, Founder of Radiate
Website: https://www.365daysofabundancequotes.com
Email: angelblssngs888@gmail.com
Social: https://www.facebook.com/NancyItokazu888
Tags: Life Coach, Therapist, Speaker, Mentor

November 9
SOFIA PINKY MAGANA

Daily gratitude is the key to an abundant life.

THOUGHT

Practicing gratitude on a daily basis will shift your focus from scarcity to creating a more abundant mindset of having enough and giving space to receive. Daily gratitude reminds us to appreciate the present moment and the blessings, big or small, that we take for granted.

What we focus on grows. I think that when we take time each day to acknowledge and give thanks for even the smallest joys, like a warm cup of coffee, a kind word, or simply a hug from a loved one, I find it helps develop a sense of fullness and prosperity. Daily gratitude has quickly changed my moods and helps open us up to receiving more abundance. You can't have a scarcity mindset and an abundant mindset at the same time.

Practicing gratitude brings awareness of the richness of our current life and helps align ourselves with a constant flow of positive energy that attracts even more incredible blessings into our lives. Gratitude will quickly transform our perception, helping us see that abundance is not just about material wealth but about the richness of experiences, relationships, and moments that make life truly meaningful.

QUESTION

What can daily gratitude create for you?

AUTHOR CONTACT INFORMATION

Sofia Pinky Magana, Owner of Loving Future Me
Website: https://www.pinkysofia.com/
Email: iampinkysofia@gmail.com
Social: https://www.instagram.com/pinkysofia/
Tags: Financial Coach, Life Insurance, Retirement

November 10

SHAD HARDY

We are born curious.
We grow up to understand. We age to guide.

THOUGHT

Curiosity drives our knowledge-seeking engine from birth. It is our instinct that fuels early learning and development and helps push us to walk, run, and explore as infants. It finds answers to questions like, "Why is the sky blue?"

As we move further into our formative years, our curiosity deepens into understanding. The combination of curiosity and understanding gives humans the power to solve problems. If we are lucky, that formula gets nurtured into something bigger than we are as individuals.

What's interesting about this early cycle of curiosity leading to understanding is that it universally sets us up for guidance in our older, wiser years. As we contribute to society in our own ways, this interconnected cycle creates growth and, eventually, legacy. Legacy builds on itself, building wisdom to make each generation a little bit better.

Curiosity. Understanding. Guidance. This cycle of human growth drives global progress. Being born curious, growing to understand, and guiding others as we age is a well-lived life. A single person can change the world.

QUESTION

Do you think a ripple on the surface can change the course of an ocean?

AUTHOR CONTACT INFORMATION

Shad Hardy, Founder of Innovita Med
Website: https://www.innovitamed.com
Email: shadhardy@gmail.com
Social: https://www.linkedin.com/in/shadhardy/
Tags: Thinker, Innovation, Technology

November 11
LACI WADDILL

*You ultimately make your own choices in life.
Dream Big. Lean into God. Trust in happiness.*

THOUGHT

I've finally reached a point in my life where I can say I am genuinely happy. For over eight years, I thought I was happy—married and running a thriving business. During the challenges of 2020, I focused on work while my husband felt alone. I met someone who helped me realize my marriage was over, and I began journaling and seeking counseling. I faced a difficult choice: stay in my comfort zone or embrace the unknown.

I surrendered to God, praying for guidance. Choosing to leave my husband and go through a divorce was painful and publicly devastating. Many family members distanced themselves, and I struggled with feelings of selfishness. Taking a step back from my business allowed me to regroup and clarify my desires. I envisioned my future, and soon after, I fell in love with my soulmate.

Everything aligned. We found our dream home, got engaged, and married the same year. I always wanted children. Here we are, starting a family with kitties, a puppy, and finally, a baby on the way. I returned to my business with a supportive team, enjoying balance and freedom. I'm grateful for my journey and the happiness I've found along the way.

QUESTION

Ask yourself: Are you happy? Do you need to embrace change?

AUTHOR CONTACT INFORMATION

Laci Waddill, Agency Owner of American Family Insurance - Laci Waddill Agency LLC
Website: www.laciwaddillagency.com
Email: laci.waddill@gmail.com
Social: https://m.facebook.com/laciwaddillagency/
Tags: Dream Protector

The Art of Connection

November 12

HOLLY BERRY

There are symbiotic relationships between design, nature, and intention.

THOUGHT

Design, nature, and intention have interdependent relationships.

A flourishing garden illustrates that abundance isn't about having more but thoughtful cultivation. It shows creativity thrives in environments rich in resources and inspiration. Just as a gardener plans each addition carefully, a designer blends elements harmoniously.

Flowers, symbols of beauty and growth, remind us creativity is both spontaneous and nurtured under guidance. Each unique flower represents a design element contributing to the whole, demonstrating that diversity in thought and style leads to rich outcomes.

Intention guides creativity, transforming raw abundance into meaningful impact. Without intention, abundant resources can become chaotic, like an untended garden. Intention ensures every design element has a purpose, enhancing overall beauty.

The fusion of abundance with intentional design yields significant results, reminding artists and designers to be mindful, cultivate their environments, and let their creative spirit flourish within the framework of purpose and vision.

QUESTION

How can you cultivate an environment of abundance and ensure your designs are impactful and meaningful?

AUTHOR CONTACT INFORMATION

Holly Berry, Founder of A Natural Design LLC
Website: https://patreon.com/HollyBerry
Email: info@aNaturalDesign.com
Social: https://linktr.ee/anaturaldesign
Tags: Natural Materials Designer

November 13
LAURA COBB

You have to suit up and show up if you want to stand up and speak up.

THOUGHT

Connection is undoubtedly our primary human need. To know that we matter and have influence in the world forces us to be seen. This risk may involve a life of deep, intimate interactions or one of isolation. There is no more significant threat to our self-worth than the vulnerability of showing the world who we are and resisting retaliation, often with criticism or invalidation.

This vulnerability is the most significant measure of courage. If we want intimate, meaningful connections, we must courageously suit up and show up in our lives so we can then stand up and speak up. We suit up by preparing for connection. We show up by being engaged in our interactions. We ask for, or are asked by another, to be seen in the world and come to know that we matter. Vulnerability seeps in, and a transformational event of connection emerges from our courage, which is the willingness to experience an event without knowing the outcome.

We cannot predict what happens after trauma, challenge, and adversity. If we do the work, plant the seeds, and find a sense of connection, happiness will come. We will find joy in life through the connections we make with others.

QUESTION

Do you have the courage to be seen and heard in the world?

AUTHOR CONTACT INFORMATION

Laura Cobb, Coach, Counselor, Advocate of Laura Cobb Consulting
Website: https://www.365daysofabundancequotes.com
Email: laura@drlauracobb.com
Social: https://www.linkedin.com/in/drlauracobb/
Tags: Coach, Counselor, Advocate, Speaker, Author

The Art of Connection

November 14

BETHANY NEWELL

A life of abundance is living your spectacular vision with brilliance, drive, and absolute clarity.

THOUGHT

Having a clear and defined vision for your life is profoundly influential in cultivating abundance. A well-designed vision serves as a roadmap. Abundance becomes ever-present when you align yourself with this vision, actively pursuing it with unwavering determination and purpose. Executing your dreams requires not only skill and brilliance but also decisive action and a steadfast commitment to your vision.

This focus and mindset attract success and achievement. Through the pursuit of transforming dreams into evident experiences, the universe responds in perfect order. Opportunities and resources are presented that enhance your vision in the direction of abundance in all areas of your life.

Creating a vision board or another tangible, visual reference can serve as a powerful reminder of your goals and desires. Regularly seeing images and words that represent your dreams is a potent tool for manifesting. Believing in the power of visualization, focused intention, positive thinking, and motivation to shape your experiences and outcomes is extraordinary. When you embrace this mindset and way of being, your vision becomes your reality.

QUESTION

Designing a vision board is a valuable practice to clarify your dreams, allowing you to see the abundant life you are manifesting. What is your vision?

AUTHOR CONTACT INFORMATION

Bethany Newell, Owner of 111402, inc.
Website: https://www.manicurist.com/
Email: bethanynewell@hotmail.com
Social: https://www.instagram.com/bethanynewellofficial/
Tags: Beauty, Design, Innovation, Lifestyle Architect

November 15
NYASHA HULSE

*Building connections in a blended family takes time.
Be brave, communicate, and remember:
love grows when we understand each other.*

THOUGHT

Blended Family: My Journey of Love Beyond Blood with My Second Mom

I used to fear having a second mom. Since I was three, I craved all the attention and didn't want to share it. My relationship with my second mom has had ups and downs, but she helps me grow. One time, I did something mean: I covered her face in our family pictures on the fridge. It hurt her, but we worked through it, apologized, and grew closer.

Through this experience, I learned that relationships can be tricky but rewarding. My dad's love is protective and unconditional, while my second mom's love feels different because I have to work for it; we need to create our bond. I am jealous of how my dad loves her and feel left out. Their love reminds me of the Bible, where it says they are now one flesh, partners in life.

I see the importance of communication. Apologizing isn't just saying "sorry"; it's about understanding each other. If you're struggling in your blended family, it's okay to feel lost sometimes. You have the power to create a loving family, and it all starts with you!

QUESTION

How can you show love and understanding in your blended family, even when things get tough? What small steps can you take to connect better with your step-parent or siblings?

AUTHOR CONTACT INFORMATION

Nyasha Hulse, Best Selling Author of Nyasha Hulse
Website: www.ruthdorsainville.com/dnalegacygroup
Email: rdorsainville@gmail.com
Social: https://www.facebook.com/ruthdorsainvilletv
Tags: Nyashahulse, Blendedfamily, Kidentrepreneur

November 16

RUTH DORSAINVILLE-HULSE

An angel mom loves beyond the ordinary, healing hearts with sacrifice.
The Light placed you to build a family and lasting change.

THOUGHT

Blended Family: The Role of an Angel Mom in Love and Unity

In the early days, I asked my new daughter about her vacation. She complained, "It was boring; we didn't do much." My husband quickly reminded her of the first-class flight and helicopter tour. Later, when he asked her to help with dishes, she refused, and he ended up pleading with her. This episode was one of many times I saw him parent out of guilt, fearing she'd pull away if he didn't give her everything.

Finding my role as a new mom wasn't easy. I remember feeling lost and meeting discouraged stepmoms in support groups. Choosing to invest in myself, I now help blended families find unity and healing.

Being a stepmom can be overwhelming, but God chose you. You are an Angel Mom, a healer of broken homes. By nurturing yourself, you'll have more to give to your chosen family and can create a life filled with love and unity.

QUESTION

How does being an "angel mom," placed in a family to heal and build through sacrifice and grace, resonate with your experiences navigating blended family relationships and creating lasting bonds?

AUTHOR CONTACT INFORMATION

Ruth Dorsainville-Hulse, Speaker of DNA Legacy Group
Website: www.ruthdorsainville.com/dnalegacygroup
Email: rdorsainville@gmail.com
Social: https://www.linkedin.com/in/dorsainvilleruth/
Tags: Ruthdorsainville, Career, Blendedfamily, Speaker, Author

November 17
BRUCE HULSE

It's not your fault; it's your responsibility.
This statement is especially true as a husband
and father in a blended family.

THOUGHT

Blended Family: Creating Harmony in Uncertainty

Growing up with two moms, I never imagined how that experience would prepare me for the challenges between my 12-year-old daughter and my wife. Balancing their needs isn't easy. My daughter, once the center of my world, struggles with change. In contrast, my wife longs to feel recognized in our family.

One difficult moment was when my daughter hid a cell phone, breaking our rules. When my wife found it, an argument followed. My daughter felt exposed, wanting privacy, while my wife felt disrespected.

No solution was painless, but I knew the way forward was to ensure they both felt heard. I let each of them express themselves, reinforcing boundaries and supporting my wife. Growing up with two moms taught me the importance of listening. In our blended family, I've learned to prioritize my wife while loving my daughter unconditionally. Our marriage is the foundation, and my commitment is an example to my daughter of what a strong partnership looks like. Someday, she will understand when she, too, has a family.

QUESTION

What if a single moment of clarity changed everything? How can a man honor both his wife's and daughter's voices, ensuring they feel heard while staying true to his commitment to prioritize his wife?

AUTHOR CONTACT INFORMATION

Bruce Hulse, Coach of Bruce Hulse Consulting
Website: www.ruthdorsainville.com/dnalegacygroup
Email: Bruce@clearottawa.com
Social: https://www.linkedin.com/in/bruce-hulse-0044a8126/
Tags: CEO, Speaker, Coach, Bestselling Author, Entrepreneur

November 18

KIMBERLY YVONNE HUMPHREYS

*When we awaken to the abundance within us,
we will naturally radiate abundance.*

THOUGHT

True abundance is not defined by material wealth or external possessions but by the deep sense of fulfillment that arises from within. When we recognize that we are inherently abundant—filled with endless potential, creativity, and love—we shift our focus from lack to possibility. This mindset allows us to see the richness in everyday moments, relationships, and experiences. Abundance naturally flows when we align ourselves with this internal wealth, attracting more of what resonates with our true essence instead of anchoring our thoughts on accumulation and affluence.

Once we get to the mental space where we can be abundant in our existence, shouldn't we strive to share the peace we gain with those around us? The poorest people are the ones clinging to their wealth in ivory towers, fearful of those they see as jealous or spiteful, hiding away to sustain an empty lifestyle they value over relationships and family. Find a way to reach into your heart and radiate your natural abundance because you know it was there all along, and avoid the trap of false abundance.

QUESTION

How can you shift your focus today from what you perceive as missing to the abundance that already exists within you?

AUTHOR CONTACT INFORMATION

Kimberly Yvonne Humphreys, Founder of HeartJoy
Website: https://heartjoytoday.com/
Email: kimberly@heartjoytoday.com
Social: https://linktr.ee/heartjoycoach
Tags: Self-Love Coach, Speaker, Workshop Leader

November 19
YVONNE SCHIMMEL

Abundance is in your head, you can think, so you can create.

THOUGHT

How I went from broke to abundance:

After my divorce, I was broke. Like, "start-from-scratch" broke. I had to rebuild everything.

My biggest dream was to get away for a few months. But how was I going to afford it?

Reading Esther Hicks' book, I realized I needed to focus on the why.

Every morning, I'd take my neighbor's dog for a walk in the forest. And during those walks, I'd vividly imagine myself in America.

Fast forward six months, and guess what? I had all the money I needed. It didn't just come from my 9-to-5 job. Out of nowhere, clients started showing up for therapy sessions (a side gig I'd practically given up). I got an unexpected tax refund, a gift from my parents, and an insurance payout after someone hit my car (and somehow, they paid more than the car was worth). The universe was basically throwing money at me.

Why? I finally stopped micromanaging how everything would happen. I just got clear about what I wanted, why it mattered to me, and how it made me feel. The universe did the rest.

QUESTION

So, my question for you: what are you metaphorically creating, an abundance of beautiful flowers or an abundance full of weeds? Your thoughts, your future!

AUTHOR CONTACT INFORMATION

Yvonne Schimmel, Founder of Healingworldwide
Website: https://healingworldwide.help
Email: info@healthworldwide.help
Social: https://www.linkedin.com/in/yvonneschimmelofficial/
Tags: Remote Bodyscan Therapist, Nutritionist, Genetic Coach, Healer

November 20

JOHN VERRICO

I don't need to blow out your candle to make mine burn brighter. Together, our combined light can help each other eliminate the darkness for all.

THOUGHT

Why do we often feel like we are competing with others and constantly comparing ourselves with them? We may envy something they have that we don't, or perhaps we think we are better than they are. We compare our body shapes, our lifestyles, and our "stuff." But not everything in life is a competition. In the end, we all want to survive and thrive, but it doesn't have to be at someone else's expense.

We live in a world of great abundance and one of dire poverty at the same time. A few hoard all the resources while others are in need. When a storm is approaching, some people buy up every gallon of milk and every roll of toilet paper from the store – more than they could possibly use themselves, not caring that others also need those supplies.

I remember, as a child, my grandmother would say, "Eat your peas. Children are starving in Africa." I hated peas and thought, "Just send the peas to Africa." I realized later that she meant I should be grateful to have food of any kind because there are people who don't have any food at all. This reality also instilled in me an ethic of sharing and not being wasteful.

Share your light; don't compare its brightness. Every lumen counts.

QUESTION

Imagine what the world would be like if everyone shared their resources, their talent, their love, and their light. What abundance can you share with the world today?

AUTHOR CONTACT INFORMATION

John Verrico, Founder of John Verrico - Share Your Fire, LLC
Website: https://www.johnverrico.com
Email: John@JohnVerrico.com
Social: https://www.linkedin.com/in/johnverrico/
Tags: LeadershipCoach, Speaker, ShareYourFire, Motivate

November 21
TAMMY WORKMAN-LOPEZ

*Often, we think we know the problem,
but true leadership requires us to dig deeper;
to turn overwhelm into opportunity
and burnout into brilliance.*

THOUGHT

Imagine feeling overwhelmed and burnt out, constantly pushing yourself with perfectionistic self-talk, nagging limiting beliefs, and working until you're exhausted. This journey is all about tackling these challenges. You'll work on building resilience, setting boundaries, and thinking positively.

By helping you master emotional intelligence, set strategic goals, and develop a clear vision for your future, we create a roadmap to not only personal success but professional excellence. The journey is about reclaiming your energy, clarity, and success, ensuring you thrive in every aspect of your life. Whether you're dealing with physical tension, struggling with self-worth, or balancing the pressures of personal and professional life, my approach provides the support and strategies you need to excel.

Together, we'll transform your challenges into strengths and guide you toward a fulfilling and balanced life. At SparksHope, we don't just focus on overcoming obstacles; we empower you to realize your full potential and achieve sustainable success.

QUESTION

*Are you ready to transform 'overwhelm and burnout'
into 'opportunity and brilliance?'*

AUTHOR CONTACT INFORMATION

Tammy Workman-Lopez, Owner of Mindset Reset
Website: www.SparksHope.Life
Email: tammystarworkman@gmail.com
Social: https://linktr.ee/coachtammystar
Tags: Speaker, Author, Entrepreneur Coach, Couples Coach

November 22

MARTINA WAGNER

Abundance is within you; it awakens when your imagination dares to believe beyond what your eyes can perceive.

THOUGHT

Abundance isn't something we just have; it's something we create from within. Your thoughts, beliefs, and imagination shape every part of your reality. The way you see yourself, the world, and your potential defines what you experience. When you realize abundance is already within you, everything begins to change. You stop seeking outside, and you finally understand that everything you need is already there - within you and in your reach. This powerful shift suddenly opens infinite possibilities.

True abundance is seeing the richness in every moment. By focusing on what you have, not what you lack, you open up to limitless opportunities and unique experiences.

Imagination is the key. When you visualize your dreams and believe in their possibility, you tap into the infinite energy of the universe. Essential oils like "Abundance" and "Believe" help you stay aligned with your vision, empowering you to manifest with ease and joy.

With only a few weeks left this year, it's time to prepare for your most abundant year yet to come. Let me help you step into this energy now and make the next year your best. Believe in the abundance within, and watch how it transforms your life. Ready?

QUESTION

What if the abundance you seek is already within you? Are you ready to believe in possibilities beyond what your eyes can see and step into your true potential - into your highest one?

AUTHOR CONTACT INFORMATION

Martina Wagner, Founder and CEO of Martina Wagner SuccessPartner4You
Website: www.successpartner4you.com
Email: office@wagner-martina.org
Social: https://www.linkedin.com/in/mag-martina-wagner-07a3176b
Tags: SuccessPartner4You, Speaker, Elite Coach

November 23

LYNN BANIS

In loss, connection becomes our lifeline—a bridge from solitude to shared strength.

THOUGHT

Losing a partner is like waking up in a world that no longer feels familiar. The routines, the shared goals, and the silence in a room take on a new, poignant weight. Many of us find ourselves withdrawing inward, thinking that the only way to handle grief is to keep it contained, to hold it tightly so no one else has to see the mess of it all. However, isolation, while feeling protective, often deepens the pain, reinforcing the belief that no one can understand. Yet, it's in these very moments of deep sorrow that connection becomes a lifeline, an opportunity to reach out, not just to escape the loneliness, but to find a new purpose and a path forward through the community of others who share a similar journey.

A connection doesn't erase loss or remove pain, but it opens a path toward healing, transforming sorrow into shared strength. When we connect deeply with others, we create space for healing to unfold naturally without rushing the process. This process is the art of connection in times of loss. This art requires courage and openness that offers understanding without expectation, and that transforms the pain of what we've lost into the resilience of a community rising together.

QUESTION

Who in your life has helped you through difficult times, and how did their support help you feel connected and resilient?

AUTHOR CONTACT INFORMATION

Lynn Banis, PhD, Founder of Widows Rising Together
Website: https://app.widowsrisingtogether.com
Email: lbanis@ameritech.net
Social: https://www.linkedin.com/in/lynn-banis-36987b2aa
Tags: LifeAfterLoss GriefRecovery Author

November 24

LADY JEN DU PLESSIS

Live your Legacy while you Build it!

THOUGHT

Commitment to happiness and success is my ambition. The "work-life balance" myth is pervasive and an illusion. Why wait for success, only to miss out on life? Live today, for today!

My breakthrough came the day I stopped proving myself to everyone. I was constantly making excuses for being late, missing deadlines, and not showing up, all in pursuit of success. One evening at dinner, I took a client's call. Pacing on the curb, I saw my family through the restaurant window, creating memories while I tried to balance work and life. In that moment, everything changed.

I began envisioning each day with excitement, knowing my efforts would be meaningful and aligned with my purpose. By integrating my values—Faith, Family, and Integrity—into daily routines, I unlocked a synergy that transformed my business goals and personal fulfillment. I intentionally focused on both work and play, whether completing a big project or spending quality time with my husband. I didn't strive to be superhuman; I aimed for intentional focus.

Through adjusting my daily activities to fit my intentions, my work life became joyful and inspiring, fueled my energy, satisfaction, and the freedom to play. That's balance!

QUESTION

How could you set an intention today to work with purpose and then play with passion by taking one actionable step toward abundance and gratitude to start living your legacy now?

AUTHOR CONTACT INFORMATION

Lady Jen Du Plessis, CEO of Kinetic Spark Consulting, LLC
Website: https://www.jenduplessis.com
Email: admin@jenduplessis.com
Social: https://linktr.ee/jenduplessis
Tags: JenDuPlessis, Speaker, Leadership, Mentor, Author

November 25
DAVID DOERRIER

Talking and Telling ain't Training or Selling

THOUGHT

As I reflect on the quote, "Talking and Telling ain't Training or Selling," it brings back memories of lessons from my mother, especially on my birthday, November 25th. She always made my favorite meal: homemade spaghetti sauce and a vibrant angel food cake. These weren't just meals; they were acts of love and connection. Through these moments, she taught me more than just cooking; she showed me the importance of engaging with people on a personal level, much like effective communication in public speaking.

My mom's cooking wasn't just about following a recipe, just as effective communication is about more than conveying information. After long days at work, she got tired of hearing, "When are we going to eat?" Instead of getting frustrated, she taught me to cook, instilling the value of effort and understanding. She also emphasized saying "please" and "thank you," which, like engaging an audience, transforms interactions into meaningful connections.

Whether in public speaking or cooking, the goal should always be to inspire and leave a lasting impact, just as my mother did in the simple yet profound ways she nurtured me.

QUESTION

Are you more focused on what you want to say or on how your audience will receive it?

AUTHOR CONTACT INFORMATION

David Doerrier, Founder of Present Your Way To Success
Website: https://presentyourwaytosuccess.com/
Email: david@daviddoerrier.com
Social: https://www.linkedin.com/in/daviddoerrier/
Tags: Facilitator, Public Speaking, Training, Speaker

November 26

MAMIE-JEAN LAMLEY

True Abundance is the ability to dream so big that you can include others' dreams in it!

THOUGHT

Reimagine abundance by appreciating what you have while daring to dream so big that you get to fit others' dreams into it! Take time to embrace gratitude as the catalyst for endless possibilities and notice the beauty in forever moments—a smile, a touch, a compliment, nature's wonder—and let those moments fuel your journey. Leverage your success by redefining your ability to uplift and inspire those around you, empowering you to take control of your definition of success. Take a leap of faith and unleash your potential through purpose and passion. Dare to disrupt the ordinary by envisioning a future where your dreams create ripples of change across communities. Ignite your future with hopes and dreams that impact the world. Be open to trusting the authenticity of others. Embrace vulnerability as a strength, and let it deepen your connections and enrich your experiences. Find solitude in self-mastering the act of receiving. This mindset invites you to live a life that will align your actions, dreams, and legacy for an abundance-filled life.

QUESTION

What small steps can you take today to align your mindset with the abundance you seek?

AUTHOR CONTACT INFORMATION

Mamie-Jean Lamley, Founder and President of i3 Empowerment Solutions
Website: https://www.i3empowermentsolutions.com/igniteyourpassion
Email: Mamie@empowermentonfire.com
Social: https://my.timetrade.com/book/PBPCN
Tags: Founder, Empowerment

November 27
DAVID GOLDBERG

*Speaking about a positive change...
Positive speaking gets them listening!*

THOUGHT

It seems we're hardwired to speak negatively. And it's unfortunate because it turns people off. However, with just a little awareness, it's easy to rephrase things positively.

For example, if someone asks, "Hey, wanna go out tonight, grab dinner, and see a movie?" You could respond, "Sorry, I can't—I have to work." But then you'd both feel bad. So rephrase it like this, "Yeah, I'd love to!...and how about tomorrow because I work tonight?" Then you'd both feel good!

Or instead of telling a colleague, "Your project is coming along well, but I have a question." How about saying, "Your project is coming along well, and I have a question!" Simply changing "but" to "and" shifts the tone from, "Uh oh, where'd I go wrong?" to "Nice!...they want to help me!"

Even everyday statements like, "Don't forget to get bananas! Sounds nicer with this positive spin, "Hey, thanks in advance for getting bananas! :-)"

So before speaking, consider what could come across negatively and rephrase it positively. You'll see the difference—I'm positive:)

QUESTION

Will you do it? Will you catch yourself before you speak negatively and rephrase it positively? Try it. It makes your conservations happier and healthier.

AUTHOR CONTACT INFORMATION

David Goldberg, Owner and Speaking Coach of EdgeStudio.com
Website: https://EdgeStudio.com
Email: David@EdgeStudio.com
Social: https://www.linkedin.com/in/davidwgoldberg/
Tags: Speaker, Coach, Trainer, Training, Voiceover

November 28

BRENT GODDARD

*The abundant life forgets itself and fills its heart,
time, and will with others.*

THOUGHT

Life experience has taught me this singular lesson: abundance is not about me. I teach my college students how to apply this. Get a job: how do I position myself as the best solution to the employers' problems? Win a contract: how do I address their needs? Start a business: how can I fill a gap to make lives better? Get the promotion: how do I help the company and my boss succeed? Happy marriage: how can I help my spouse be happy and fulfilled? Great leadership: how do I invest in others?

Jesus exemplified this, saying: Blessed are you, the poor, the meek, the mourning, the persecuted. Love one another as I have loved you. Simple, yet so complex. We are naturally self-centered. When consulting on writing proposals, I counted how many times companies referred to themselves versus the customer. Generally, even the documents of proposal professionals were 10 to 1 about themselves. But the customer doesn't care how great you are; they want confidence that you will make them great. Abundance and happiness are in what you give, how you serve, and who you love. And to learn this elusive discipline? Practice. Practice in your conversations, emails, texts, tweets, and finally—your thoughts.

QUESTION

Examine your interactions with others; how can you focus your words, actions, and thoughts on understanding, involving, and encouraging those around you?

AUTHOR CONTACT INFORMATION

Brent Goddard, Co-Founder of Nutrition Rescue
Website: https://www.facebook.com/brent.goddard
Email: brentlgoddard@gmail.com
Social: https://www.facebook.com/brent.goddard
Tags: Humanitarian Entrepreneur, CSR Adjunct Professor

November 29
MARLAINA WILLIAMS

Abundance is the physical manifestation of our soul's true destiny.

THOUGHT

This powerful statement reminds us that the inner abundance we cultivate influences and manifests our external reality. Nurturing inner wealth through love, gratitude, and mindfulness awakens neurochemical responses that empower us to find joy and meaning in life. To thrive, we must transcend the limitations we impose on ourselves and embrace our innate power as creators of our destinies.

By harnessing the power of our senses, we can cultivate a rich experience of abundance within ourselves. Take the time to truly feel the warmth of connections, hear the joy in laughter, and appreciate nature's beauty. True abundance transcends material wealth; it arises from vulnerability, self-acceptance, and love. As we envision these vivid moments, our minds blur the lines between imagination and reality, igniting our drive to recreate those chemical responses.

Abundance is not merely an external experience; it's a state waiting to flourish from within. Ignite the spark of abundance in your heart and embrace this perspective to deepen your connection with yourself and all of life's treasures.

QUESTION

How can I pause in my daily routine to truly appreciate the moments of joy and connection that surround me? How can I actively express gratitude for these experiences, deepening my sense of abundance?

AUTHOR CONTACT INFORMATION

Marlaina Williams, Founder, RN, BSN, Holistic Healer of Creative Fire Alchemy
Website: https://creativefirealchemy.com
Email: marlaina@creativefirealchemy.studio
Social: https://www.facebook.com/CreativeFireAlchemy/
Tags: Holistic & Functional Healthcare Practitioner

November 30
NANCY SIEVERT

Three keys to success: chasing your passion, carving your niche, and crucial financial insights.

THOUGHT

The first key to abundance is defining and pursuing your passion, which transforms your business/career aspirations into a joyful journey. By immersing yourself in what you love, every task feels invigorating, and your enthusiasm naturally drives you to excel. Passion creates unwavering commitment leading to innovative ideas and exceptional outcomes, as you're more inclined to go above and beyond when your heart is in it.

Next, carving your niche is essential. By honing in on a specific area where your passion meets market demand, you create a unique space for yourself. Focusing on your niche distinguishes you from competitors and allows you to cater to a dedicated audience that values your expertise.

Finally, in business, crucial financial insights are vital for sustainability. Before launching, understanding startup costs, potential revenue streams, and setting realistic financial goals for the first and second years are imperative. This foresight enables you to navigate challenges with confidence, ensuring your passion project remains profitable. Embracing these three keys cultivates an abundance mindset, turning aspirations into reality while fueling personal and financial growth.

QUESTION

Today, are you ready to take your first step to improve your financial health and begin the path to success you've always dreamed of?

AUTHOR CONTACT INFORMATION

Nancy Sievert, President of F&S Advantage Ltd.
Website: https://www.fandsadvantage.com
Email: nancy@fandsadvantage.com
Social: https://www.linkedin.com/in/nsievert/
Tags: Business Coach, Financial Systems Strategist

December 1
EMMELINE SAAVEDRA

Life simplified is power multiplied.

THOUGHT

Life teaches us the best lessons. At times, the price is high, and at times, they come for free!

I have come to the point where I am living my best life. They call it having "arrived."

Getting here was packed with a lot of chaotic internal work, thinking, and prayers for an enlightened mind, body, and spirit. Running a start-up business makes it even much more challenging, often dealing with a lot of lack and a lot of prayers for God to see me through it all.

Finding peace and joy in the process also takes work. Heart and gut work over brain work: any day and every day. What I have learned growing up in a family of entrepreneurs overseas was always to work hard, be smart, and always do and think ahead of the next person. The path to an enriching life is a journey of sacrifices and hard toil.

Boy, was I surprised - after 58 years! The answer to it all is: Find faith in God, in the energy of the universe, and honor the higher power! So simple, so available, and yet I missed it early on. And, it is perfect as it is - however long it took, and what's here right now is what matters.

Life can be simple and yet powerful. With profound faith, peace, and joy will always follow, as does success.

QUESTION

Are you living your best life now? If yes, what is your secret?
If not, what can you take on new, and what can you give up?
What will bring you peace and joy? What kind of life do you dream of?

AUTHOR CONTACT INFORMATION

Emmeline Saavedra, President, Owner of Champion Dentists
Website: https://www.championdentists.com
Email: emmie.timeisnow@gmail.com
Social: https://www.facebook.com/championdentists
Tags: Dental Consulting, Dental Practice Growth Advisor

December 2

GERI GEASLAND

My photos are my transport to my best moments!

THOUGHT

"Look B'andon, I found another one!" Chad pointed his tiny, chubby hand at the bright yellow plastic egg. His little brother toddled over excitedly. "You can have this one," Chad said, putting the egg in Brandon's basket. The two wandered around the yard, continuing their Easter Hunt.

I remember sitting on the porch watching them, feeling wonder and contentment. So much joy to have these little monsters in my life. I run my hand over the photo again, remembering. The kids, the beautiful day, the feelings I had. That picture with their little Easter buckets and their cute little outfits is a captured moment in time. And this is just one picture in the photo album.

Each picture tells a story, igniting a memory in my mind. I can hear their voices and remember where we were and what they said. I have over thirty albums.

The kids are all grown now with families and busy lives of their own. Those tiny hands are big and strong and capable now. That's as it should be. My job was to raise them to be capable and independent. I am so very, very proud of them. I sit in the rocking chair, my hand flat on the old photo book. And I remember: So many, many precious memories.

QUESTION

What have you done this week to make good memories with the ones you love?

AUTHOR CONTACT INFORMATION

Geri Geasland, Owner and Creative Talent of Broken to Beautiful
Website: https://www.amazon.com/-/e/B0DHFRHSH4
Email: gerilynng50@gmail.com
Social: https://www.facebook.com/geri.lynn.378
Tags: Poet, Artist, Author

December 3
SUSAN KERBY

*Abundance isn't something to chase;
it is an experience to embrace. When I align with my soul,
I open the door to an enchanted life of true abundance.*

THOUGHT

Abundance doesn't come from striving or searching outside of myself. It comes from tuning into the wisdom within. In this soul alignment, I find freedom. Instead of waiting for some future moment to feel abundant, I recognize that abundance is here and now, woven into the fabric of every experience, even in times of great challenge.

I experienced this when my husband and I faced bankruptcy after our business lost 80 percent of its sales in 2008. It felt like we were losing everything. As I asked God, "Why me?" I realized I had a choice: suffer or trust and be open to miracles, even in that trying time.

What I lost was my debt, what I gained was my freedom.

Our attorney said, "Take what money you have; learn a new way to earn money." I'd been well-trained to speak and influenced over 15,000 lives while volunteering to speak for an international training company. Yet, what would I say? I invested in mentorship to find my message. "Speaker training? Really?" I argued with God. I heard, "I'll bring you my messengers; you have them be good." Now, I help world-class speakers and aspiring messengers transform the world with their message.

Blessings abound when we stop chasing and start witnessing.

QUESTION

*What if you could embrace the abundance of miracles around you now?
Can you see every situation as an opportunity calling you forward to
speak your truth and transform your world? Abundance awaits.*

AUTHOR CONTACT INFORMATION

Susan Kerby, Speaking Mentor for Messengers of Awaken To Your Calling
Website: https://awakentoyourcalling.com
Email: susan@susankerby.com
Social: https://www.facebook.com/Susan.Barry.kerby
Tags: Speaker, Speaking Mentorship, Speak Your Truth

December 4

ROY MOORE

Perseverance is life, determination is fuel, and victory is our goal. Let's go and get it!

THOUGHT

This quote was created initially to be my mantra as I drove into the office while serving on active duty in the U.S. Marine Corps. At the time, I was an Operations Manager for a headquarters team that supported over one thousand people. My days were long and riddled with interesting personnel challenges. My drive home ranged from 90 minutes to three hours. My wife's office was over 90 miles away, and we had a newborn.

Things were challenging, and I needed to find a healthy, sustainable method to increase my mental resilience and focus. The feeling of abundance resonated throughout my entire day, enabling me to find simplicity within complex issues and an appreciation for the small things that make life grand. Over time, the mantra took on additional meaning as I unwittingly began incorporating its meaning into coaching sessions and speaking engagements, successfully helping others create a shift in their paradigms. Today, this mantra and quote is even more applicable than it was ten years ago.

QUESTION

When you feel stressed, remember it is not the external factor creating the tension but rather your perception of the situation. How do you modify your thinking to create enlightened mental shifts?

AUTHOR CONTACT INFORMATION

Roy Moore, Founder and Owner of RPM Fitness, LLC
Website: https://www.rpmfitness.com
Email: roy@rpmfitstrong.com
Social: https://www.instagram.com/rpmfitstrong
Tags: Life Coach, Leadership Coach, Fitness Coach

December 5
CARRIE VAN AMBURGH

Abundance 2025 For one to live an Abundant life, one must be Grateful.

THOUGHT

Life on planet Earth is rapidly changing. The way we move forward has altered the very fabric of the cosmos. The electronics that were created for more productivity, ease of function, and social marketing have taken hold of many people, and their lives have come to a standstill. Many have allowed these devices to control how they think, learn, spend, and create.

To have abundance, peace, love, and gratitude, we must put aside these intrusive devices. Get out into nature, feel the earth beneath our bare feet, run in the ocean, allow the wind in our hair, feel the warmth of the healing sun on our faces, and give in to our inner child.

Abundance is waiting for us all. Whether it be spiritual, financial, professional, or relationship, we must return to a kinder, gentler path, one where we are able to hear nature and be still with ourselves.

QUESTION

Do you crave an Abundant life?
What changes are you willing to make to be Abundant?

AUTHOR CONTACT INFORMATION

Carrie Van Amburgh, Founder of Itscarriei.com
Website: https://itscarrie.com
Email: carrieilene@gmail.com
Social: https://mybook.to/artofconnection5
Tags: Founder, Owner, Writer, Producer, Speaker

December 6

MARC BEILIN

Using the abundance, gratitude, and emotions we have within us will create durable relationships.

THOUGHT

We all subconsciously live in a world of attraction, and projecting the abundance in our lives shows other people our innate qualities. Abundance cannot be measured by possessions; it is only by how we embrace what the world throws our way, the people we encounter, and the blessings we can count each day. By abundance, I mean, is the richness of every relationship, every act of kindness, and the ability to find gratitude in others, not any form of affluence.

On days when I struggle to find abundance, I circle back to the gratitude in my life, and "wow," the abundance stares back out at me. I have gratitude for my family and friends regardless of what else they bring to the table. Having abundance is having joy in your life and then looking for what follows instead of thinking those things bring abundance.

QUESTION

If abundance doesn't exist in every relationship in your life, then ask yourself: What do you need to do differently? Where does it matter?

AUTHOR CONTACT INFORMATION

Marc Beilin, Founder and Creator of On the Marc TV
Website: https://www.onthemarctv.com
Email: marcbeilin@quantumideastech.com
Social: https://www.linkedin.com/in/marc-88a600173/
Tags: Platinum Connector, Branding Media Influencer

December 7
DANIEL FAUST

Being thankful is a choice that will produce fruits like transformation.

THOUGHT

As an entrepreneur and living a military life, trials will come. It is not an if but a when. In my season of life, I have had many, including deployments, moves, job loss, attempted suicides, threats of divorce, homelessness, and lots of financial struggles. Every time one of those trials comes up, you have two choices: ungrateful bitterness or joyous thanksgiving.

These are polarizing opposites. The great thing is that if you make a negative choice, you are not stuck. You can choose a joyous thanksgiving. Why choose a joyous thanksgiving? Because of your perspective, outlook, and future changes.

Joyous thanksgiving says the situation is horrible but won't define me. It says I will find the lesson in it. It says my value and worth are not defined at that moment but by who I am. It says I can see this as more than a scar and will find the beauty. It won't be easy, but beauty can come out of ashes.

QUESTION

What will you choose? Ungrateful bitterness or Joyous Thanksgiving?

AUTHOR CONTACT INFORMATION1

Daniel Faust, Veteran Transformation Coach of Learn & Live
Website: HTTPS://learn-n-live.us
Email: daniel.r.faust@gmail.com
Social: https://www.facebook.com/@daniel.faust.33
Tags: Military, Veteran, Marriage, Family, Leadership

December 8
LESLIE KUNTZ

Be genuinely grateful for all that you have at the moment, and you will hold the key to unlocking the door to all that you can imagine having.

THOUGHT

Love, peace, joy, health, happiness, and abundance are the mantras I wake up to and fall asleep to as I say my daily prayers. I try to live in the moment of now, being aware of my attitude and how I react to the world around me, finding gratitude and goodness in all that I do. Being human makes this a challenge on some days more than others.

I have found that when I feel myself going into a negative spiral, I try to stop those thoughts immediately by resetting myself, stating: I am Grateful for the Love, Peace, Joy, Health, Happiness, and Abundance in my life now.

As my experiences change, so can my mantra. Being out of balance and not in harmony causes more frustration, and if I do not stop and reset myself, it can affect my demeanor (vibration) my whole day by returning even more of the same. The bottom line is the more I become aware of my thoughts and actions, the easier it is to maintain a higher vibration from which to create a fantastic life of an Abundance of Love, joy, peace, health, and happiness one day at a time!

QUESTION

Can you hold the vibration of gratitude with which to attract and create an abundant life? It all begins and builds upon being aware of your state of mind and the thoughts you hold at the moment.

AUTHOR CONTACT INFORMATION

Leslie Kuntz, Owner of Creative Properties
Website: https://www.365daysofabundancequotes.com
Email: LeslieKuntz1@yahoo.com
Social: https://mybook.to/artofconnection5
Tags: Author, Angelic Orb Photographer, Speaker.

December 9
BETH ROBINS

Make your life a beautiful story!
It is your birthright to create a life you truly love!

THOUGHT

Five hundred twenty-five thousand, six hundred minutes. That is the exact amount of time we each have in one year of life. We could all live to be 99 years old. Some will live 99 years; others will live one year 99 times.

Think about your own life right now. I'll bet there's part of you longing for more. Once upon a time, there was a big, audacious dream tugging at your heart. Somewhere along your journey in life, it got tucked away and forgotten. Perhaps someone talked you out of it. Perhaps that someone was you!

What happened to your dream? Know this. That dream is uniquely yours. It is a gift from the Divine given only to you to live an extraordinary life! It is your birthright to see it come to fruition! You were blessed with unique gifts, talents, and skills to align your spirit with that intention.

Take a moment and imagine yourself living that dream. Imagine it all worked out, and now it is your real life. You have the power within you to achieve anything you set your heart to. It is more significant than any circumstances around you! You need the right tools to open the door, keep focused on your why, and allow the Divine wisdom that it will work out into your consciousness!

QUESTION

You have the power within you to make your dreams come true! Is it not worth investing your time and resources? What is one action step you can take today to get the ball rolling? If not now, when?

AUTHOR CONTACT INFORMATION

Beth Robins, Owner of Balanced Life Productions
Website: https://www.BalancedLifeProductions.com
Email: blp416@gmail.com
Social: https://www.facebook.com/BALANCEDLIFEPRODUCTIONS/
Tags: Life Coach, Author, Speaker

The Art of Connection

December 10
BRITTON MURREY

A great idea means nothing without execution.

THOUGHT

Entrepreneurs are often full of big ideas, ambitious goals, and detailed plans. And what truly sets the successful ones apart isn't how great their ideas are—it's how well they execute them. It's easy to get lost in planning or constantly chasing new ideas, but little of it matters if you don't take consistent action.

The reality is that success doesn't depend on how high you set your goals but on the strength of the systems that support them. Your progress is determined not by your aspirations but by the daily habits, processes, and structures you put in place. No matter how brilliant your vision is, without solid systems to back it up, even the best ideas will struggle to get off the ground. Entrepreneurs who build solid and repeatable systems are the ones who turn their ideas into tangible results.

Success isn't about perfect plans. It's about taking action and letting your systems carry you through the inevitable challenges along the way. Ideas inspire change, but systems make change possible. Remember, a great idea means nothing with execution.

Scan the QR code to access our free guide on how to start building a system that tackles your big ideas.

QUESTION

What systems can you build today to ensure your ideas and goals turn into lasting outcomes?

AUTHOR CONTACT INFORMATION

Britton Murrey, PMP Founder, CEO of Unbound Strategy Group
Website: https://unboundstrategy.co
Email: britton@unboundstrategy.co
Social: https://www.linkedin.com/in/britton-murrey/
Tags: Growth Strategy, Business Coach, Marketing, GTM

December 11
KAREN CLARK-REDDON

At the moment you think that you have lost everything, pause and remind yourself that you will always have everything you need and more!

THOUGHT

Stay in the present because everything happens for a reason. Have you experienced peace and happiness, but some unexpected incident turns your entire world upside down? Imagine being at home, sitting peacefully in your most comfortable chair. Can you feel the peace and tranquility?

Just as you pick up your favorite cup to take a sip, the ceiling in your home caves in from a crack that you have ignored, and brown liquid and ceiling debris pour down on you nonstop. You jump up completely soaked and muddy. You are in disbelief. Do you run out of the house? Do you try to salvage anything? You are paralyzed in the moment, trying to clear your racing thoughts.

This damage is a huge loss, but is it the end of your journey? No! After the shock wears off, you slowly begin to think about what you still have left. You did not lose everything. You are safe, and you have options.

You have money in the bank, so you can secure a place to stay. Your neighbors come to your aid and offer to help you through this disaster. Only moments ago, you were uncertain as you watched all of your material possessions get destroyed. Now, you see that everything is not lost; you have all that you need.

QUESTION

How have your life experiences changed or confirmed the idea that everything happens for a reason and that you already have everything that you need to be your best self?

AUTHOR CONTACT INFORMATION

Karen Clark-Reddon, Owner of Devonshire - A Perfect Events Company, LLC
Website: https://www.devonshireperfectevents.com
Email: coordinator@devonshireperfectevents.com
Social: https://www.facebook.com/aperfecteventscompany
Tags: Event Planner, Corporate Events, Strategist, Party

December 12

TIFFANY M. MYLES

Abundance leads you to limitless possibilities that align with your mindset from endless gifts from the universe.

THOUGHT

Abundance is derived in many shapes and forms that can be empowerment and lead to embracing resilience. The ripple effects shine into having positivity to access while experiencing personal growth, wealth, and awareness of unexpected places. The concept of abundance are unbreakable strengths that shape self-affirmation and mental well-being with unlimited opportunities as you leave a legacy of fulfillment while developing unique paths for generations. Learn to be Practical, Get real, and Have nothing to fear.

A famous quote is, "You have nothing to fear except fear itself." You can avoid the trap of fear by learning a different mantra, "Fear is an option; danger is real; learn to cope with the first while learning to overcome the second." Developing competencies to walk on unfamiliar paths to success is how you find the endless possibilities that the Universe wishes to gift you, so keep growing and seeking unexpected places, and start with your mindset!

QUESTION

How can you shift your thought process into limiting beliefs that you see more of in your daily life in the smallest ways?

AUTHOR CONTACT INFORMATION

Tiffany M. Myles, Founder and Owner of Amora Notary Services, LLC
Website: https://www.365daysofabundancequotes.com
Email: notaryisign@gmail.com
Social: https://www.linkedin.com/in/notaryisign/
Tags: Speaker, Entrepreneur, Advocacy, Notary, Coaching

December 13

ANGEL MARIE MONACHELLI

By feeling & rehearsing abundance, you align your energy with limitless possibilities, igniting the perfect vibe for your vision to Shine in reality!

THOUGHT

As a Reiki Energy Healer and Spiritual Sage, I've taught that our thoughts and emotions aren't just fleeting—they profoundly shape the lives we experience. Abundance is not merely about material wealth; it's an energetic frequency with which we can align. Just like tuning a radio to the right station, we can access abundance through mindfulness, visualization, and energy practices as simple and powerful as conscious breathing.

Yes, I am known as a Breath Pusher and a Water Pusher—two essential elements of life, sustained by the flow of positive energy. When we nurture these foundations, we ignite the vitality and joy that keep us thriving.

Practicing abundance is clearing energy blocks and opening the path for our dreams and goals to Shine. When energy flows, possibilities become limitless.

I chose "Ignite" and "Shine" for the titles of my books because that's precisely what happens when we align with abundance. "Ignite" sparks that fire within as energy healing reawakens our body's natural healing abilities. And "Shine" is all about letting our true, radiant selves come through.

Reiki realigns our energy, opening us to manifesting our highest visions with greater ease and flow.

QUESTION

How have mindfulness and intentional thinking helped you overcome your blocks to abundance? Everything is energy, so let's chat and explore how you can have it all! You deserve it! Let's connect!

AUTHOR CONTACT INFORMATION

Angel Marie Monachelli, CEO of Angel Marie Inc.
Website: https://angelmarieinc.com/
Email: azlightworkersgifts@gmail.com
Social: https://www.linkedin.com/in/angelmariemonachelli/
Tags: Reiki, Spirituality, Shineon, Meditation, Crystals

December 14

MAUREEN POIRIER

Abundance is taking a leap of faith and following the call of the divine, for God is a God of abundance.

THOUGHT

In 2017, I found myself heading across the ocean to Hawaii from Arizona with three suitcases and a backpack. I was looking forward to reconvening with my Prius in Hilo, Big Island, which was shipped three weeks prior. I have $11 in my pocket, enough for one month's rent, and some empty credit cards I knew I could use if needed. I was leaning into the unknown, trusting the guidance I had received to take this journey, heading to live in a place I had never visited. A week into my journey, an opportunity found me at Starbucks that led to my current career.

Knowing I was on a spiritual journey, I trusted the process and leaned into the insight that I was on the right path. I financially struggled for the first three years, yet I continued to hold tight to my faith.

I am grateful for the journey; rich provisions have been gleaned from this adventure and career over the past 7.5 years. It has richly blessed me, and I am grateful to be able to share it with others who are also altered by this platform.

God was pointing me to a life of abundance, and it was in leaning into the internal nudge, trusting the call, and taking a leap of faith that I discovered the abundance on the other side.

QUESTION

Where in your life could you take a leap of faith and lean into abundance?

AUTHOR CONTACT INFORMATION

Maureen Poirier, Director, Trainer, Agent of Director
Website: calendly.com/maureenpoirier8/
Email: MaureenPoirier8@gmail.com
Social: https://www.linkedin.com/in/maureen-poirier/
Tags: National Speaker, Best Selling Author, Director

December 15
ALEJANDRO LOPEZ HERNANDEZ

En la vida, la verdadera riqueza no son posesiones materiales, sino el amor y conexiones que cultivamos con aquellos que nos abrazan por lo que somos.

THOUGHT

Nací en un pequeño pueblo de México, donde la comunidad era humilde y muy unida. A pesar de los recursos limitados, no nos faltó nada en el amor y la conexión. Cuando me mudé a los EUA cuando era adolescente, mi perspectiva cambió dramáticamente. Aprendí que el éxito aquí a menudo se define por el trabajo duro y la ganancia financiera, con el sueño americano como objetivo final. Perseguí este sueño, acumulando posesiones materiales para validar mis logros. Sin embargo, pronto me sentí desilusionado; cuanto más adquiría, menos satisfecho me sentía.

Más tarde conocí a mi esposa y supe que ella era diferente. Su historia reveló un viaje de resiliencia que fue esclarecedor. Enamorarme de ella me abrió los ojos a la riqueza de valores no materialistas que había pasado por alto. Con ella, descubrí la satisfacción basada en una conexión genuina y una intimidad emocional. El amor y la aceptación en nuestra familia me transformaron, mostrándome que la verdadera alegría proviene de relaciones enriquecedoras, no de posesiones. Darme cuenta de ello fue profundamente gratificante y llenó mi vida de un propósito y una felicidad que los objetos materiales nunca podrían proporcionarme.

QUESTION

¿Cómo ha cambiado tu comprensión de la verdadera realización del viaje desde la ambición material hasta el descubrimiento del valor de las relaciones significativas?

AUTHOR CONTACT INFORMATION

Alejandro Lopez Hernandez, Co-Owner/CEO of A3D Services
Website: https://www.a3dservices.com
Email: alejandro@a3dservices.com
Social: https://www.instagram.com/a3d_services/
Tags: Janitorial Services

December 16
LUCIE ROSA-STAGI

Abundance thrives in energetic collaboration!

THOUGHT

Abundance is so much more than material wealth. It's what we create when we uplift other people. It's what happens when we collaborate and open doors for other people to be seen and heard, and we help them connect so that they may succeed. I believe the best way to describe the abundance journey is walking an intentional path of competency cocreation.

If we help enough people to be successful, then we can consider ourselves successful as well. By working together, we not only build something meaningful for ourselves but also create lasting value that can be passed on. The pinnacle form of abundance is communal legacy. It's all about empowering others, learning to give, and knowing when to receive as well, the ultimate form of prosocial exchange for the benefit of all. Think this way: I have to do this, so while I do it, why not teach another, benefitting all?

QUESTION

Do you like to collaborate with others?

AUTHOR CONTACT INFORMATION

Lucie Rosa-Stagi, Co-Founder of Launch Lab Academy
Website: https://www.launchlabhub.com/home
Email: rosastagilucie@gmail.com
Social: https://beekonnected.com/LucieRosaStagi
Tags: Personal Branding, AI-Powered Personal Branding

December 17

CHRISTOPHER ARNOLD

Any principle designed to create connection can also be used for manipulation–the difference lies in the sincere intentions of the heart.

THOUGHT

I've always wanted to be successful. Even as a child, I would read self-help books to learn the secrets of success. When I first read Dale Carnegie's *How to Win Friends and Influence People,* I joked that it should be called *How to Manipulate Friends and Take Advantage of People.* Reading the principle, "Smile," I imagined living with an insincere grin on my face all of the time. I didn't realize that I was already being manipulative because I was using leadership principles to satisfy my self-interests instead of genuinely connecting with others. When this strategy didn't bring me success, I became critical and isolated myself from those who might have helped.

I was applying the correct principles, but I was using them with insincere intentions. My head and my heart were disconnected. In a moment of clarity, I asked myself, "What's preventing me from smiling authentically most of the time?" This clarity led me to discover that I needed to connect with my own heart before I could deeply connect with family and friends, my purpose, and true success. Years later, I founded my leadership coaching practice, and now, I help business leaders connect their hearts with their strategies.

QUESTION

What's preventing my heart from being fully aligned with the principles I'm using to connect with others?

AUTHOR CONTACT INFORMATION

Christopher Arnold, Founder and Principal Advisor of Care Deeply Consulting
Website: https://caredeeply.com
Email: christopher@caredeeply.com
Social: https://linkedin.com/in/arnoldchris
Tags: Leadership, Healthy Conflict, Accountability, Bcorp

December 18
MARY GILBERT

Abundance is an individual perspective each of us deems important, focusing upon our blessings and the many positive aspects of our lives.

THOUGHT

Our world is a very diverse place. The concept of abundance varies considerably based on where you are, both physically and mentally. In the Western world, the focus many have is based on appearance and physical belongings, their "stuff." These individuals based their self-worth purely upon things accumulated. For these individuals, the concept of abundance is fragile because without their "stuff," they have no sense of self-value.

Many of these people fail to see the value of health, family, friends, and personal accomplishment in their perspective of abundance. In contrast, in lands that are deemed less technologically advanced or less affluent, the perspective of abundance is vastly different. These people find abundance and joy in simply living. They find value in day-to-day survival and being part of their family and tribe.

As I get older, my perspective of abundance continues to shift. Things I was programmed to view as necessary no longer support my current perspective. The joy in simplicity, time freedom, and good health far outweigh more "stuff." Being able to do what I want, when I want, and with whom I want feeds my soul and allows me to experience true abundance.

QUESTION

What shapes your definition and maintenance of abundance?

AUTHOR CONTACT INFORMATION

Mary Gilbert, Arizona Mortgage Broker, MH Loan Services
Website: https://www.mhloanservices.com
Email: mary@mhloanservices.com
Social: https://www.linkedin.com/in/mary-gilbert-351a2b20
Tags: Mortgage Broker

December 19
ERICKA AVILA

*Fear is an option; courage is an option;
quitting is an option; persevering is an option!*

THOUGHT

No one will ever honestly know your heart, pain, past, or desires. I say this to you with the fire that burns in my soul: "Persevere and seek what you wish to experience in this life."

We have the privilege to live and collect experiences. Our perceptions will define them as good and bad or convenient and inconvenient. The common theme is that they're all experiences, and they're all a part of your beautiful collection. The meaning you place upon your experiences is entirely up to you. I invite you to reflect on this moment.

Where are you?

How do you feel?

What do you desire in this moment?

What will you do about it?

Maybe today is the day you take a step in the direction of what you desire. Send that email? Make that call? Apply for that job or promotion. Sign up for that class. Say I love you! Whatever it may be, this is your invitation to take action.

QUESTION

What legacy will you leave behind for generations to come?

AUTHOR CONTACT INFORMATION

Ericka Avila, Founder of Return To Yourself Wellness
Website: www.ReturntoYourself.org
Email: ericka@returntoyourself.org
Social: https://www.instagram.com/return_to_yourself_wellness/
Tags: Author, Speaker, Mindset Mentor, Instructor, Owner

December 20

JOAN PATTERSON

*Abundance appears and fear
disappears when you are grateful.*

THOUGHT

The wheel of my van hung helplessly in mid-air. I had pulled off the road to check my GPS and the destination was nearby. But when I pulled back onto the road, I was stopped by a loud thump and could go no further. What seemed a level area was a curb. Fearing towing costs and expensive undercarriage repairs, a call to 911 brought local police and firefighters. Men in heavy fire-retardant jackets and hard hats strode to my van to examine the problem. I was filled with gratitude when they announced a tow truck would not be needed. They constructed a pillar of blocks under the dangling wheel as I traded places with one of the firefighters behind the wheel of my van.

The night was damp and chilly, but I was warmed by gratitude at their willingness to leave their

comfortable, warm homes and help someone in need. He started the engine and slowly backed my van onto solid ground. He checked the road for signs of leaking fluid and found no damage to the undercarriage. I could safely go on my way. Abundance isn't always material things. That night, gratitude abounded for the faithful men who came to help. Maybe nothing special to them, but insurmountable to the recipient, me.

QUESTION

How would you use gratitude to eliminate your fear and increase your abundance?

AUTHOR CONTACT INFORMATION

Joan Patterson, Owner
Website: https://joanpatterson.org
Email: joan@joanpatterson.org
Social: https://www.linkedin.com/in/joan-patterson-96103a327/
Tags: Author, Speaker, Encourager, Service Dog, Dog

December 21
NICOLA SMITH

*To let abundance flow, I learn to let go.
Holding on won't make it stay. What's meant for me will find its way.*

THOUGHT

Abundance is about flow, not hoarding. It's an energy born of the universe itself—ever-expanding, moving outward. Aligning with this energy is more about letting go than holding on. It's about leaving one on the shelf, trusting there's always enough. Resting in this 'enough-ness' connects me to more significant resources and creativity, allowing me to create more—from a place of trust.

Letting go isn't about being passive; it's about actively choosing to release control and trust the unfolding of my life. This conscious choice opens me to new possibilities. It's not about being careless but about understanding that abundance isn't something I can grasp and hold onto. I experience it through trust, gratitude, and presence.

When I let go, I step into the natural rhythm of my life. I make room for new experiences, insights, and opportunities that align with who I truly am. This shift from fear to trust transforms my life and allows more abundance.

So, I choose to live in the flow of abundance. To trust that the universe is always expanding, always providing, always enough. As I align with this energy, I know that I am inviting more abundance my way, and this feels good.

QUESTION

*In which area of your life could you let go a bit and lean into trust?
What does more abundance look or feel like in this area?*

AUTHOR CONTACT INFORMATION

Nicola Smith, Founder of The Next Level 'training for the mind'
Website: https://thenextlevel.co.nz
Email: nicola@thenextlevel.co.nz
Social: https://www.linkedin.com/in/executive-coach-mindset
Tags: Mindset, Coach, High Performance, Speaker

December 22

CAYDENCE WONG

There's more to explore beyond the clouds.

THOUGHT

I ran into a field of flowers, a hazy pink. They surround me, pulling me into a tight hug. I dance around admiring the masterpiece. The flowers swayed as the wind blew left, then right, then still. You could hear the bees buzzing and nature's calling. It's incredible, but I often feel lonely. This place is my backyard.

Suddenly, it started raining, then thundering. I dashed across the millions of flowers. I gasped. One golden flower was eye-catching, but I had to get inside quickly. My clothes were drenched, but I didn't seem to care. It was mesmerizing and golden, unlike the others. I picked up the mysterious flower, and it burst out glitter in all colors, such as red, pink, gold, and silver. It flew into the air with me to see the big cities, the life I had never seen: Immense skyscrapers in dashing blue and so many cars in a variety of colors. I never knew there was such an abundance of colors beyond my boundaries.

QUESTION

What have you explored beyond your boundaries?

AUTHOR CONTACT INFORMATION

Caydence Wong, CEO of Caydence Wong
Website: https://www.365daysofabundancequotes.com
Email: rainbowgummyworm45@gmail.com
Social: https://mybook.to/artofconnection5
Tags: Student, Fan of Minnie Mouse, Daughter, Sister

December 23
DANIEL SCHNEIDER

Peace of mind holds more value than any wealth; it's the foundation for true success and fulfillment.

THOUGHT

Growing up, I faced a challenging childhood with undiagnosed ADHD and the absence of my father. My mother, a single parent, did her best to protect and nurture me, but without a father figure, I often rebelled against authority. The Israeli military, which I joined at 18, was a turning point. Although I struggled with rigid structure, I eventually adjusted to it. My time in the IDF taught me resilience and perseverance.

I spent years traveling and searching for my identity, grappling with failed marriages, unstable jobs, and unsuccessful ventures. At the age of 40, I realized that I was the common denominator in my life's challenges. This epiphany was catalyzed by a song lyric from the Zac Brown Band: "There is no dollar sign on peace of mind; this I've come to know." These words resonated deeply and changed my perspective.

I learned that success is not measured by material wealth but by inner peace and self-awareness. This realization propelled me to build a stable and fulfilling career. At age 55, I am the proud owner of Empower Training Academy, Inc. Embracing my journey, I discovered that overcoming adversity and finding inner peace were crucial for achieving my dreams.

QUESTION

How can you shift your focus from external success to inner peace, and what steps can you take today to start this journey?

AUTHOR CONTACT INFORMATION

Daniel Schneider, Sr. Consultant of Empower Training Academy, Inc.
Website: https://www.empowertrainingacademy.com/
Email: daniel@empowertrainingacademy.com
Social: https://www.linkedin.com/in/danielschneideraz/
Tags: Sr Consultant, Speaker, Business Coach

The Art of Connection

December 24

PHYL FRANKLIN

*The only way that you will fail is if you give up;
if you keep trying, you will succeed.*

THOUGHT

Abundance is all around us—unlimited opportunities, possibilities, and connections waiting to be tapped into. I choose to live with an abundant mindset because it allows me to see beyond challenges, knowing that with persistence, the possibilities are endless. That's why I never give up. Every setback is just a setup for growth. Every "No" brings me one step closer to "Yes." The key is to stay focused, keep moving forward, and trust that success is within reach.

I also encourage you never to prejudge anyone. You don't know someone's potential, journey, or what they might bring into your life or business. Everyone has a unique path and untapped potential, and to prejudge someone would be to limit the abundance of opportunity they might bring. By remaining open, I allow myself to see possibilities where others see limitations. It's not just about being positive—it's about believing that every interaction can lead to something greater, something more significant.

Living in abundance means knowing there's enough success, joy, and wealth. If you never give up and never prejudge, then you align yourself with that abundance, and in doing so, you open doors that were never seen before.

QUESTION

Are you ready to embrace abundance and unlock the limitless potential around you? What opportunities might you be missing by giving up too soon or prejudging others before seeing their actual value?

AUTHOR CONTACT INFORMATION

Phyl Franklin, Independent Distributor of Whosoever
Website: http://cellularutilization.com
Email: phyl247@me.com
Social: http://cellularutilization.com
Tags: Cellular Utilization, Nano, Hydrostat, Encapsulation

December 25
SHAWN JONES

The most valuable abundance assets one can hold are experiences.

THOUGHT

Experience is a unique treasure that cannot be bought, lost, or replaced like material possessions. It profoundly enriches our lives, shaping who we are through personal triumphs, professional hurdles, and moments of joy. These experiences impart wisdom that far exceeds monetary value, providing resilience and perspective that are hard to replicate.

Life experiences form our foundation, giving us opportunities for growth and learning. With each lesson, whether positive, negative, or otherwise, we learn to adapt and overcome challenges. We can easily face challenges and find our purpose. They become integral to our identity, influencing our core values and interactions with the world.

Ultimately, the measure of our lives lies not in possessions but in the wealth of experiences we gather. Each interaction and moment of joy contributes to a meaningful story that showcases our growth and resilience. Thus, experiences emerge as life's true treasures, illuminating our path and deepening our self-awareness.

QUESTION

Taking inventory of your abundance of experience assets, what areas in your life could be added to, and how would living your life be different by adding these assets?

AUTHOR CONTACT INFORMATION

Shawn Jones, Integrative Practitioner of Infinite Core Healing & Coaching
Website: https://www.infinitecorecoaching.com
Email: jones@infinitecorecoaching.com
Social: https://www.linkedin.com/company/infinite-core-coaching
Tags: Integrative Practitioner, Coach, Speaker

December 26

ADRIANNE SIZE

*Abundance shows up in many forms throughout life.
It has been said that abundance is a state of plenty.
A supply of whatever is desired.*

THOUGHT

What is the first word or image that comes to mind when thinking of abundance? Is it wealth, health, feelings of gratitude, fulfillment, or having everything ever wanted or desired? Does lack of abundance first show itself? Focusing on positive possibilities and living as if they already exist, rather than limitations one may already be experiencing, can significantly change the type of abundance experienced. If one finds oneself stuck in limiting abundance, look for the lesson being presented. Is it learning compassion, patience, calmness, or just letting go? Lessons can be long and challenging. Some lasting a lifetime before discovery! Find it! Give forgiveness if necessary. Accept your responsibility in this lesson. Give gratitude for all the lesson(s). Permit yourself to move forward into the newly discovered possibilities with hope and excited anticipation. See them. Live them. Adjust along the way as necessary. The following mantra I have found helpful:

"I am happy!

I am grateful!

As above, so below!"

QUESTION

How do you want to see, live, and experience your life of abundance?

AUTHOR CONTACT INFORMATION

Adrianne Size, Founder and Owner of Arizona Spiritual Energy Healing
Website: https://www.arizonaspiritualenergyhealing.com
Email: arizonaspiritualenergyhealing@gmail.com
Social: https://www.linkedin.com/in/adrianne-size-b337b67
Tags: Shaman, Reiki Master / Teacher, Life Coach

December 27
RUTHERFORD PASCAL

Our society doesn't fully comprehend the greatness of everyday life. We need artificial dates and holidays to celebrate what we should feel daily.

THOUGHT

Believing in your beliefs is the cornerstone of unlocking the abundant life you aspire to. Your beliefs fuel your confidence, drive your actions, and ultimately shape your reality. When you embrace the courage to doubt your doubts, you release yourself from the invisible chains of fear, insecurity, and self-imposed limitations.

This critical shift in mindset enables you to view challenges not as obstacles but as opportunities and setbacks as stepping stones to greater achievements. Each small victory reinforces your confidence, building momentum toward your goals. True abundance isn't about material wealth alone; it's about cultivating a life rich in purpose, fulfillment, and joy. It begins with the courage to believe in your worth and potential, even when the path ahead seems unclear.

By trusting in your ability to persevere, innovate, and adapt, you transform your dreams into realities and inspire others to do the same. Remember, abundance isn't a destination, it's a journey, one that starts with a single, powerful belief: you are capable of more than you imagine.

QUESTION

What if we only judge each other on their gifts and talents? How joyful and productive would we be?

AUTHOR CONTACT INFORMATION

Rutherford Pascal, Founder and CEO of Glass Walls Leadership
Website: https://glasswallsleadership.com/
Email: rutherfordpascal@gmail.com
Social: www.linkedin.com/in/rutherford-pascal-42381b3
Tags: Speaker

December 28
COURTNEY BROWN

*When you let yourself open up and you receive
the true abundance of creativity, you feel the true power
that is meant for you to see and make so.*

THOUGHT

When I get in the mindset of abundant thought to create my products, I see them, I feel them, and I make them so. I want to thank my father for giving me an open mind and the willingness to see things in an out-of-the-box way that not everyone else sees. He also gave me the strength and common sense to stick with a project until it is complete.

When you open yourself up to your creative side, for me, there is no better place to reside. I feel so happy and filled with joy. It helps me to be in a place where I can create for the better of our fellow beings. I know that in this space of abundance, if you stay open to it and do not let life or others get in the way. You can create and share your abundance with others.

My father also taught me how to be a man of value and that you can have a great life and teach, share, and grow without giving up your true beliefs. My father has lived a life that I am genuinely proud of. I am truly proud to call him Dad. So, abundance to me is living, growing, creating, sharing, and being open to all that is out there for us. Thank you, Dad.

QUESTION

*What will it hurt if you leave yourself open to an abundant life where
you think of others more and you less? Will you make a change in the world and
leave it a better place for the future? Let's hope!*

AUTHOR CONTACT INFORMATION

Courtney Brown, Ultimate Cart and Dolly Owner, Developer, Designer
Website: https://www.ultimatecartanddolly.com/
Email: courtney@ultimatecartanddolly.com
Social: https://www.linkedin.com/in/courtney-brown-ucd
Tags: Business Owner, Product Designer, Developer

December 29
STEPHEN TURNER

Abundance is like glasses: wear them to see the world clearly, or forget them and struggle through the day with vision loss.

THOUGHT

Imagine waking up in the morning and reaching for your glasses. Without them, everything is blurry and unclear. You might still make it through the day, but you'll constantly struggle to see, squinting to make sense of your surroundings. With your glasses on, however, the world sharpens, and everything becomes easier and clearer. This clarity is how the mindset of abundance works. It's a perspective we adopt; It's a conscious choice to see the opportunities and potential in the world around us.

When we "wear" the lens of abundance, we notice the small wins, appreciate the good in people, and see challenges as chances to grow. We view our circumstances not as limiting but as full of possibility. However, if we neglect this mindset, it's like going through the day without our glasses. Life appears tougher than it needs to be. Opportunities feel scarce, frustrations take over, and we miss out on what's right in front of us.

Abundance is always there, but it's up to us to see it. This simple shift can transform how we navigate life, making everything seem more manageable and filled with promise. The more often we choose the lens of abundance, the clearer and brighter our world becomes.

QUESTION

What lenses are you choosing to wear today—are they helping you see the abundance and opportunities in your life, or are they blurring your vision with limitations?

AUTHOR CONTACT INFORMATION

Stephen Turner, President of The Turner Group
Website: https://thesteveturner.com
Email: Newhomesalesandmarketing@gmail.com
Social: https://www.linkedin.com/in/newhomesalespro/
Tags: Marketing, Consultant, Entrepreneur, Real Estate

The Art of Connection

December 30

ALLISON HAMMOND

How did we find abundance in our lives?
We had an estate sale!

THOUGHT

We had a big house, lots of collections, filled storage closets, furniture never used, etc. We were living in maybe 20 percent of it all. We have one son who we knew did not want all of our things. Our solution was to have an estate sale.

When we engaged an estate sale professional, we were the first "living" customers they had ever had. They priced, advertised, and conducted the sale, and when it was over, our house was pretty much empty.

Walking into my empty house was emotional. I cried and hugged two of my dolls that had not been sold. I heard my echoing footsteps as I walked through the rooms. It was like peeling off a bandaid.

And yet, I had an overwhelming sense of calm as I realized that the material things that we left were enough. We were moving on to an abundant life of simplicity.

Now, we live abundantly in a smaller house, have a smaller yard, and have fewer things to care for. We have abundant time for each other, our favorite pastimes, family, and community involvement. We enjoy experiences more than things.

We live so much more abundantly with less.

QUESTION

How do you find abundance in experiences?

AUTHOR CONTACT INFORMATION

Allison Hammond, Founder of ResponsAble People & Company
Website: https://www.responsablepeople.com
Email: allison@responsablepeople.com
Social: https://www.linkedin.com/in/allisonbakerhammond/
Tags: Facilitator, Leadership, Author, Speaker

December 31
AMETHYST KINNEY

*Abundance and cannabis,
who would have thought!*

THOUGHT

Abundance and cannabis, who would have thought? There are so many benefits from cannabis for increasing abundance. If we overcome the stigma of cannabis, we can increase abundance in our everyday lives.

Health in abundance is essential for an abundant lifestyle. If we are unhealthy, we strain to do even the most routine tasks, which hinders success. Have you ever thought that your health could be aided by cannabis? The naturally healing plant offers medicinal relief on many levels. Some people lack health in abundance due to a chronic illness, while others need to sleep more than three hours each night. People who suffer from chronic pain know all too well that any relief from that pain will increase their abundance significantly.

Community abundance is received from cannabis on multiple levels. The taxation on cannabis offers help to communities to support local law enforcement, local community colleges, local community road and highway repairs, and much more throughout the community. We usually think about our abundance, but when the community receives abundance, we all benefit more as individuals.

Millions of people are benefiting in abundance from cannabis, and you can too.

QUESTION

*How can we overcome the stigma of cannabis
by showing how it can increase abundance?*

AUTHOR CONTACT INFORMATION

Amethyst Kinney, Founder and CEO of Blue Dream Entertainment
Website: https://www.bluedreamentertainment.com
Email: amethyst@bluedreamentertainment.com
Social: http://linkedin.com/in/amethyst-kinney-1692855a
Tags: Cannabis, Entrepreneur, Woman-Owned Business, Educator

Endorsements

John Verrico - john@johnverrico.com
Gratitude is supremely important to our daily well-being and helps us overcome the drama, trauma, turmoil, and strife that may pop up in our lives. This collection of daily affirmations from more than 300 brilliant thinkers came at just the right time. This is going to sit at the bedside for daily reading.

Susan Finley - spidersuezee@gmail.com
The Art of Connection is not just a book; it's wisdom, inspiration, and gratitude for life, and I am genuinely grateful for the Genius of Robert Jones in the creation of this spectacular and enjoyable master collaboration of over 300 authors! :) This book has enriched my life on so many levels!!!!:) SueZee Finley

Len DeCarmine - len@mindfulmanmethod.com
This book has become my go-to for inspiration in daily life. I love flipping through the pages, soaking in the wisdom from various quotes. This book shares a powerful common thread from influencers to entrepreneurs and everyone in between - they illuminate the beauty of gratitude and the power of connection in our lives. Whether you're new to practicing gratitude or already experienced, "365 Days of Gratitude Quotes" is a must-have. Invest in your journey of appreciation and connection today.

Jennifer Farrar - jennifer@healingpeacewithin.com
In the first few pages, my mind is already blown. Gratitude is one of the highest states of being. This book introduces you to all new ways to be grateful and have gratitude in your life. I love reading other people's stories and how to have gratitude even in the face of difficulty in life. It inspires me to live more, love more, and be more!

Kathleen Carlson - kathleen@straightupsuccess.com
This book is full of gems! I Love this book. It is full of inspiration, words of wisdom, and great quotes. I like to start my day randomly picking a page to start my day with gratitude. We all have so much to be grateful for. This book is the perfect rolodex for a group of heart-centered business folks.

Lori Osborne - lori@bizbolster.com

This is such an amazing compilation of an equally amazing group of authors! I am so honored to be part of this history-making series. And I absolutely love reading all the quotes around gratefulness from Entrepreneurs, Business Owners, and Influencers. This should be a DAILY read for everyone!

Mary Gaul - mary@successmagnified.com

"The Art of - Connection: 365 Days of Gratitude Quotes by Entrepreneurs, Business Owners, and Influencers" is a treasure trove of inspiration and insight into the power of gratitude in both personal and professional realms. As a contributor to this enriching collection, I can attest to the profound impact each daily quote holds. With thought-provoking questions and powerful stories accompanying each quote, readers are gently guided to explore the depths of their gratitude and find meaning in even the simplest moments of life. Whether it's the joy of belonging, the beauty of meaningful connections, or the abundance that surrounds us, this book serves as a beacon of light, reminding us to live each day with intention and appreciation. I highly recommend it to anyone seeking to infuse their days with positivity, purpose, and gratitude.

Mary Jo Gremling - maryjogremling@gmail.com

What do you get when you gather reflections on gratitude from over 300 entrepreneurs, business owners, coaches, and influencers? You get an amazing collection of wisdom from a wide variety of perspectives. One of my favorites is by Krys Pappius: "Gratitude is the antidote to the sinkhole of comparison." In four brief lines, Krys showed me an entirely new view and gave me a valuable life tool. This book is one you can refer to again and again. Inspiring, challenging, and uplifting!

Affiliate Recognition

The following affiliates brought at least twenty contributing authors into this book. We wish to acknowledge their valuable support of the Art of Connection book series:

John Verrico is a seasoned communication professional with over 40 years of experience in public relations and leadership. As a motivational speaker and trainer, he specializes in employee morale and organizational communication strategies. John Verrico has also been featured in various interviews and discussions, sharing his expertise in communication and leadership.

SueZee Finley is a Sound Therapist, PEMF Specialist, and Laughter Yoga Leader dedicated to promoting wellness through sound therapy. She founded Acoustic Therapeutix and the Happiness Now Network, offering retreats, workshops, and a podcast focused on well-being.

Marc Beilin is the CEO of On The Marc TV, an international best-selling author, and a business mentor. He serves on the boards of various organizations that aid entrepreneurs in global brand expansion. Marc Beilin has also been featured in various interviews and discussions, sharing his expertise on entrepreneurship and brand development.

Laura Lee Kenny is a Wealth Mindset Coach and Certified Financial Planner with over 25 years of experience. She is also an international best-selling author dedicated to guiding clients toward financial success and personal growth. Laura Lee Kenny has been featured in various interviews and discussions, sharing her expertise on financial planning and wealth mindset.

The following affiliates brought at least ten contributing authors into this book. We wish likewise to acknowledge their support:

Ken Rochon Jr. is a seasoned entrepreneur, author, and speaker who specializes in event photography and marketing amplification. As co-founder of The Umbrella Syndicate, he enhances event engagement through social media strategies. Ken is also a published author and host of the 'Amplified' radio show.

Lori Osborne is a public speaker, best-selling author, and Founder and Chief Solution Architect of BizBolster Web Solutions. She specializes in empowering small businesses by enhancing their online presence through effective website strategies.

Thank You!

If you enjoyed the transformational pages from the authors in the Art of Connection 365 Days of Abundance Quotes of Entrepreneurs, Business Owners, and Influencers, please go to Amazon and show them some love by leaving a review. Scan the barcode above with your phone camera or click on the link below.

https://www.amazon.com/dp/B0DSK5HGYZ

Become an Author with us!

Would you like to be a contributing author in the next book in the Art of Connection series? Scan the barcode above or go to the link below to sign up for our introductory inclusion!

https://365daysofresiliencequotes.com

Made in the USA
Middletown, DE
18 April 2025